GREAT ACTING

GREAT

LAURENCE OLIVIER

SYBIL THORNDIKE

RALPH RICHARDSON

PEGGY ASHCROFT

MICHAEL REDGRAVE

EDITH EVANS

JOHN GIELGUD

NOËL COWARD

edited by HAL BURTON

ACTING

HILL AND WANG · NEW YORK
BY ARRANGEMENT WITH THE BRITISH BROADCASTING CORPORATION

Published in the United States of America
by Hill & Wang, Inc.

Library of Congress catalog card number: 67-23522

First American edition November 1967

Printed in Great Britain

CONTENTS

ILLUSTRATIONS

The photographs were chosen to show each actor in as wide a range of parts as possible. To show comparison groups of related parts (e.g. Shakespeare, Restoration comedy, Chekhov, twentieth-century plays) have been put together, although within these groups a rough chronological order is usually followed. Marginal notes in the text give the page and letter of illustrations referred to.

The following list gives the theatre at which each of the productions illustrated was presented. All the theatres are in London, unless otherwise stated. The Old Vic Company (O.V.) was playing at the New Theatre from 1942 to 1950. E.S.C. = English Stage Company.

LAURENCE OLIVIER 33 C–F Birmingham Rep.; 34 A,B New, C O.V., D Phoenix; 35 O.V.; 36 A,B Stratford, C–E O.V.; 37 A–C,E O.V., D Stratford; 38–9 National; 40 A St James's, B Saville, C,D E.S.C.

SYBIL THORNDIKE 42 A,C Gaiety, Manchester, B Little, D Criterion; 43 A New, B Princes, C Lyric, Hammersmith, D O.V., E Empire; 44 A,C O.V., B,E New, D Vaudeville; 45 A–C O.V., D Lyceum, Edinburgh; 46 A,B,D Duchess, C Apollo; 47 A Haymarket, B,D Australian tour, C BBC Television, E Vaudeville; 48 A New, B Holborn Empire, C Christchurch, Oxford.

RALPH RICHARDSON 73 B Birmingham Rep., C Doran Shakespeare Co., D Royal Court; 74–5 O.V.; 76 A,B,D O.V., C Stratford; 77 A,B Haymarket, C O.V., D Stratford, E Foreign tour; 78 A Malvern Festival, B Duchess, C Haymarket, D New, E O.V.; 79 A,B,D Haymarket, C Globe; 80 films.

PEGGY ASHCROFT 81 C Savoy; 82 A,B O.V., C,D New; 83 A Haymarket, B,D Stratford, C O.V.; 84 A,D–F Stratford, B O.V., C Haymarket; 85 A, C–D Stratford, B Aldwych; 86 A Queen's, B Aldwych, C New, D E.S.C. at Queen's; 87 A O.V., B Lyric, C Haymarket, D E.S.C.; 88 A–C His Majesty's, D,E E.S.C., F Aldwych.

MICHAEL REDGRAVE 113 C Liverpool Rep; 114 A,B,E O.V., C Haymarket, D,F Queen's; 115 A,C Queen's, B Phoenix; 116 A Garrick, B St James's, C O.V., D Guildford; 117 A,D O.V., B Stratford, C Aldwych; 118 Stratford; 119 A Embassy, B–D National; 120 films.

EDITH EVANS 121 C Haymarket; 122 A,B,D O.V., B,C New, E Piccadilly, F Stratford; 123 A,C Stratford, B O.V.; 124 A Globe, B Malvern Festival, C Cambridge, D Birmingham Rep.; 125 A Strand, B Royalty, C,D O.V.; 126 A,B New, C O.V.; 127 A Aldwych, B Wyndham's, C,D Haymarket; 128 films.

JOHN GIELGUD 146 A,B,D O.V., C Regent; 147 A–C New, D Lyceum; 148 A,B Queen's, C Piccadilly, D Stratford; 149 A,C,D Stratford, B Phoenix, E O.V.; 150 A Stratford, B Palace, C New, D Haymarket; 151 A,C,D Phoenix, B Queen's; 152 A Lyric, B Queen's, C New, D Aldwych; 153 A Regent, B Criterion, C,E Globe, D New.

NOËL COWARD 154 C Prince of Wales, D Garrick, E St James's; 155 A Everyman, B,C New; 156 Phoenix; 157 A,B Ethel Barrymore, N.Y., C Haymarket; 158 Haymarket; 159 A Ambassadors, B National, C,D Queen's; 160 films.

ACKNOWLEDGEMENTS

Grateful thanks are due to the actors for lending their own collections of photographs, and to Mander and Mitchinson for their help and research.

Acknowledgement is due to the following for permission to reproduce illustrations: Maria Austria (Particam) 150B; BBC 85A,D; Cecil Beaton 82D, 83A, 84C, 118A, 124C, 150D, 151A; BHE Film of the National Theatre Production 39C; Michael Boys 47E; British Lion Film Co. Ltd 40D, 80B,C, 160C; British Theatre Museum Collection, London 35D, 153D; Anthony Buckley 44D; Central Office of Information (Crown Copyright reserved) 34A,B, 48D, 77E, 82C, 122B, 147B; Columbia Pictures Corporation Ltd 160B; Daily Express 158C; Eileen Darby 88A,B,C; Zoë Dominic front cover, 38A, 88F, 116D; Foulsham and Banfield Ltd 43A, 154D; Gordon Goode 85C; Guy Gravett 87D, 88D,E; Keystone Press Agency Ltd 48A; Lenare Ltd 73D; Life Magazine 117C; Mander and Mitchinson Theatre Collection 41B,C, 42B,D, 43E, 47B,D, 48B, 76A, 81B,C, 122A, 124A,D, 125A, 146A,B, 147D, 153A, 156B, 157A,B; Angus McBean 34C, 35A,B,C, 36A,B, 37D, 38C, 39A,B, 40A, 45A, 46B,C, 76B,C,D, 77A,B,D, 78C,D, 79A,C,D, 83B,D, 85A,D,E,F, 85B, 87B, 114C,E, 117B, 118B,C,D, 119B,C, 122C,D,F, 123A,B,C, 127A,B,C, 147C, 148D, 149A,B,D, 150A, 152D, 153C,E, 158A, 159B,C,D; Lewis Morley 38B; Odham's Syndication Ltd 41A; Oxford Illustrated Journal 48C; Radio Times 47C; Radio Times Hulton Picture Library 33B, 34D, 44A,E, 45C,D, 47A, 78A, 114F, 124B, 125B, 126B, 127D, 146C, 148A,B,C, 151B, 152B,C, 153B, 155A, 156A,C; Rank Organization 120A,B,C, 128B; Houston Rogers 46A,D, 78B, 79B, 86A,B,C, 87C, 113C, 114D, 115A,C, 122E, 126A, 149C, 150C, 151C; Edwin Smith 149E; Stage Photo Co. 73B; Studio 59 Ltd 40B; Thomson Newspapers Ltd 43C; John Timbers 40C; The Times 44B; Twentieth Century Fox 80A; United Artists 128C; John Vickers 36C,D,E, 37A,B,C,E, 44C, 45B, 74A,B,C, 75A,B,C,D, 77C, 78E, 83C, 84B, 87A, 116A,B,C, 117A,D, 119A, 125D, 126C, 151D; Warner Pathé Ltd 128A,D; Whitecross Studios 86D, 119D (photos by Sandra Lousada).

PREFACE

The art of acting is highly intuitive and it is for this reason that the actor does not really like to talk about acting. But when he does he can be shrewd and illuminating. While he is giving you an analysis and a critical appraisal of how he sets about his work, he is, quite unwittingly, telling you a good deal about himself.

Some knowledge of the actor's craft will certainly not diminish the illusion created by an actor's performance, because no actor can explain the mystery at the heart of acting, how he invests himself with the personality of another human being when he is on the stage. An actor is the child of his time, he expresses himself in terms which are understandable and acceptable to the audience of his day and age. For that very reason there are fashions in acting styles; what appears realistic to one generation may seem ham to the next, and vice versa. The generation of actors who preceded the contributors to this book was led by Gerald du Maurier. He never played in the classics but appeared nearly always in high comedy, melodrama, or romantic pieces. He perfected for himself a sophisticated, highly polished, realistic style of acting which was admirably suited to this type of production. The leading actors and actresses of the day, who satisfied the taste of a philistine upper-middle-class audience, seldom had a chance to play in any work with intellectual content because of the plethora of light comedies which filled the boards.

When John Gielgud therefore brought Shakespeare back to the West End of London with *Hamlet* (1930) and *Romeo and Juliet* (1935) he had something very different to offer. The acting of his young and vital Company was emotionally charged and intelligently controlled; it was robust, flexible, and sensitive. Consequently the range of parts he and his colleagues were able to play was prodigious – (witness Gielgud in *Hamlet* and *The Good Companions*; and in later days Laurence Olivier in *Richard III* and *The Entertainer*). Star actors were expected during this period of the twenties to fifties always to be heroes and heroines (the day of the anti-hero had not, as yet, dawned) and no groups of actors were better endowed either physically or vocally to give those stage characters so much humanity, poetry, and elegance. In classical plays the emphasis placed on the use of the voice was such that the sound of the spoken word was as important as the sense behind it: acting in the grand manner was still a possibility – in fact it was 'a consummation devoutly to be wished'.

The dramatist who is most discussed after Shakespeare is Chekhov, and this is not surprising, as the actors who gave these interviews have been responsible for a number of memorable productions and performances of his plays. The masterpieces of Chekhov are the perfect antidote to the Shakespeare canon; his plays require a style of acting which gives the player a chance to add a new dimension to his interpretative skill. He is not so much telling a story as exploring a character and creating a mood. Three of the most notable productions of our time have been Komisarjevsky's *Seagull* (1936), Michel Saint-Denis's *Three Sisters* (1938), and Laurence Olivier's *Uncle Vanya* (1964). They were notable not only for individual performances but for the ensemble playing which had a lightness of touch, superb orchestration, and an equitable and mercurial balance between comedy and melancholy.

There are two observations which apply equally well to all the actors in the series. They possess not only good judgement but the companion gift of self-analysis. These qualities

7

have helped them, on most occasions, to choose the right part at the appropriate moment in their lives. An actor with star quality is much sought after, but he is seen only in a very small percentage of the plays he is offered by theatre managements, producers, or playwrights. An actor makes his reputation not only on the plays in which he appears but also maintains that reputation on the parts he turns down. This seems to be the only explicable reason why the contributors to this book have such untarnished reputations, after so many years' variety of work in this most precarious of professions.

These interviews also reveal devotion to an iron self-discipline – a discipline which enables them to be at their best, both physically and mentally, at every performance: the entertainment of the public is first and foremost in their minds. They know that while they are on the stage they must be in full control of themselves and their audience. They also know that if a play or a performance lacks heart it is moribund from the start. D. H. Lawrence said, 'the human heart needs, needs, needs splendour, pride, assumption, glory, and lordship'. These particular actors give those qualities to the theatre in abundance, and their audiences are grateful for it.

This publication differs from most books on the Theatre because it contains a highly personal account of our twentieth-century stage as seen from the actor's, not the audience's, point of view: the story is told by the players who helped to make that history. They are, therefore, in a position to record how some of the most important productions were initiated; and, at the same time, to give precise details of the actual process whereby many of the great characters they played were conceived and performed. It should become a valuable source book for future theatre historians.

At the time when most of these actors were making their débuts, the theatre was still the most potent form of entertainment in this country. They entered the profession with the foreknowledge that they would probably spend the rest of their days performing before a live audience eight times a week. Though subsequently most of them have had distinguished careers in the Cinema, we still think of them as essentially stage actors. It is interesting to note that their working lives embrace so many of the principal events in the history of our twentieth-century Theatre. Sybil Thorndike was a member of the first English Repertory Company in Manchester during the first decade, and Laurence Olivier was appointed director of the National Theatre in 1964. In the intervening years the idea of forming a company of actors, all of first rate quality, to play in more than a single production, working together for the best possible realization of an author's script, especially the classics, became increasingly important by virtue of the results it produced. The stars were often willing to sublimate themselves to create an ensemble and an overall style, but they still imparted to the company their own particular stature. The chart at the back of this book will remind theatregoers that whenever two or more of them came together at the head of a company to play Shakespeare, Chekhov, Sheridan, or Wilde, it was always a memorable occasion.

Revivals of Shakespeare's plays became popular from the early 1930s onwards and they were a strong contributory factor in moulding these actors into the kind of players they eventually became. But without the existence of the Old Vic, it is doubtful if all of them would have reached their full stature. This unique theatre, under the management of Lilian Baylis, was able to offer all of them in turn the right parts at the precise stage in their development when they needed the big Shakespearian roles to stretch their latent powers to the uttermost limits. Once the actor had proved himself in a series of these great parts and a discerning audience had applauded his effort, he never looked back.

Noël Coward contributed a postscript to the series. He talks about his experience of comedy acting with an authority which no other actor can command; his appreciation of his craft is both fundamental and practical. His views, clearly, vividly, and humorously expressed, have intrinsic value, because as an actor Noël Coward is the last of a line of great entertainers who stem from the late Victorian and Edwardian Theatre. The fact that he has recently produced one of his best known comedies, *Hay Fever*, with the National Theatre Company, thereby joining the ranks of the classics, entitles him to have the last word.

Television Centre
May 1967   *Hal Burton*

LAURENCE
OLIVIER

Laurence Olivier, the Director of the National Theatre, talked to Kenneth Tynan, theatre and film critic and Literary Manager of the National Theatre, on the stage of the Old Vic and in a Television Studio. Mr Tynan's comments are in italic.

Can we begin with All Saints Choir School? Acting seems to have been a very important part of the curriculum there.

Yes, yes it was. We had an extremely lively, highly artistic priest on the staff. That church, All Saints, Margaret Street, is a high Anglican Church. It was Anglo-Catholic, as we used to call it in those days. I went there about 1916, I suppose. And the priesthood was likely, in those days, to indulge in the flamboyant. They preached very dramatic sermons, they were very effective, they were a bit theatrical, and they were not in the least bit ashamed of it. It was part of the colour of the denomination as opposed to the rather dull, staid, dark-grey of the nonconformist, the low church, with a very simple altar and a plate in the middle and just possibly two candlesticks, possibly not. But we had six blazoned candlesticks, a crucifix, the Host with a lamp in front of it, and we had everything known that you could possibly extract from the Prayer Book except Benediction. That was not allowed because it wasn't in the Prayer Book. But these lads, these priests, used to love to think that they hob-nobbed with Sybil Thorndike, and of course be overjoyed even to have met Forbes Robertson. The theatre was immensely respectable; Irving gave it a tremendous canopy of respectfulness. The priests of this rather colourful denomination were delighted if they felt there was any talent in their choir, and indeed there was talent. I believe we were about the best choir in London, musically; we certainly had a very good following.

Many famous actors came to see the performances. When you were ten years old Ellen Terry said, 'The boy who plays the part of Brutus is already a great actor.' Do you remember playing Brutus?

Oh yes, I do, I do indeed. My father had a story about Forbes Robertson. I never believed it, but my father used to tell it, so I'll tell it, for what it is worth. He said that he met Forbes Robertson on that occasion and, as he put it, Forbes Robertson had tears in his eyes when my father said, 'My little boy isn't bad, is he?' or something, and he said that Forbes Robertson said, 'My dear man, he *is* Brutus.' Well, I don't see how I can have been at ten. Still . . . Then *she* came, we finally got hold of Ellen Terry. I remember the horror when we were told that Ellen Terry was finally coming to see us, and I piped up in my little schoolboy voice and said, 'Who is Ellen Terry?' It was greeted with terrible laughter by everybody – but I just didn't happen to have heard of the dear old thing.

Your father was a high Anglican clergyman wasn't he? Did he have a great deal of influence on your life?

Oh yes, very much, very much. You see, both my brother and I started at least with a great sense of ritual, because the high Anglican church did all it could in the way of ritual.

It made the services extremely attractive, very romantic. Our first entrée to the altar was when we were 'boat boys', we carried the boat full of incense and marched down in procession beside the thurifer. The ultimate ambition of any acolyte was to be the thurifer, the man who swung the incense and made extraordinary juggling cavortions, occasionally; depending on the height of his theatricality and his nature, he could make the censer do wonderful things if he really chose. From being a boat boy you got to serve the altar and then you got into the choir and, after you'd been in the choir for some years, as a young man, you occasionally went back as an acolyte and became a member of the staff of some church. That happened to me, as a matter of fact; when I was a student at the Albert Hall I was an acolyte, again at All Saints, Margaret Street.

And it was these elaborate rituals, perhaps, that gave you the idea of acting?

plate 33b

Yes, oh yes, and my father's great prowess in the pulpit, like Geoffrey Heald, who produced us in these plays at All Saints, Margaret Street, and who was the Petruchio to my Katharina when we played at Stratford-on-Avon. We must have been very good because we were invited to play a special matinée at Stratford-on-Avon on Shakespeare's birthday itself – that must have been in 1922 – and we played there in the old theatre. I can always show off and boast that I played in the old theatre before it was burnt down.

Did your father approve of your going on the stage?

Well, as a matter of fact my relationship with him had been extremely distant all my youth – I was terrified of him. He was a very frightening father-figure, a Victorian father-figure. I absolutely worshipped and adored my mother who died when I was thirteen years old, and I often think, and say, that perhaps I've never got over it. Anyway, my father had to take over, not knowing me very well. I think to him I was rather an unnecessary child. He could look at my sister eating a lot of porridge and my brother eating a lot of porridge with comparative equanimity, but when I was eating a lot of porridge it annoyed him intensely. My sister says I simply got on his nerves, poor man. I don't blame him at all because I was probably very fat and absolutely brainless. However, when my mother died he had to take care of me; my brother was at school and my sister was, I think, already half-way out in the world. But finally, when my brother went to India as a rubber planter, I was filled with the glamour of what he was doing. When we had seen him off on his boat at Tilbury and got back home to Letchworth where my father was rector, I said, 'Well, when can I follow Dickie out to India, father, please, about one or two years – I don't want to go to the university.' And my father said, 'You're talking nonsense, you're going to be an actor.'

And this was a complete surprise to you?

Yes, it was. I was amazed that he'd thought things out for me at all and that he'd thought things out that far. I secretly knew that he was right, that I ought to be an actor, and I was very surprised that he had the perspicacity, and the observation of my character, to know that finally I was going to be that – no matter what I thought I wanted to be, a priest, a mercantile marine, or anything else.

And so after this direct exhortation from your father you went off to the Central School and there you met an extraordinary woman called Elsie Fogerty. What kind of a woman was she?

A very powerful woman, very powerful. I remember she said two things, one which was quite illuminating, and one brilliantly illuminating, brilliantly observed. I must tell you that it was my last term at my school, which was St Edward's, Oxford, and I had to come up to take the scholarship, because my father assured me that if I didn't get not only the scholarship, but the bursary as well, which was £50, I couldn't go; and I wasn't going to get a start in the theatre at all unless I went to this school first, I was quite sure of that. And so I went up for my examination. The school was in one of those horns at the side as you look at the Albert Hall, the horn on your right was the stage of the school and there were three or four rooms going round each cusp, as it were. And I remember going into the Albert Hall, asking where the Central School was, being directed to it and looking in at the Albert Hall on my way and seeing this enormous arena, and I really thought that afternoon I was going to have to be down there, all by myself, and that the place was going to be full to hear me do my examination. I really thought that, ingenuous and stupid as I was.

However, I made my way to the school and I was perfectly delighted to see that I was only going to be put on a stage which was about ten yards away from where Elsie Fogerty was sitting behind a table, waiting for me to begin. I did the seven ages of man. Afterwards she said, 'Come down, boy, come down', and she sat me beside her and she said 'I think you've got a little too strong an idea of the importance of action.' It's rather funny that anybody could say that about me then, aged seventeen. She said, 'It is not really necessary to make fencing movements when you are saying "Sudden and quick to quarrel".' And then she did a marvellous thing, an unforgettable thing, she said, 'You have a weakness here', and she took her little finger and placed it vertically down the middle of my forehead. It's funny, I must have shown some sort of shyness, and been beetle-browed, and she said, 'You have a weakness here and remember that.' Well, *something* made me slap on all that putty on my face for years and years afterwards, and I dare say it was that.

After the school you began looking for work. Had you any idea then what kind of actor you wanted to be?

No, no, I hadn't honestly. I knew that experience was necessary and that's what I was after. I actually started as a professional before I left the Central School, even in the first holidays. I got a little job in Letchworth, of all places: I was a general understudy and A.S.M., and that sort of thing. I started right away. I was very vague, very vague. I had a sort of burning ambition; I didn't know how to place it or what to do with it. I think possibly one of the most strongly contributing factors towards such an ambition was my upbringing, and although I was treated with immense sweetness, kindness, thoughtfulness, consideration, generosity by all my family, the fact is, I think, that the atmosphere of genteel poverty is probably the most fertile ground for ambition that there can be. 'Because', you seem to say, 'I want to get out, I'm going to get out, when I get out of this I will show them, I will show them, I will show them', without having the faintest idea how you're going to show them or what you're going to show them: I simply had this driving – 'I'm going to be a simply smashing actor.' Probably I wanted emotional parts more than any other because, in those days, one always wanted emotional parts. One assumed all the idiotic opinions of one's colleagues in the school, you know, 'Of course, Gladys Cooper's rotten, of course Gerald can't act.' Actually, Gerald du Maurier, brilliant actor that he was, had the most disastrous influence on my generation, because we really thought, looking at him, that it was easy; and for the first ten years of our lives in the theatre, nobody could hear a word we said. We thought he was being really natural; of course, he was a genius of a technician giving that appearance, that's all.

Your first important job was at Birmingham, wasn't it? The Birmingham Rep.?

That was a very sought-after thing if you were a serious actor. There were two types of actors, one very much less than the other. There was the sort of old boy type of actor, 'Get a jolly good juvenile part, old boy, on the road, old boy, for £12 a week, old boy, that's the life, old chap, and eventually you get forty quid a week, old man.' That was one very strong influence in the theatre, of going into the theatre for what you could get out of it, and for the sort of success you could make, the sort of clothes you could wear, the sort of golf you could afford to play. Now there was a short list of people who were after, dare one say, higher things, and I suppose my nature made me belong to that group, and I was after things like the Birmingham Rep. But I was pretty damn stupid.

I got a job at one time, before I joined Sybil Thorndike – bless her, and bless Lewis Casson, too; they gave me a wonderful chance early on. But before I got to that, I got with a troupe called the Lena Ashwell players. We used to play in swimming baths in Deptford, Ilford, Watford, Islington, Shadwell, paying one's own fares – I was nearly starving getting £2 10s. a week. We had to dress in the cubicles and sometimes in the lavatories, and so we became known as the lavatory players. Well, I had an opportunity with them when I was playing Flavius in *Julius Caesar*. There was a couple of very dreary wreathes pinned to the curtain, and the great thing to do was to tear them down angrily, and, if possible, tear down the curtain as well, to see the naked behinds of the girls dressing at the back: that was a big laugh. And one day Marullus was standing on a little beer box as a rostrum and saying 'Knew you not Pompey', and he had long pants and they came off underneath his toga and folded over this beer box so that he couldn't move, couldn't get off. Well, I laughed so much I had to leave the stage: and the next morning I was fired. Now, you'd think that was warning enough, but no, no, no, not for me. In my first job at Birmingham, two years later, which I would have given my ears to get, where I had dreamt of being, where I knew would be found the absolute foundation of any good that I could ever be in my profession – in my very first part I was nearly fired for giggling. I gagged – stupid little idiot that I was. Thank God, there was a very sweet man at the head of that organization, a great man, Barry Jackson, and he had mercy on me and allowed me to stay. I was very nearly fired.

plate 33d, e   *Among the parts you played there were Uncle Vanya, Tony Lumpkin and Harold in Tennyson's play of that name. Which do you think you were best in?*

Harold was actually at the Court. One of the great advantages of being with Barry Jackson was that he not only had the best repertory theatre (although people who went to Liverpool, Diana Wynyard, Robert Donat, would claim that Liverpool was the best), but he also had three theatres in London, the Royal Court, the Kingsway, and the Regent. The Regent is now a cinema opposite Euston Station but it was accounted a West End theatre. The original production, I believe, in London, of *The Immortal Hour* was at the Regent Theatre. He had these three theatres as well as his own theatre in Birmingham, so one had a very good chance, if one got on at all, of getting a showing in London, and that was one of the main reasons for wanting to go there, apart from the experience you could pick up at the Rep. He also ran tours from all the successes that he had,

plate 33c   like *The Farmer's Wife*. *The Farmer's Wife* had three concurrent tours for five years and, you knew, if you got in there, you weren't going to be out of a job if you were any good at all. Well, Harold was the first part I suppose I played in London. But Uncle

plate 33e   Vanya I played when I was nineteen. I think I must have shown promise and emotional content in my performance.

14

Coming to the West End, you played Stanhope in 'Journey's End' and Beau Geste, which were very showy star parts. It looked at this time as if you were not so much interested in the classics as in being a very successful West End actor. Is there any truth in that?

I couldn't pin my ambition down, it was all over the place. Of course I wanted to be a West End actor, of course I wanted money. I wanted violently to get married, I wanted to have all the earmarks of success; they appealed to me as they appealed to everybody else. I think I sort of knew, you know, without wanting to sound too prophetic, that I was going to climb towards something, to reach some heights, and I knew that the path to such heights was a stony one. But in the meantime I was very happy and content to be a young West End actor of a leading type, as in *Beau Geste*, for instance, and *The Circle of Chalk*. Then a little after that I went to New York and played my first leading part there; it took me a long time, actually, to get round and back to the really serious intention. I think I needed a lick at the luxury of those lush valleys; I needed a taste of that before I really set my face higher up.

On your way up you had a happy association with Noël Coward. You played what's known as the other part in 'Private Lives'. How did you find working with Coward?

plate 34d

Thrilling, very inspiriting. He was terribly funny, very witty. I think Noël probably was the first man who took hold of me and made me think, he made me use my silly little brain. He taxed me with his sharpness and shrewdness and his brilliance, he used to point out when I was talking nonsense, which nobody else had ever done before. He gave me a sense of the balance of right and wrong. He would make me read: I never read anything at all. I remember he said, 'Right, my boy, *Wuthering Heights*, *Of Human Bondage*, and *The Old Wives' Tale* by Arnold Bennett. That'll do, those are the three best. Read them.' I did. I also read *The Forsyte Saga*. I began to read a bit of Dickens. I remember way back Geoffrey Heald, my mentor in the choir school, had said, 'If you're going on the stage, read Dickens, and you'll never lack for a characterization, because you'll read some part in Shakespeare, or by any other author you like, and you'll say, "Oh, that's Mr Snodgrass", or "That's Mr So-and-So", you'll always have a picture, an image in your mind for a make-up or a mannerism or a characteristic.' However, Noël was a tremendous influence, he made me a little bit more sensible than I had been up till then, I think.

Noël did a priceless thing actually, although it sounds a very minor thing. He taught me not to giggle. Now having been fired twice, as I told you, he saw that I was a giggler and said, 'Right, I'll cure you', and he brought me round to his dressing-room one day and said, 'Look, if you ever giggle again, I'm going to make you very sorry indeed. I'm going to train you not to giggle. Now, you've got three months in London, you've got four months in New York with this play. By the end of that time, that's seven months, I'll have cured you.' And he said, 'I'll tell you how I'm going to do it. I'm going to make you giggle. I'm going to make you, make you, make you, make you, make you giggle.' And what he and Gertrude Lawrence didn't get up to, to make me giggle in that breakfast scene at the end of *Private Lives* is nobody's business. For one thing he invented a dog called Roger. . . . Then, when Gertrude Lawrence as Amanda had to splutter over the coffee, I had to slap her too hard on the back. One day she choked and turned round and said, 'You great clob.' And Noël said, 'Clob?' and she said, 'Yes, clob.' And Noël said, 'The man with the clob foot.' You know, it sounds too silly, but on the stage those things are as funny as they are in church.

Wasn't it around that time that Clare Eames said something rather penetrating about your acting?

Well, it was a bit before *Harold*, actually. She gave me, wrought for me, my first notice at the Court Theatre, in a play called *The Adding Machine* by Elmer Rice. I was introduced to Clare by my old friend Denys Blakelock. I went to Clare to study the East Side New York accent, which incidentally I discovered is like no other in the world. And so I made a very careful study of it and I taught a bit of it to Beatrix Lehmann, who was my partner in the play. It was a tiny little scene we had in a graveyard, and Clare had very carefully taught me the accent, absolutely precisely, every word of it. Now my producer, little W. G. Fay, an angelic Irishman, very kind, very good, just didn't understand this accent, kept trying to cure me and said, 'You must stop doing it like that', and I'd say, 'I know how you want it, Mr Fay, I just don't seem to be able to do it', and of course, I went back to it. But that accent fetched a notice from St John Ervine which was a great glorification to me. There was another thing Clare said to me during the process of our acquaintanceship. I used to talk about a straight part or a character part and she said, 'What's the difference? Don't tell me there's such a thing as a straight part. There isn't a part in the world that isn't a character part.' And it was she who gave me that attitude.

Earlier on, you said something about action; you have a reputation for indulging in strenuous physical action on stage whenever you can. Can you remember when you first started that?

I remember first trying it. I was, of course, absolutely swept overboard by Douglas Fairbanks and John Barrymore in films, and indeed, John Barrymore playing Hamlet at the Haymarket was tremendously athletic. I admired that greatly, all of us did. In fact a lot of the silent film stars were very full of muscle and torso; I remember Milton Sills, Ramon Navarro in *Ben Hur* – they all had to show very manly biceps and chest, it was part of their glamour. One thought of oneself, idiotically skinny as I was, as a sort of Tarzan. It appealed to the girls, it gave one a tremendous special kind of glamour. In films, of course, it was all physical glamour, it had to be – Rudolf Valentino, Fairbanks – it was physical prowess, the brilliant use of the sword, the wonderful way of leaping over ridiculous heights, which probably they never used to do at all.

How do you keep yourself fit?

I keep myself very fit now, I have to. I go to a gym twice or three times a week, not merely to look tremendously muscular, but I have to keep fit for my job. I'm determined to hold on to my job. I love it. But it is no use pretending it doesn't involve a certain amount of overwork, because it does. I've seen a lot of contemporaries get a bit under the weather with such work and I'm determined not to. Some idiotic, childish reasoning tells me that a strong body means a strong heart and I daresay it will look after me.

Coming back to 1935, you appeared in a play called 'The Ringmaster', for the first time under your own management. Do you think you're a good manager?

That's a very hard question. It wasn't actually my management, it was Gilbert Miller's, but he made me a partner in it because I bought the play. But for the next play I did, I did have my name over as 'Laurence Olivier presents'. I loved it, sure, but it was my generation's wish to be that; the great ambition was to be an actor-manager, to have the responsibility, in fact to be your own boss, it was as simple as that. Yes, I loved it. I think I'm a fairly good manager now, I've learnt a lot about it. I ran the St James's theatre for eight years. I didn't run that at all well, not at all well. I made mistake after mistake, but I dare say those mistakes taught me something.

16

At that point, in 1935 or thereabouts, did you think your career was a success or a failure?

It was just beginning, you know, it was just sort of turfing up into something. I was directing my first play about then; that was another thing I'd always wanted to do, to direct. About this time, as a matter of fact, an accident happened which made a big difference to me. I had just got engaged by H. M. Tennent and Hugh Beaumont to play in a play by Frederick Lonsdale with Edna Best, and I had obviously been thinking a lot about 'higher things' – you know, Shakespeare. It was beginning to eat at me a bit. My present standard of work, my present kind of work was beginning to dissatisfy me rather violently. And it only took two days of rehearsal of this play to make me give the part up. Now it was a very unfortunate circumstance, it always is when an actor wants to give a part up. He has to rely greatly on the kindness and the understanding of the manager. Well, H. M. Tennent was an awfully good sort of man and the author, Frederick Lonsdale, was extremely kind and I said, 'I'm terribly sorry, I somehow no longer feel this is my sort of work. I don't know why I'm saying this, but I feel I ought to be playing Romeo now.' Actually, I had a sort of ambition to put Romeo on myself. And unfortunately – because it made a difference of opinion and a misunderstanding between Binkie Beaumont [Managing Director of H. M. Tennent Ltd since Tennent's death in 1941] and myself for three or four years – about two days after this happened, Bronson Albery sent for me and said John Gielgud wanted me to alternate with him the parts of Romeo and Mercutio. So it looked as if I knew perfectly well that this was going to happen to *plates 34a, b, 147a, b* me, when I left that other play. It took Binkie years to believe that it just happened to be circumstantial and wasn't really a plan at all.

Which of those two parts did you prefer playing?

Oh, Romeo, Romeo.

That surprises me. I should have thought you were a natural Mercutio.

Well, yes, perhaps that's why. But I saw myself as Romeo; I was fighting a cause when I was playing Romeo. I've admired John Gielgud all my life with complete devotion; I've never thought of myself as quite the same actor as he is, not the same sort of actor. I've always thought that we were the reverses of the same coin, perhaps. I've seen, as if you had a coin, the top half John, all spiritual, all spirituality, all beauty, all abstract things; and myself as all earth, blood, humanity; if you like, the baser part of humanity without that beauty. I've never been so interested in that side, though naturally I've had to develop something of it in order to be an actor at all. But I've always felt that John missed the lower half and that made me go for the other. I suppose I must have sensed a sort of possible rivalry between us, that might last all our lives, I don't know. But whatever it was, when I was playing Romeo I was carrying a torch, I was trying to sell realism in Shakespeare. I believed in it with my whole soul and I believed that Johnny was not doing that enough. I thought that he was paying attention – to the exclusion of the earth – to all music, all lyricism, and I was for the other side of the coin. I dived for that.

Some of your early reviews reflect that. James Agate once said, 'Mr Olivier does not speak poetry badly, he does not speak it at all.' Is that the kind of attitude that you encountered?

Yes, it was. Oh yes, I got terrible notices for it. It shattered me. I remember headlines like 'A beautiful Juliet, *but* . . .' and that sort of thing. But I don't know. I'm not such an ass as to say the critics were all wrong about me, the way they were all wrong about Ibsen or Wagner or anything like that, but it is possible that they were a little wrong. It is possible that I went too far in *my* attitude. But I don't know that I've ever consciously changed and I could, I suppose, sit here and say, 'Well, they've come round to me now, therefore I was right': but it wouldn't be quite honest or true. I'd been taught as a child to make Shakespeare my own language and that's the way I believed it should be, and that's the way it still is with me. But until you can put the reason you are doing something into words, it doesn't offer you quite such a strong belief in it.

plate 35a

It was Michel Saint-Denis who put it into words for me. When I was working with him on *Macbeth* he said, 'It must be absolutely true, and you must find the truth *through* the verse, and you must not discard the verse and pretend it's prose, and you mustn't be carried away by the verse into utter unreality; therefore, you must find the truth *through* the verse.' Cedric Hardwicke once said that theory is the backwash of success, and it's true. If you are successful in something, people ask you how you did it, and you have to find a reason. You might have been perfectly snug and comfortable in the dark about the true reasons for your instincts doing certain things. I remember Charles Laughton

plate 35d

coming and giving me a reason when I was playing *Henry V*, and he came round to my dressing-room and said, 'Do you know why you're so good in this part?' And I said, 'No, please tell me.' And he said, 'You are England, that's all', and so when people came round and said to me, 'Tell me how', I said, 'It's simple, I am England.' It's very useful to know why, in so many words.

plate 35e

In 1937 you accepted an invitation from Tyrone Guthrie to go to the Old Vic, and you opened with a full-length 'Hamlet'. How confident were you? It must have been an awful moment.

Yes, it was. But you know it was all or nothing, it was just all or nothing, and so the only thing to do was to open smack out with a part that I knew I'd be very sternly criticized in. John Gielgud had proved himself to be the Hamlet of his generation and I knew that I was putting myself up in a kind of stupid rivalry. But I thought, if I don't have a bash, I'll never learn anything at all and obviously Hamlet is a part of such enormous length and depth that you're bound to learn something through having played it. After eight weeks of it, you'll probably know a bit more about it than any of the commentators in the variorum; probably, because you've had experience of it. For instance, I had a very sharp lesson on the first night, because in those days we didn't have much time to rehearse at the Old Vic. The rehearsal schedule had to be necessarily rather a short one and I actually faced the audience on the first night of *Hamlet* in its entirety, never having had a run through of the part, never knowing what it was like to go from one scene to another, never having had a chance to teach myself where I should take a rest, where I would need the breath, where I could afford to let myself go.

How did you find that remarkable woman Lilian Baylis?

I took to her at once, she was marvellous. I was dragged along to see her by Tyrone Guthrie, to be presented as a possible leading man, and I went to see her in her office at the Old Vic which is now my dressing-room. I've still got her desk, I got it out of storage for sentiment's sake. She sat behind her desk, the dog in the corner snarling at me; I found that she was perfectly all right, no trouble at all. We got on very well, famously. During the dress rehearsal of *Hamlet*, which went on till five in the morning, I said, 'My thoughts be bloody or be nothing worth.' The rehearsal stopped again and she chuckled from her box and said, 'I bet they couldn't be bloodier than they are, dear boy', or something like that. Our relationship was always very good. She used to come to my dressing-room

18

between the shows and wrap me up in Mrs Sterling's eiderdown to give me good thoughts and that sort of thing. I once came to her with what I thought was a brilliant idea and I said, 'Lilian, I've got an idea; why don't we have a bar in the theatre, that would attract people much more. Why can't we have a bar?' She looked at me as though I'd shot her and said, 'My dear boy, don't you realize if it hadn't been for drunken men beating their wives, we'd never have got this place.'

LAURENCE
OLIVIER

In this production of 'Hamlet' I believe you and Tyrone Guthrie worked out a rather original approach to the character.

Yes. That was inspired by Professor Ernest Jones, who wrote a book, the title of which I'm afraid I can't remember. But it was concerning itself among other things with *Hamlet* in the light of the Oedipus complex. He made a really watertight case about this and we believed in it thoroughly, and although I will not go so far as to say that that's all the play is about now, I did in those days. I thought it was the absolute resolution of all the problems concerning Hamlet. At least, it gave one a central idea which seemed to fill the great vacuum left by all the crossed ideas about Hamlet, what he really was, what he really wasn't, whether he was a man of action, whether he wasn't a man of action. He could safely be a man of action under the auspices of that particular idea, that he couldn't kill the king because, subconsciously of course, he was guilty himself. Although I now think there are many more things in *Hamlet* than that, I still would stay with the idea that, if there is such a thing as the Oedipus complex, which we know perfectly well there is, it was not entirely absent from the royal court of Denmark.

That means leaving out the political side of the play. Did you find that you had to bend the text to accommodate the Oedipus complex?

Oh no, not in the very least. In the film, of course, it was editing rather than bending the text. It had to be brought down to two and a half hours from four and a half hours, and that makes an enormous difference to the content. Of course, you can't reach it entirely, you can't get the whole marvellous majestical sweep of the play, you can't get the same tremendous effect out of it as an audience can, having seen it in its entirety, because, in its entirety, it has a much better rhythm than if it's cut. As for the film, I know I was criticized for spending so much time going up staircases and all that sort of thing, but you do feel a need, in making a film, of pictorial introductions to sequences. It's a long time ago, 1947, and it was very much the way of films in those days.

But you aren't really a contemplative or philosophical actor. Was that why you cut so many of the soliloquies in the film?

No, no. Let me say this. When I made *Henry V* I really thought I was inventing a new form of entertainment, by using Shakespeare in the way I did in that film. When I made *Hamlet* I was determined to be much more of a film-maker than I had been in *Henry V*. How successful I was, God knows, but the soliloquy I cut out then, to my horror or rather my sadness, was, 'How all occasions do inform against me', and I cut it out with infinite regret, because to me it's far the most valuable soliloquy in the whole play. He says to the audience, 'Ladies and gentlemen, I can't do this and I don't know why.' And therefore it's the most valuable indication of what's in his heart. I cut it out in the film because I was trying to be a film-maker, and I was more keen to make good film than good Shakespeare. I thought it was the right way round, probably mistakenly, I don't know. But I cut it out – I'd already shot it, but I cut it out from the final cut – because,

19

from a film-maker's point of view, it was not the time to get discursive, and so I cut it for that purely filmic reason.

Suppose we go back again to 1937. How did you get on with Tyrone Guthrie as a director?

Oh, very well, very well indeed. There are different kinds of directors. People who direct actors have different ideas as to what their part really is. When I was young, the director was very much of a martinet, rather a colonel, or a sergeant-major who roars.

Like Basil Dean?

Yes, Basil Dean. We felt, all of us, that he was very, very unkind to us, and we were very frightened of him. Actually he wouldn't harm a fly, but he managed to get his effects out of us. I don't think he was ever happy unless he had the leading lady in tears at least once a day. Certainly he nearly had me in tears, when he was rehearsing me, several times. But, bless his heart, not that he meant any harm; it was his way of going about it and sometimes it works, sometimes it's good. I'm rather grateful for that bit of education now, because sometimes you've got an actor or an actress and you think, 'Well, nothing's happening, have to try this old-fashioned business on them'; and I've seen it work occasionally, quite well, even today. Then there is the sort of director in whom you have complete faith. I remember the first time I worked with Michel Saint-Denis, he struck me like that. I thought, 'I'll believe in you, boy, whatever you say, I'll believe in you.' *plate 35a* He directed me in my first *Macbeth* in 1937, and for him, for me, for Lilian Baylis, for the Old Vic, for everybody concerned, it was utter disaster. But in spite of that, when he *plate 36d* came to direct me in *Oedipus Rex* eight years later, again I found myself just putting myself in his hands, delighted to be. I still had utter faith; and that time, of course, it had a very splendid result.

Which of the two sorts of director was Guthrie?

Guthrie was much more the next sort of director, a companion, a partner; and although he had brilliant conceptions of crowd scenes, of shape, of grouping, of pace, of those sort of external things, he never seemed to touch the heart of the matter very much except symbolically. He seemed to me, in those days, to be a wee bit nervous of the intimacies, a bit shy of great human emotion. I may be misjudging him, but I remember in *Henry V* he would say to me and Jessica Tandy, 'You two go and do the love scene by yourselves, will you, I can't be bothered with that.' All I know is that finally, through friendship, I discovered him to be a marvellous person and on one occasion he gave me the most priceless bit of advice I've ever had from anybody, and that was a great surprise to me. Guthrie and John Burrell had restarted the Old Vic and Ralph Richardson and I opened *plate 37b* our first play, *Arms and the Man*, at the Opera House, Manchester. Ralph and I had been got out of the Navy in order to do this work, and we opened and it was all right. The next day Ralph and I went along to the pub, next to the stage door, and we had half a pint, or something. On the way back he bought a paper and, looking over Ralph's shoulder going along the street towards the Midland Hotel, I remember seeing, 'Mr Ralph Richardson was a brilliant Bluntschli. Mr Laurence Olivier, on the other hand...', and I thought, 'That's it. That's it. I've had this now for nearly twenty years. I'm going back to the Navy. I can't stand it. . . . I cannot stand criticism, I can't bear it any more.' Well, that night Tony Guthrie came to see the performance, and as we came out of the stage door and turned the corner underneath the canopy outside the theatre Tony, from his great height, looked down at me and said, 'Liked your Sergius very much.' And I snarled and said, 'Oh, thank you very much, too kind, I'm sure.' And he said, 'No, no. Why, what's the matter?' And I said, 'Well, really, don't ask . . . no, please.' And he said, 'But don't you love Sergius?' And I said, 'Look, if you weren't so tall, I'd hit you. How do you mean, how can you love a part like that, a stupid, idiot part? Absolutely nothing to do but to conform, to provide the cues for Shaw's ideas of what was funny at the time. How can you possibly enjoy or like a part like that?' And he said, 'Well, of course, if you can't love Sergius, you'll never be any good in him, will you?' Well, it clicked, and something happened, I suppose, that gave me a new attitude, perhaps an attitude that had been completely lacking in me, up to that time, towards the entire work of acting.

In those first two seasons at the Old Vic before the war you played, amongst other things, Henry V, Macbeth, Iago, and Coriolanus, and Coriolanus was acclaimed as a great performance. Did you think it was your best performance of the series?

plates 34, 35

No. I'd obviously got much more proficient by that time. I'd been on the stage now thirteen years, and I think my voice had got quite good in that time. Coriolanus doesn't require very great cerebral heights in the artist performing him. He's a very straightforward, reactionary son of a so-and-so and it's quite easy to get on to him, his thoughts are not deep. You've just got to appreciate what he is and make quite sure that he is a patrician first and foremost, and that his pride is of the nature that he is too proud even to accept praise. I'd got quite a lot of spunk and guts in the way I marched on to the stage and if I fell about and did somersaults they were quite well done. I think, honestly, the critics thought it was about time they were kind to me.

Eighteen years later, at Stratford, you did a new version of 'Macbeth' and, four years after that, of 'Coriolanus'. Did you change your approach to the parts at all?

Not in *Coriolanus*. I had a very brilliant director, Peter Hall, working with me. I don't know if anybody noticed any difference at all – how could they remember eighteen years before? We found what we thought were a few secrets about the part and it was chiefly these – the business of his not being able to accept praise, a fault in him of pride. In rehearsal we dolled around with the idea that he was not even a good soldier, that he was a phoney: we discarded that idea. He must have been a good soldier or nobody would ever have followed him into battle. He must have been a successful soldier, because he was incapable, through a false pride, of accepting success in the normal human manner.

plate 36b

But *Macbeth* is another problem altogether. I don't care how bosh a shot you have at it. I mean if you're twenty-seven years old you can't do it, although you can recite it, you can go through the motions, you can give them a hell of a fight at the end, you can reach all sorts of poetic passages perhaps. You can reach the humanities to a certain degree, but only to a certain degree, because you have to be of a certain age of life's experience to play parts as enormous as that; you have to know about humanity, you have to know a lot about human relationships. *Macbeth* is a domestic tragedy. You must understand and perceive that Macbeth knows at once, the minute he sees the first witch he knows what's going to happen. The interesting part of the play is that the man has imagination and the woman has none. The man sees it all, she does not. That's what gives her the enormous courage to plot the whole thing, force him into it, persuade him, cajole him, bully him, tease him into it. And he allows himself gradually, bit by bit, to be teased into it. But he knows the answer, he knows the result, and she doesn't. It's the passage of two

plate 36a

people, one going up and one going down. And there comes a moment in the play when he looks at her and he realizes that she can't take it any more, and he goes on and she goes down.

When I saw the performance, it seemed to me that your Macbeth was a guilty man long before he killed Duncan. He was consumed with his own guilt, and, by killing Duncan, almost overcame his guilt, and was able to become a much more powerful monster.

Yes, in a way he knew, he knew. Another thing time gives you is more chance to think about things, to work things out in any Shakespearian tragedy. For instance, we worked it out that it was perfectly obvious that, as Lady Macbeth says about the king 'If he had not resembled my father as he lay', Duncan was her father's brother, so that she really was in direct line of succession. And probably the moot, or whatever they were called in Scotland in those days, turned her down because she was only a snip of a girl. They said 'We can't give the crown to her, we'd better give it to the brother'; that happened constantly in those days. But she was in direct line of succession, I'm sure. She then marries the splendid young Montgomery of the time and they would have shared the pillow with many an intimate thought, 'Of course, dear, you're the fellow who ought to be the next king and, after all, I'm the daughter of the last one.' When they first meet Lady Macbeth says to her husband, 'Your face, my thane, is as a book, where men may read strange matters.' They've talked about it and so when he tries to put it off, he says, 'We will speak further'; it's something they both know about. We also had in that production a bit of business which I think was a little illuminating. When Macbeth came on to Duncan, he and Banquo together having won their great battle against the Thane of Cawdor, there was a coronet on the pillow; and as we came on, I looked at it and sort of registered, 'Oh, already, fine.' Then it goes to Duncan's son as the Prince of Cumberland: blow between the eyes. But he knows, and as I say, the minute he sees the first witch, he knows the end of the story, I'm quite sure.

There was a lot of physical infighting in that part. Which of the big classical roles involves the most physical strain?

That's one of the worst. Titus Andronicus is an enormous strain, Richard III is a very big physical strain. It depends upon the loading that the author gives one. Othello is the worst because of the loading.

How do you mean, loading?

Well, in the easiest of the great parts – and when I say easy, don't misunderstand me: Hamlet, although it's enormously long, is so placed in the play that he's given a few rests, he hardly ever has to cap climax upon climax – in *Othello*, for instance, in the second half of *Othello*, you have the big scene about the handkerchief, a little rest, then almost at once you're right into an enormous scene finishing up in the fit. You go straight on from the fit to Desdemona's entrance and to the slapping of the face, straight from that to the greatest scene of all, the scene where he screams at her and calls her a strumpet. Now, that is an abominable strain. It's said, rather jokingly, that the author said to Richard Burbage, 'Now, I'm going to write a part that you really can't play', and it does seem almost impossible sometimes.

You once wrote, 'However much an actor may loathe a character, he must try to comprehend the cause of his evil. It is no good being so horrified that he rejects the character out of hand, he must have a real

*knowledge of the human heart and must promote its understanding.' Have you found it difficult to find
aspects of yourself in the evil characters you've played?*

If somebody asked me to put in one sentence what acting was, I should say that acting
was the art of persuasion. The actor persuades himself, first, and through himself, the
audience. In order to achieve that, what you need to make up your make-up is observation and intuition. At the most high-faluting, the actor is as important as the illuminator
of the human heart, he is as important as the psychiatrist or the doctor, the minister if
you like. That's putting him very high and mightily. At the opposite end of the pole you've
got to find, in the actor, a man who will not be too proud to scavenge the tiniest little bit
of human circumstance; observe it, find it, use it some time or another. I've frequently
observed things, and thank God, if I haven't got a very good memory for anything else,
I've got a memory for little details. I've had things in the back of my mind for as long as
eighteen years before I've used them. And it works sometimes that, out of one little thing
you've seen somebody do, something causes you to store it up. In the years that follow
you wonder what it was that made them do it, and, ultimately, you find in that the
illuminating key to a whole bit of characterization.

I suppose it was your performance of 'Richard III' at the Old Vic, towards the end of the war, that *plate 37a*
*set you on the summit of our classical drama. Did you know at the time that it was going to be one of
the key performances of your career?*

No, no. A lot of things contributed to it. One thing that may lead an actor to be successful
in a part, not always, but it may, is to try to be unlike somebody else in it. At the time
when I first began to think about the part Donald Wolfit had made an enormous success
as Richard only eighteen months previously. I didn't want to play the part at all, because
I thought it was much too close to this colleague's success. I had seen it, and when I was
learning it I could hear nothing but Donald's voice in my mind's ear, and see nothing
but him in my mind's eye. And so I thought, 'This won't do, I've just got to think of
something else.' And it was the childishly approached differences, really, that started me
on a characterization that, without comparing it with Donald's at all, at least made it
different. I think any actor would understand this desire on my part not to look the same
as another actor. Now this can get you very wrong sometimes, and land you in very hot
water indeed; at other times it may land you on to a nice fertile beach, thank you very
much.

First of all I had heard imitations of old actors imitating Henry Irving; and so I did,
right away, an imitation of these old actors imitating Henry Irving's voice – that's why
I took a rather narrow kind of vocal address. Then I thought about looks. And I thought
about the Big Bad Wolf, and I thought about Jed Harris, a director under whom I'd
suffered *in extremis* in New York. The physiognomy of Disney's original Big Bad Wolf was
said to have been founded upon Jed Harris – hence the nose, which, originally, was very
much bigger than it was finally in the film. And so, with one or two extraneous externals,
I began to build up a character, a characterization. I'm afraid I do work mostly from the
outside in. I usually collect a lot of details, a lot of characteristics, and find a creature
swimming about somewhere in the middle of them.

Perhaps I should mention now what everybody's been talking about for years, and
that's the Actors' Studio and the Method. What I've just said is absolutely against their
beliefs, absolute heresy. And it may be, as long as you achieve the result of, don't let's
call it naturalism, don't even let's call it realism, let's call it truthfulness, that it doesn't

matter which method you use. But in exercises like Shakespeare or Greek tragedy it is an enormous task, because you've got so many facets, so many angles and so many considerations to contend with, in order to achieve the reality or the truthfulness that is necessary. Some people start from the inside, some people start from the periphery. I would say, at a guess, that Alec Guinness is what we would call a peripheral actor. I think I'm the same. The actor who starts from the inside is more likely to find himself in the parts he plays, than to find the parts in himself; perhaps not necessarily in himself, but simply to find the parts, go out to them and get them, and *be* somebody else.

Who would you say was a typical example of the interior method?

Well, I think personally that most film actors are interior people. It is necessary for them to be so truthful under the extraordinary microscopic perception of the camera; it's very seldom that you get a film actor who dares to characterize very thickly.

Since we're talking about externals, which do you regard as your most important physical attribute, your voice, your hands, your eyes, which?

Well, once upon a time you asked me that question and I said the eyes. That was some years ago. It depends what you are – really it's a fusion of every single part of you that has to go into it. The mime actor doesn't need the voice; the film actor hardly needs the voice, hardly needs the body, except to use it as a marvellous physical specimen in such roles as demand that attribute. The stage actor certainly needs the voice, certainly needs all the vocal control, all the breath control, all the techniques of the voice, certainly needs all the miming power imaginable, certainly needs the hands, certainly needs the eyes – he needs them all.

When you were playing Richard, was there a moment when you knew you were there, that all was set fair for your future?

Well, I'd been on the stage now for twenty years. I'd just finished making *Henry V* and, I don't know how, or why, I just went into it with the same distrust of the critics, the same fear of public opinion as I had always experienced. I went on to the stage frightened, heart beating, came on, locked the door behind me, approached the footlights and started. And I – I just simply went through it. I don't think anybody in the company believed in the project at all. I think everybody was rather in despair about the whole production. And nobody particularly believed in my performance, none of us particularly believed in any of our performances; I don't think even our producer, John Burrell, believed in *plates 37b, 74a, b* it much. In the first three plays which we presented, Ralph Richardson had brought *Peer Gynt* off brilliantly, *Arms and the Man* was a success on its own, and now there was this rather poor relation, with a part that people had seen quite a lot of. And so I didn't know – I didn't know; I was just once more going to have, as we say, a bash. I had developed this characterization, and I had got a lot of things on my side, now I come to think of it, from the point of view of timeliness. One had Hitler over the way, one was playing it definitely as a paranoiac, so that there was a core of something to which the audience would immediately respond. I fancy, I may be quite wrong, but I fancy I possibly filled it out, possibly enriched it a bit with a little more humour than a lot of other people had done, but I'm not sure about that. I only know that I read a few notices, stayed up till three and drank a little bit too much.

My next performance was the next-day matinée, for which I was all too ill-prepared. But there was something in the atmosphere. There is a phrase – the sweet smell of success

– and I can only tell you (I've had two experiences of that), it just smells like Brighton and oyster-bars and things like that. And as I went down to the prompt corner, darling Diana Boddington, my stage manager, and still one of our stage managers at the National, sort of held out her hand and said, 'It's marvellous, darling', or something like that, and I said, 'Oh, is it?', and as I went on to the stage – the house was not even full – I felt this thing. I felt for the first time that the critics had approved, that the public had approved, and they had created a kind of grapevine, and that particular audience had felt impelled to come to see me. It was an overwhelming feeling, a head-reeling feeling, and it went straight to my head. I felt the feeling I'd never felt before, this complete confidence. I felt, if you like, what an actor must finally feel: I felt a little power of hypnotism; I felt that I had them. It went to my head, as I said, to such an extent that I didn't even bother to put on the limp. I thought, I've got them anyway, I needn't bother with all this characterization any more. It's an awful story really.

You said there was another occasion when you felt this whiff in the air. When was that?

That was after *The Entertainer*. It was when we'd finished the run at the Court and we revived it a few months later at the Palace, and my dear old friend George Relph and I went down to the theatre together, walked on to the stage and said together, 'Smell it, it's okay.'

plate 40d

In the 1945–6 season there was 'Oedipus' and I can remember a notice I wrote in which I tried to answer some of your critics who were saying that you had tricks, vocal mannerisms and physical mannerisms. I said that these tricks might exist, but that they were unique and only you could pull them off. Do you think you have mannerisms?

I'd like not to think so, of course. I know I have because I see them, and when they're pointed out I feel them. But what are mannerisms? Mannerisms are cushions of protection which an actor develops against his own self-consciousness. An actor comes on to the stage on a first night and hangs his head, or does something or other, and for that second it's a comfort to him, it gives him a little moment of reality at this terrifying moment; and it goes into the works. In the future, if he's not very careful, he resorts to it on any first night, and those things collect and collect up, and you've got about twenty-four, thirty-seven things that you finally can't do without. Those are mannerisms.

One of them, for instance, is your habit of lilting an upward inflection at the end of a line, like 'God for Harry, England and St George' in 'Henry V', when your voice suddenly soars up. It's very exciting.

I don't think that was for any feeling of protection. I thought it was a good thing to do; I probably thought it was exciting. You must remember that parts of that size are not usually parts into which you can segregate any one part of your personality. I did do a very special, rather limited characterization in *Richard III*, that thin voice and all that, in order to present myself in an entirely different light from anything else I was doing that season. But Shakespeare, as a rule, does not tolerate a very sharp light thrown across his work. You get into great trouble if you think of a special or topical theme for a Shakespearian production; he just doesn't tolerate it. I remember Michael Redgrave once did a very brave and courageous thing at Stratford: he played Richard II as an out-and-out queer with all the effeminate mannerisms. He simply said, 'Richard II was a homosexual, in my opinion, and I'm going to play it like that.' Well, it worked, it worked brilliantly; but I don't think, and I've never talked to him about this, that it worked all the way

plate 118c

25

through, because at the end Shakespeare says of Richard III, Richard II, Hotspur and a lot of parts you could have taken a very sharp characteristic slant upon, 'I'm not tolerating that, you're now going to become St George.' So you can't do it, you have to stop all that characterization.

Did you ever find that you had to change your performances when you translated a Shakespearian character from stage to screen?

Not very much. Only out of respect for the technique of the medium, I think.

Now let's talk about 'Othello'. At the beginning you were very reluctant to play the part at all. Why was that?

plate 37d

Well, I knew it was a terror. I knew from past experience that it was almost impossible. When I was on tour in Europe one time doing *Titus Andronicus*, and Anthony Quayle was playing Aaron, we had a little interval together, about five minutes. It was very hot in that part of Europe and we didn't bother to go to our dressing-rooms, with those huge stages, we sat at the back on a sofa and used to talk a little bit, gossip a little bit. One day he said to me, 'Is this a very bad one for you, this Titus Andronicus?' and I said, 'Yes, awful, awful,' and I said, 'But you've played Macbeth too. I think you'll agree that Macbeth is the worst.' And he said, 'You haven't done the black one yet, have you?' And I said, 'No – why? Is that terrible?' He said, 'Terrible. The worst parts, the most difficult ones to bear, are the ones that are complaining all the time, the ones that moan. Macbeth is all right because he is positive,' he said, 'but you know what you hate about Titus, he's always going "oh, oh, oh, look at – fancy them doing that to me, oh, oh, oh." And how many ways are there of saying 'oh, oh'. It's very tough on your imagination, it's very tough on your resourcefulness of variations of all kinds, and, therefore, it's also a very great strain physically. He said, 'Othello is all of that and you have to black up as well.'

plate 77c

You'd been involved in the play just before the war when Ralph Richardson played Othello and you played Iago. Was there anything off beat about that production?

Yes, very much indeed. Tony Guthrie and I, as I told you before, had studied the works of Professor Jones. Now Professor Jones was quite sure that it wasn't the Oedipus complex. The trouble was the part of Iago, not the part of Othello. Nobody has ever really disputed what makes up Othello, but they've certainly wondered about Iago, what makes him such a thoroughly beastly fellow as he is; and Jones's theory was that Iago was subconsciously in love with Othello. Well, Tony Guthrie and I were completely sold on this idea. Ralph wouldn't hear of it at all. However, there came one moment in rehearsal, so the story goes, and I don't remember this, but this is the story that is told – that losing all control of myself, I flung my arms round Ralph's neck and kissed him. Whereat Ralph, more in sorrow than in anger, sort of patted me and said, 'Dear fellow, dear boy', much more pitying me for having lost control of myself than despising me for being a very bad actor.

plates 38c, 39c

When you came to play Othello yourself, did you feel physically equipped for it in every respect?

No, I didn't. That was another thing that had troubled me. I didn't think that I had the voice for it. But I did go through a long period of vocal training especially for it, to increase the depth of my voice, and I actually managed to attain about six more notes in the bass. I never used to be able to sing below D, but now, after a little exercising, I can get down to A, through all the semitones; and that helps at the beginning of the play, it helps the violet velvet that I felt was necessary in the timbre of the voice. And then, from the physical point of view, I went through, and I still do, a very severe physical training course.

What was there in your conception of the part that made it different from the conventional Othellos that we're used to seeing?

Well, you know that very rough estimate of the theme of Shakespearian tragedy. It's constantly said that Shakespearian tragedy is founded by Shakespeare upon the theme of a perfect statue of a man, a perfect statue; and he shows one fissure in the statue, and how that fissure makes the statue crumble and disappear into utter disorder. From that idea you get that Othello is perfect except that he's too easily jealous; that Macbeth is perfect except that he's too ambitious; that Lear is perfect except that he's too bloody-minded, too pigheaded; that Coriolanus is too proud; that Hamlet lacks resolution; and so on. But there seems to me, and there has grown in me a conviction over the last few years, that in most of the characters, not all, but in most of them, that weakness is accompanied by the weakness of self-deception, as a companion fault to whatever fault may be specified by the character in the play. It's quite easy to find in Othello, and once you've found it I think you have to go along with it; that he sees himself as this noble creature. It's so easy in the senate scene for you to present the absolutely cold-blooded man who doesn't even worry about marital relations with his wife on his honeymoon night, to reassure the senate that he's utterly perfect, pure beyond any reproach as to his character, and you can find that, and trace it, constantly throughout. He's constantly wishing to present himself in a certain light, even at the end, which is remarkable. I believe, and I've tried to show, that when he says 'Not easily jealous' it's the most appalling bit of self-deception. He's the most easily jealous man that anybody's ever written about. The minute he suspects, or thinks he has the smallest grounds for suspecting, Desdemona, he wishes to think her guilty, he wishes to. And the very first thing he does, almost on top of that, is to give way to the passion, perhaps the worst temptation in the world, which is murder. He immediately wants to murder her, immediately. Therefore he's an extremely hot-blooded individual, an extremely savage creature who has kidded himself and managed to kid everybody else, all this time, that he's nothing of the kind. And if you've got that, I think you've really got the basis of the character. Lodovico says it for us: 'Is this the noble Moor . . . whom passion could not shake. . . . I am sorry that I am deceived in him.'[1]

There is also a sense of a caged animal in your performance. I remember writing that you communicate more than almost any actor I know a sense of danger, you feel at any moment that the great paw may lash out and someone's going to get hurt. Are you conscious of this power you have over audiences – and over other actors for that matter?

I'm not very conscious of the workings of it. I feel consciousness of the desirability of having that ingredient in my work, very much so. *Othello*, of course, screams for it. It's the only play in the whole of Shakespeare in which a man kills a woman, and if Shakespeare gets an idea he goes all out for it; he knows very well that for a black man to kill a white woman is a very big thrill indeed, to the audience, and he doesn't pull any punches. As an alchemist Shakespeare gets hold of that one all right. Therefore, if you feel that thing in yourself, that sort of easily released or closely guarded animal inside you, you must use it in this part of all parts.

[1]*Othello*, IV, i, 275, 277, 293.

Perhaps we'd better move on to your excursions into contemporary plays. Things like 'The Sleeping Prince' by Terence Rattigan, John Osborne's 'The Entertainer', Ionesco's 'Rhinoceros', and 'Semi-detached'.

plate 40b, c, d I absolutely adored them all, particularly *The Entertainer*. I think it's the most wonderful part that I've ever played. I loved *Rhinoceros* a little less well. I didn't find it quite such a good work. It was very interesting, very interesting and I was just mad for it because it was another modern part. I adored *Semi-detached*.

Why do you think it wasn't a success?

I like to think it wasn't my fault, but it may well have been. I think it was a very cruel play, and I remember coming moaning to you once and saying, 'I don't know why it is they don't like this piece', and you said, 'Well, it's extremely cruel and you are making the audience suffer, and that's the idea of the play; but you can't always do that and get away with it.'

What I meant was that it was the first time you'd played a complete swine without any redeeming charm or pathos.
Are there any actors who have had a particular influence on you?

Yes, lots of them. I've mentioned Fairbanks and Barrymore whose *Hamlet* I first saw when I was seventeen years old. Noël Coward in his way influenced me a great deal, he taught me a very stern professionalism. Alfred Lunt taught me an enormous amount, by watching him, in the field of really naturalistic acting; he had astonishing gifts, an astonishing virtuosity in overlap, marvellous. That was when I first saw him in 1929 in *Caprice* at the St James's Theatre.

Overlap meaning what?

Oh, overlapped conversations with his wife, Lynn Fontanne. They must have rehearsed it for millions of years, it was delicious, absolutely delicious to watch, and they carried on their own tradition in that way for many, many years. Valentino made me see that narcissism is important. Of all the people I've ever watched with the greatest delight, I think, in another field entirely, was Sid Field. I wouldn't like anybody to think that I was imitating Sid Field when I was doing *The Entertainer*.

Well, there were little things in it.

Little things, but Sid Field was a great comic and Archie Rice was a lousy one. But I know when I imitate Sid Field to this day, I still borrow from him freely and unashamedly. I watch all my colleagues very carefully, admire them all for different qualities. I think the most interesting thing to see is that an actor is most successful when not only all his virtues but all his disadvantages come into useful play in a part. The man who, I think, gave me the best sort of thoughts about acting was my friend Ralph Richardson. I watch Rex Harrison for timing. I watch all my colleagues for different qualities that I admire, and I imitate them and copy them unashamedly.

You talked about actors using their disadvantages. Which of your own qualities, for instance, do you dislike most as a person?

Well, I've got an awful way of flinging my hands about which I detest, and I try to control it. But sometimes, as I say, sometimes a part requires all you've got, weaknesses and all, and I just let myself go; I let it all happen and hope for the best.

Talking about narcissism, are you competitive as an actor?

Not with anybody else on the stage, and not with younger actors or anything like that. No, no, no, I never feel that. I never have been, I'm glad to say; I'm very thankful for it. No, the teamwork on the stage is a great essential to me. The actors must understand each other, know each other, help each other, absolutely love each other: must, absolutely must.

How aware are you of other actors on stage, of what they're doing, where they are, how their performances are going?

Oh, very much, very much. You can upset each other without meaning to very easily. If you suddenly have a mental aberration and forget a line, or forget a word, and you see it's upset the actor, it upsets you too. And, sure enough, if one actor starts drying up, another will and another, it becomes a sort of round the company drying up; it catches on like a terrible disease. I couldn't act competitively with anybody. I couldn't do the thing that Kean did to Macready and act him off the stage. I think it would be terribly wrong and I don't think I would have the power to do it anyway.

In an unguarded moment you once said that you need to be a bit of a bastard to be a star. Is that true?

Well, I think that came out of the fact that, at one time, I may have thought that somebody lacked the necessary *edge* to be a star. I think you've got to have a certain edge, that might be traced to being a bit of a bastard, inside. You've got to be a bit of a bastard to understand bastards, and you've got to understand everybody. I think the most difficult equation to solve is the union of the two things that are absolutely necessary to an actor. One is confidence, absolute confidence, and the other an equal amount of humility towards the work. That's a very hard equation.

Do you think actors ought to be influenced at all by their private convictions and political ideas? For instance, would you accept a really first-rate part in an anti-negro play?

Only if, in the character concerned, I was able to show something that was true about people, and that's quite possible. I wouldn't like politics to take hold of a play more directly, more obviously, than is done by Anton Chekhov, the great prophet of the revolution. But the way he did it was always an illumination of the human heart, to show the people the knowledge of themselves more clearly, a little sadly, a little despairingly. But he doesn't go out and make red, black, white, or blue win, or anything like that, or say they're right or wrong.

Are there any major parts, Shakespeare or others, that you'd still like to have a crack at?

No, no, there aren't. really. It sounds very self-satisfied. I don't mean to sound like that, but the fact is that, as you said, I have got other work. I think that work gives me enough opportunity to do what I'm able to do. As one gets older, quite naturally, one's range becomes more limited. I mean age does show, we can't help that. If you're a kid of seventeen you can't play King Lear properly – you might make a very good shot at it, but if you're a kid of fifty-eight then I'm afraid you can't play Romeo any more; therefore the field does narrow. It's bound to narrow as the grey hairs creep in or they disappear altogether. Your limitations are bound to show more, therefore you're more inclined not to bother so much about carving yourself up into different facets, to suit different characterizations when different characterizations aren't going to be all that different. I'm afraid, as time goes on, one's ambitions are necessarily narrowed by Dame Nature.

You developed into the kind of actor you are when there were no real permanent ensembles, subsidized ensembles, in this country. Do you think you would have developed in the same way if you had joined a company of that kind when you were beginning?

Well, in a way, from time to time, that has been so with me. I was with the Birmingham Rep. for two seasons. I was at the Old Vic for two years. I was with Ralph Richardson, engaged on work for the Old Vic at the New Theatre, for five years, when we tasted the blessings of a permanent troupe. When a foreign company, such as the Moscow Art Theatre, which is used to the idea of a permanent ensemble, arrives upon our shores, and we see their work, it is that hot breath of unity that always seems to me to be more important than the star system. Ultimately it is more important to an audience than the star system, though goodness knows how many years it's going to take us to make that clear to them.

When you were asked to be director of the National Theatre, was this the first thought in your mind, to create that sort of company?

Yes, oh yes, because I had, in smaller ways, formed companies before. Next to directing a film, which I'm sorry to have to say is the most exciting thing I've ever done, next to that, forming a company, helping it along, serving it, leading it if you like, but not necessarily so, is the most exciting thing a man can do.

But just a minute. You've suddenly thrown a bit of a bombshell by saying that directing a film is the most exciting thing of all. Why is that?

Well, I suppose for a craftsman, who is always all the time made conscious that his craft is purely interpretive, who isn't given the opportunity to create, except in so far as the author will allow him to create within the precincts of the character that he has drawn for him, I suppose being a film director is the nearest one gets to feeling like a creator, because the film is entirely the director's medium.

At the Old Vic, of course, you're an administrator and an actor and you direct plays. Do you find being an administrator interferes with the active theatrical work?

I think I act and direct all I need to, all I want to. I love the job. I was very frightened of it when I started it, but I looked around as honestly as I could, and I hope without self-deception, and thought perhaps I was the fellow with the best sort of experience to start the thing going. I was determined that there should be a National Theatre in our country. I think that a National Theatre is probably the only way of making the theatre a part of people's lives. It will take a bit of time. It's easier for the ballet or the opera to win to itself an audience. There are certainly people who will only go to see the ballet if Fonteyn or Nureyev are dancing, and there are people who will only go to see the opera if Tito Gobbi is singing; but there are quite a wadge of people who will go, because they love opera, because they love ballet; and television does not quite obliterate the need for them to see these media. Now the theatre is served, or drama is served, more constantly by television than any other form of expression; they switch it on and there's always a play or a film. If a big star is playing in the theatre, they'll go to see the star, but they don't feel the same urge, the same necessity, to see drama for drama's sake.

30

Now my earliest feelings about acting were suffused with an intense wish to fascinate the public in the art of acting. I suppose when I was seven years old I found it the biggest fun, the idea of pretending to be somebody else, of making an audience believe that I was somebody else: it was a fascinating idea, a very childish one, but it fascinated me. And I suppose most of my young life was concerned with trying to fox people, who came in to see me at the Birmingham Repertory Theatre, that I was quite a different chap from the chap they saw last week. No doubt that encouraged a lot of use of putty, noses, whiskers, all sorts of paraphernalia; but I think it was really a genuine wish to make an audience watch an actor as keenly, and with as much interest and enthusiasm and fascination, as they watch a player on the soccer field, or as they watch a billiard champion, or as they watch a boxer.

Is there a special sort of actor you were looking for when you formed the National Theatre Company?

Very good ones, very good ones. Versatile ones; people who had their heart in the right place; unlazy ones, deeply enthusiastic, courageous, gifted with all sorts of attributes. I must say that the nature of the work, as I said before, does demand physical – not perfection, but physical prowess. It does demand great strength, much more than people think. It demands much more physical tone. When you get an actor who is gifted with immense strength, his co-ordination is so much better than a weedy type of actor. We've got an actor, Colin Blakeley; he played Philoctetes in a Greek tragedy which didn't succeed very well. But to see this man put one foot up on a rostrum above him, and get up like a lion in the most wonderful gesture of his body, that's the sort of thing we ought to be able to do, to be very physically adept.

The younger actors in the company – do you ever find any difference of approach between them and you?

Well, I suppose if they come into our company now, they look about them, see how the land lies, and try to fit in. They're not going to start, their very first week, by trying to create a revolution. No, I found it much more in America where, as I say, they've got an extremely difficult attitude, due to this revolution in thoughts on the drama, created by Lee Strasburg and the Actors' Studio. Lots of such revolutions start as a gesture against the *status quo*. Stanislavsky probably was the first actor, for all we know, who said, 'This won't do; this operatic false kind of acting won't do; we must get back to absolutely bone realism.' And he rehearsed plays for nine months, he made people live the parts, live all day long in their make-up and clothes, and become the people, become the characters concerned. I think Brecht also was revolutionary against what was going on in Germany at the time. Now, that intense realism is very important to understand, but it's not the final and complete answer to the actor's work. I think you and I, sitting here in this television studio, might be giving performances of somebody interviewing somebody, and if anybody was watching us and we were acting these parts, they would say, 'Yes, that's absolutely real all right, there's nothing phoney about that': and there isn't. Now, the place where these Method actors work in New York is a very small place, and they act almost on these terms from what I've seen, and from what I gather from many other people who've watched their work; and this is very important, to feel absolutely bone real, and that it is you and me talking together. But that is not the big problem in acting, not in theatre acting. It is the big problem, if you like, the only problem, in film acting where the camera comes in and gets you, or the microphone comes in and gets you. But in theatre acting the problem is to express what you are expressing at this close distance fifty yards away – that is the problem. Therefore this particular revolution that's been

31

going on in America, which isn't a revolution against any particular type or style of acting, is really a revolution against nothingness, against the situation in which actors could achieve no exercise for themselves. What I dare to say, possibly, is the disadvantage of this system is that it tends to indulge the actors concerned in that work.

Our situation now is that we've got plenty of openings for actors in this country. Our subsidized theatre has opened up so much. But if you could look ahead, say five or ten years hence, what changes would you look for in our own company at the Vic? What would you like it to have developed into?

I'd like better conditions first of all: I'd like a better theatre, better conditions in order to increase our activities, so that eventually, perhaps, the art of the actor may finally be regarded as an important part of the life of the people.

A 1919 In fancy dress

B 1922 Katharina, *The Taming of the Shrew*

C 1926 Richard Coaker, *The Farmer's Wife*

D Tony Lumpkin, *She Stoops to Conquer*

E Vanya, *Uncle Vanya*

C–F 1926–8 Birmingham Rep.

F Guy Sydney, *Something to Talk About*

A & B 1935 Romeo and Mercutio, *Romeo and Juliet*   C 1937 Hamlet

D 1930 Victor Prynne, *Private Lives*, with Adrianne Allen, Noël Coward, and Gertrude Lawrence

A 1937 Macbeth

B 1938 Coriolanus

C 1937 Sir Toby Belch, *Twelfth Night*

D 1937 Henry V

E 1937 Hamlet,
with Esmé Church (Queen)

B 1959 Coriolanus,
with Edith Evans (Volumnia)

A 1955 Macbeth,
with Keith Michell (Macduff)

c 1945 Justice Shallow, *2 Henry IV*   d 1945 Oedipus   e 1945 Hotspur, *1 Henry IV*

A 1944 Richard III,
  with Joyce Redman (Lady Anne)

B 1944 Sergius, *Arms and the Man*,
  with Joyce Redman (Louka)

C 1946 King Lear   D 1957 Titus Andronicus   E 1945 Puff, *The Critic*

A 1965 Tattle,
Love for Love

B 1963 Captain Brazen, *The Recruiting Officer*

C 1964 Othello

A 1962 Astrov, *Uncle Vanya*, with Sybil Thorndike (Marina)   B 1964 Halvard Solness, *The Master Builder*

C 1964 Othello,
with Maggie Smith (Desdemona)

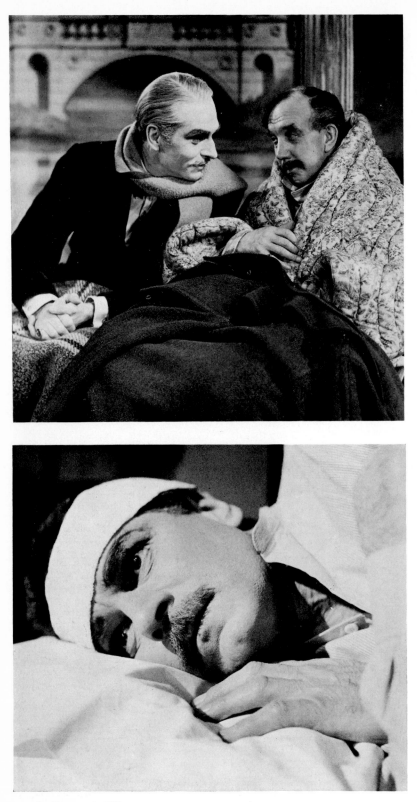

c 1960 Berenger, *Rhinoceros*

D 1957 Archie Rice, *The Entertainer*

A Aged 4

B Aged 13

C Aged 17

A 1913 Hester Dunnybrig, *The Shadow*, with Jules Shaw

B 1920 *Grand Guignol*: Lea, *Private Room No. 6*, with George Bealby

C 1912 Malkin, *The Whispering Well*, with Jules Shaw

D 1923 April Mawne, *Advertising April*

A 1923 Imogen, *Cymbeline*   B 1926 Lady Macbeth   C 1927 Chorus, *Henry V*

D 1938 Volumnia, *Coriolanus*, with Laurence Olivier   E 1925 Queen Katherine, *Henry VIII*

43

A 1944 Queen Margaret, *Richard III*

B 1924 Joan *St Joan*

C 1945 Mistress Quickly, *Henry IV*

D 1961 Teresa, *Teresa of Avila*

E 1924 Joan, *St Joan*

B 1944 Aase, *Peer Gynt*,
with Ralph Richardson

A 1941 Constance, *King John*,
with Ernest Milton (King)

A

B

C 1944 Aase, *Peer Gynt*

D 1950 Lady Randolph, *Douglas*

A 1947 Isabel Linden, *The Linden Tree*, with Lewis Casson (left centre)

B 1938 Miss Moffat, *The Corn is Green*

D 1949 Isabel Bracken, *The Foolish Gentlewoman*, with Lewis Casson

C 1949 Aunt Anna Rose, *Treasure Hunt*

A 1951 Mrs Whyte, *Waters of the Moon*   B 1955 Mrs Railton-Bell, *Separate Tables*   C 1966 Mrs Moore, *Passage to India* (TV)

D 1955 The Grand Duchess,
  The Sleeping Prince

E 1965 Abby Brewster, *Arsenic and Old Lace*, with Athene Seyler

47

A 1924 Hecuba, *The Trojan Women*,
with Ann Casson (Astyanax)

B 1920 Medea

C 1925 Medea

D 1941 Medea, with Lewis Casson, C.E.M.A. Welsh tour

SYBIL
THORNDIKE

Sybil Thorndike talked to Michael MacOwan in the sitting room of her London home and in a television studio. Michael MacOwan directed many classical and modern plays in London before he was appointed Principal of the London Academy of Music and Dramatic Art in 1954. He directed Sybil Thorndike and her husband Lewis Casson in two plays: J. B. Priestley's *The Linden Tree* in 1947 and *The Foolish Gentlewoman* by Margery Sharp in 1949. His comments are in italics.

plate 46a, d

Sybil, the piano means a lot to you, doesn't it? It has always seemed to me so strange that your first idea was that you were going to be a pianist, not an actress.

Yes. I would rather have been a pianist than anything. It was nerves that stopped me; it affected my wrist.

It's extraordinary to me that you should have been stopped doing anything because of nerves. I always think that, as an actress, you've got the most tremendous control.

I have got control of them gradually, but with the piano I was paralytic. I first played in London when I was just eleven years old, at Steinway Hall, and I thought I'd die, I really thought I'd die. And that lovely man Hadyn Coffin was on the same programme, and he caught hold of me and said, 'Little girl, you mustn't be nervous like this. Come up with me.' And he said, 'Look at that old man in the front row, now you play to him, and go and just play to him', and that suddenly bucked me up. Funny little podge me, on I walked in white nun's veiling, with brown stockings and shoes; I played Beethoven and was encored – oh, but nerves! No child of eleven ought to be nervous like that.

You've never felt like that about acting, have you?

I am always nervous. Acting, you see, was the outcome of something I wanted to do, and it was my relaxation from the piano. I always felt that I could do everything much better than anybody else, as an actress, from the time I was four. It's only when I've got older that I've known that I'm not quite as good as I thought I was. I'm more nervous in my old age than when I was young. I know when Ben Greet first engaged me he gave me all the small parts, and I thought, 'What's this? I can play all the big parts.' I played them all in the barn with my brother Russell. I know them off by heart. You know, you get frightfully cocky, but if you haven't got that in the theatre, if you don't feel, 'I've got something to say that nobody else on this earth knows how to say', I don't think you're any good.

Confidence.

Absolute confidence, but it gradually gets a bit worse as you get older, and you're not quite so confident; you may be more confident about what you want to say, but you're not so confident in your own powers.

Do you think that early training as a pianist has had an effect on your work as an actress?

I can't begin to tell you how much. When I look at the young actors today and the way we had to work, actors don't know what work is, compared with musicians. It's such dedicated work, music, that you don't have the time or the desire to think about anything outside your technical equipment and how you are going to express all the things that are in your inward soul; you are just mad to get yourself technically right, because you know then that everything will come through. And that's why I get so mad sometimes at young people thinking that they needn't do their voice exercises and their technical work every single day of their lives. Nothing comes through, of truth, unless you've got the machine right to get it through.

Yes, it's most important, realizing that one is a machine that has to be kept in order like any other machine.

The piano is such a taskmaster – I've worked eight, nine hours a day.

When you came to acting, the tremendous precision and demands of music were still with you?

In the early days I had such disasters vocally, through overwork, that I knew I had to get the machine right. And bodily: I mean I'm not very elegant, never have been – and I had to do something to make myself look respectable, which was always so hard for me, from my earliest years.

The most important thing of all is that you're strong. Don't you think that actors have got to be strong?

Absolutely. You've got to be like iron. Oh yes, I am. You've got to be healthy, and not mind knock-downs and not mind criticism. That's where the piano is so wonderful, because you're torn to shreds when you're working as a pianist.

And from that you learned to take an impersonal attitude to your work?

You do. And then, if you have that clarity, technically, something of yourself is able to come through, something that you want to say.

Complete freedom only comes from having accepted a discipline?

Oh, that's wonderful.

It looks as though all the things in your early life were right and fortunate, for what you were going to do, for what you were going to become.

Yes, they were. And another thing was fortunate for me – this learning from memory. You see, I worshipped my father, I thought he was practically God, and he was perfect. And I noticed – because he was in church every morning at half past seven, and I was up at a quarter past five practising – I used to notice that he always had poetry on his dressing-table when he was shaving. He learned something every day and I thought, 'What father does, I do.' I've always kept it up, and I still do, to this day.

You were quite a big family, weren't you?

There were only four of us, two boys and two girls. But, of course, Russell and I were tremendously close. We were never going to marry. We started a society, when we were nine years old, called the vigilists, and our motto was '*ora et labora*'.

Russell always meant to act, didn't he?

Russell was always going to act and write. At first I thought it was a pity to take up acting as a profession, because you ought to be more dedicated, you oughtn't to have such fun.

But you caught the acting a good deal from Russell, didn't you?

Oh yes, because when I had to give up the piano it was Russell who said, 'Come on then, let's go on the stage', and I thought, 'Oh, all right.'

But you'd already been doing quite a lot of acting.

I never went more than two months without being in a play from the time I was four. I was a mad keen amateur.

And your sister Eileen too?

And Eileen too. When Eileen was born we roped her in, and then Frank was born and he was roped in. We roped them all in, but Russell and I played all the best parts.

And your father and mother, did they like the theatre?

They were, of course, Ellen Terry and Irving fans, and the first Shakespeare I remember was father reading *Hamlet* to me from having seen the Terrys.

There's a long connection, isn't there, between the church and the theatre? They often go together.

Oh yes. We always used to think that father, in the pulpit, looked like Forbes Robertson. And another technical thing that was wonderful, father had the most tremendous long breath, only beaten by Larry Olivier. Father could do the general exhortation, 'Dearly beloved brethren, the scripture moveth us', one and a half times through in one breath; Larry could do it twice. We used to notice father in church, Russell used to nudge me and say, 'Father's doing the collect all in one breath.'

You were a very united family it seems, united in a love of music and the theatre: and in your religious feelings.

We were tremendously united in all our main interests, and, of course, religion-mad. Father always encouraged us, from small children, to argue at our luncheon table, our supper table – we were always arguing. When father came home from church, on a Sunday morning after his sermon, we tore him to shreds. We've always been interested in religion, and when people talk about religion and put on holy faces, we can't understand that, because father was never like that. I've been madly interested in it all my life.

Without some big point of reference, outside the ordinary affairs of life, the theatre is a terribly difficult world, isn't it?

Yes it is, but you find a wonderful thing in the theatre – you find friendliness, a very deep friendliness. When they talk about actors being jealous of each other, I don't think that is true. It's not nearly as true as it is of musicians. Actors are friendly, they like to see other people doing well.

To go on with your development as an actress. When you found that music wasn't going to work for you, then you went to the Ben Greet school. It was the only drama school existing then, wasn't it?

Yes, there was no other recognized school, and it was run by a wonderful little actor called Frederick Topham, who was a brilliant teacher. I was so miserable at first, but then I pulled up my socks and said, 'Well, I've got to do something to earn my living.'

51

What did you do at the Ben Greet school, because now we've got rather complicated in our training?

No complications at all. We took plays and rehearsed them and we did nothing technical at all. Anyway, I always did voice work by myself.

Really? You didn't do any voice work as part of the professional training? Or work on the body either?

Oh no, nothing. But I'd been to dancing school, you see, as a little girl. I had always danced, and Russell and I had practised with the sheets and blankets – we knew exactly what to do with togas and things, because we'd practised them on the beds at home.

And while you were rehearsing the plays, did you begin to discover some sort of basic principles for yourself?

I can't quite explain it, it was so queer. It was so utterly different from any of the more careful training now. We rehearsed plays and were told that if you make a gesture, you do it that way, and if you are going to a door you say, 'I am going out of that door.' You know, you made a round gesture. He gave you basic things, just basic rules, that I think now the amateurs are given.

Then it depended entirely on your talent?

Oh, it depended on your working, as I remember to my horror. I think I was playing Portia, and Topham said to me, 'I don't think you'll ever be a tragedienne, you're a comedienne.' And I thought, 'The blazes! I can play tragedy better than anybody', and I made up my mind. I'd always wanted to play tragedy, I don't know why he said I couldn't. I suppose I didn't suggest it.

Anyway, the Ben Greet school got you your first professional job, with Ben Greet?

Yes, I played Lady Twombley in *The Cabinet Minister* by Pinero. And Ben Greet said, 'I'll take the girl to America and I'll give the boy (that was Russell) a job in England.' And so off I went to America and it was marvellous because, when I got off the ship, a terrible little ship, terrible – I think it was condemned after that voyage – when we got off the ship, Ben Greet said to me, 'We've got a very heavy tour ahead, everybody's sure to be ill. Are you strong?' I said, 'Strong as a horse.' 'Then you'd better learn all the parts.' I said, 'I know them all.' I'd played them in the barn at home.

Did you play a lot of parts on that tour?

Do you know, everybody was ill. It was a terrible tour. I've been in every state but four in America with Ben Greet. We used to see places in the distance and drop off. Well, if you are not young and very strong, you can't always stand it. They said I put the evil eye on them, so they got ill. I played all the understudies, and when the real, proper understudies didn't know the parts, which I always prayed they wouldn't, Ben Greet would say, 'Syb, do you know the part?', and I'd say, 'Yes, I do.'

And what plays were you doing?

Oh, how ever many did we do? *Macbeth, Twelfth Night, Much Ado*; I should think we did about fifteen.

All Shakespeare?

No. Then we played all the regular old comedies, like *She Stoops to Conquer*, and *Everyman* and the old shepherd plays.

52

Oh, really. It was an unusual thing in those days, surely, doing the miracle plays?

Yes it was. Ben Greet was one of the first. Of course, Poel had done some. Ben Greet knew Poel very well, he was an enormous admirer of Poel. He wasn't of the same scholastic quality as Poel, but he was as passionately keen on Shakespeare.

And he adopted Poel's idea of going right back to the Elizabethans, looking at the text of the plays as they originally were, and trying to play them as they were originally played?

He swallowed it whole. That was my training for the open stage because we never played in a proscenium at all. We played in the open air and in halls. And if we played in theatres, we never had the curtain down.

It's taken us all this time, then, to lead us to Chichester.

They all say it's such a new thing. I was doing it when I was a girl.

That must have been a tremendous experience for you, often playing leading parts as a junior member of the company.

Yes, and playing parts way beyond me really. But I didn't think they were beyond me!

You never bothered about whether you were being good or bad?

No, I just went wholeheartedly, bang into them. Of course, I'd always got plenty of voice – that was father's training, you see, with breathing.

It's really essential to the development of an actress like you, that you're not afraid and not continually destroying yourself by thinking you're bad?

Yes, because you're caring much more about what you're doing. I've never wanted to be one person, and I've never wanted to be a star actress. I've always wanted to act people. I wanted to know what people feel, awful people too.

You've never been stuck with one kind of person, have you?

No, I haven't. I'm saying this, and it isn't mock-modest; but I've never been a wildly attractive person, which was, really, to my joy, because I was able to do all sorts of things that an attractive girl wouldn't. I loved acting and playing people. It was also a means of finding out about people, and making the audience like them. You say, 'Come on, this is what this old bitch is like, now you can understand her.'

It is a particular feature of your work, that you can play the most horrible people doing terrible things but, somehow, it never is unpleasant; when you do it, one understands them.

Now that goes deep down into what I believe, because I believe that within us we've got the germ of every other sort of person. If I can play a terrible part which I can find somewhere inside me, then, but for the grace of God, I might have been that person. I can never forget that after playing the *Medea*, I felt as though I'd been in a bath. You can get rid of all sorts of embryo awfulness and throw them off. All the foul tempers, wanting to knock Lewis's block off, wanting to spank the children, I got rid of them all. The family used to say I was angelic after playing the *Medea*. I think it was Aristotle who said, 'Purge, through pity and terror.'

plate 48

How long were you in America on that tour?

Just on four years.

Playing leading parts, at your age, in the open air, you must have got pretty tired?

Well, the thing was I lost my voice, but that was an accident. I was playing at Princeton University and Russell and I were staying with Woodrow Wilson, who was then president of the University. We were playing on the campus – I was playing Good Deeds in *Everyman* – and I opened my mouth and drew in my breath, and a piece of powder-puff which was on my veil flew into my throat and got stuck round my vocal cords and I couldn't speak. I did a lot of *acting*, but I couldn't say another word! And that began my struggle with voice. I worked for nearly three months in the open air with a false voice. Of course, I ought to have been silent then for at least a week. I went to a doctor the next day, who said my vocal cords were clear, but they were a little swollen. And then I went on working until finally it got so bad that Russell said, 'Sybil's got to go home. She must see a doctor.'

I came home and I saw a top specialist, Sir St Clair Thompson, who was King Edward's throat doctor. And he looked at my throat, and said 'Are you a brave girl?' And I said, 'Yes, I am.' And he said, 'I'm afraid you won't speak on the stage again.' Wasn't that awful! And he said, 'Your vocal cords are smothered with growths. I can't see anything, I can't see a vocal cord at all. But if you could possibly be silent for six weeks, I might see if it is curable. So go out of this room, don't speak another word for six weeks. Have a notebook and write everything down; and when you come back, into my room, in six weeks time, I can tell you if it's curable.' Not a word did I speak – I practised the piano, I went for long walks in the country. I was staying at the vicarage of course, with my father and mother. And then, when I went back to the specialist in six weeks, he looked at my throat, and I was sitting in perfect terror. He said, 'You've got the constitution of an ox, those growths have all gone, your vocal cords are clear. Now,' he said, 'you've got to be jolly careful.' Then I went to a person and worked. He was quite a quack, but he knew how to get me over the first difficulties and so I got back my voice again.

Was it very interesting, those six weeks of silence?

It was one of the loveliest times I've spent in my whole life. I read poetry and played the piano and went for long walks with my dog in the country. I've never quite got away from the joy of silence.

Of course you practically had to start again, in the theatre?

Yes, when I had got the voice right, it took me about six weeks' hard study to get it poised properly. Then Nigel Playfair gave me an introduction to the Play Actors, a Sunday Night Players Society; and so he got me into that. I played two plays for them; and the second play Bernard Shaw came to see with Nigel, and they sent for me the next day. They were going to send out a tour of *Candida* and they wanted the understudy, and they asked me if I would like to read for it. So I read it and, my dear, I put everything I'd got into it – Lady Macbeth, Everyman, Beatrice, everything; and when I'd finished with a bounce, Shaw rocked with laughing. He said, 'Splendid, my dear young lady, you go home and have a husband and children and do the housekeeping, and you'll be a very good Candida; but you'll do for the understudy.' And he said, 'You're understudying one of the most beautiful actresses I know, Ellen O'Malley', and that was a great joy – Shaw loved her very much. And at rehearsals Shaw always had me sitting next to him, at the table, and explaining everything as it went along. And do you know, he did say a lovely thing to me – mustn't sound conceited – but he did say, 'You've got something that Janet Achurch had.' He said, 'Work, you work, watch everything, and you'll do it.'

54

He could only be virulent when he'd got his pen in his hand, and on the platform in debate; he was marvellous then. But I don't think he could say an unkind thing to people, he was so feeling for them. If people were really awful, and they showed conceit, then he could squash them flat. But anybody who was trying, however feebly, he would always be very kind to.

Didn't you find it frustrating and boring understudying after you'd been doing all that work?

Well no, because we had a front piece and I played the leading part in it. It was a rather racy play for those days, by Havelock Ellis, you know, the sex man. I've absolutely forgotten what it was called, but it was a lovely little play, and that came in front of *Candida*; because *Candida* wasn't considered a full evening's length in those days.

We started off the tour under the aegis of Miss Horniman at Belfast. Miss Horniman's Manchester Company was playing the first three days of the week and we played the last three days. I went in front, on the first night, to see the Manchester Company, and I saw a young man playing Trench in *Widowers' Houses*, who was Lewis Casson. Now I was very devoted to a certain cousin of mine – really rather in love with him, and I thought, he looks like Basil. Oh, what a nice man, I like him. I loved the very incisive way he spoke. And then I went round afterwards and was introduced to him, but he never spoke a word to me; he was changing his shoes, very quick, and you know the way he talks – very sharp. Then the next day, out in the street, I met him again, and again he never spoke a word to me, but talked to May Playfair; so then nothing happened. We went off to Dublin for the next week and May Playfair and I went off to the zoo; and there, in the lion house, was Lewis Casson, trying to make the lioness go to sleep, mesmerizing her. And I thought, that was a nice thing to do. So we walked all round the place together, but he never spoke a word to me, he talked to May Playfair – they talked shop the whole time. Then we sat down to have a cup of tea and afterwards I said, 'Well, I'm going into the lion house again, because there's one lion I want to have a look at.' And Lewis said, 'I'll come too.' So he came, and we stood in front of the cages and I thought, 'I wish I were a boy. That's the sort of man I'd like to have for a pal.' Wasn't that funny? And that began it.

And then, of course, we did the rest of our tour and came back to Manchester where we were playing at the Gaiety Theatre. And then they offered me an engagement to stay on, with the Manchester regular company, to understudy the leading parts. I had to learn these parts very quickly and Lewis Casson, being a very kind man, said, 'Would you like me to help you get these parts into your head? I'm rather good at doing that.' I said, 'Oh, if only you would.' And we went up on the roof of the theatre and then we became great friends and did walks together and, well there we are, and that was it. Then, in June, I came back to London, and Lewis did some pastoral plays and asked me to be in them with him. Then I joined the Manchester company for the autumn season, and I was there when I married.

How long were you with Miss Horniman?

For about two years, but I had a baby after the first year.

Again you were in at the beginning of something very important, because the Manchester Repertory was a big step in our repertory history.

Annie Horniman had financed the Irish Players in Dublin with Lady Gregory, but then she got offended with them and started in England. Manchester was the first repertory theatre in England. It started the whole movement.

Not only the idea of repertory theatre, but the kind of plays you were doing.

Ah yes, that's rather amusing. When they talk now about kitchen sink plays, we were doing kitchen sink at the beginning of the century. They were all about working-class people, the problems of the Manchester poor and the awfulness that went on. The plays were full of social content.

From the acting point of view that was a very different cup of tea from what you'd been doing with Ben Greet in America?

Very different, but so exciting because with a classical training it enabled one to play these very real people – not absolutely realistically, because if we had we wouldn't have been heard or understood. You had to translate into Lancashire something of classicism; this was a means of heightening the atmosphere of the Manchester scene and expressing the fundamental feelings of the people. It was a time of political and social upheaval and votes for women. When I met Lewis I wasn't a socialist, but I wouldn't have cut any ice with him if I hadn't been! So there you are, we were all in it.

Was Lewis directing a lot of these plays?

No, he was only one of the leading actors then; but he directed the Greek plays. We did the *Hippolytus*. Then, of course, there was the excitement of the first repertory in London, the Charles Frohman repertory – a six months' season at the Duke of York's. That was a direct child of the Manchester Repertory Company – I think Frohman did it because he wanted to show that repertory was nonsense and the star system was best. After that Frohman asked Lewis and me to go with John Drew and star with a company through North America for a year.

When did Lewis first begin to have an influence upon you as an actress?

He influenced me from the very start, when I had to play Candida, first, as the under-study. I met him the next morning, when I only just knew him, in a fish shop with a friend. We were buying fish for our digs, and we met him and he said, 'Now here are the notes I've made.' Isn't that like him? He said, 'Very good, now', and he ticked me off. He started then, and I've never got away from the man, never got away from him. But I must say, he's helped me vocally more than anybody I know.

And in other ways, surely, because Lewis's mind is so clear and he sees right through a whole play, the shape of it as well as the details. And you must always have been what I call a splurger by nature.

Oh yes, that's very true. Lewis has got a very clear mind, a scientific mind; I haven't. I've got a jumpy mind; I jump from here to there. Of course, it meant ghastly quarrels, ghastly quarrels, but still, there you are. A good old ding-dong is what I'd been trained for by my father, and a good argument does you all the good in the world.

Then you came back to Manchester. This time Lewis was actually director, wasn't he?

Yes, he was, and we had an enormously interesting season. We did some classical plays and Shakespeare, but it was mainly the Manchester plays, the new writers. And that lasted almost until the First World War. When the war came Lewis, of course, joined up. And Ben Greet wrote to me and said, 'Do you want to come and work at this place called the Old Vic, run by a complete mad woman?' I was most intrigued. He said, 'She's as mad as you are.' So I went down to meet Miss Baylis and of course I was bowled over by her. She was wonderful, she was like nothing on earth. I'd seen a pretty good oddity in Miss Horniman, but she was nothing to Lil.

Yes. And so you were right in at the beginning of things once more, the amazing Old Vic which led eventually to the National Theatre?

Yes, I was. But oh, it was wonderful working there. Of course, I had all the big lovely parts. And then, being wartime, gradually the men were filtered out and Ben Greet said to me, 'Do you want to play boys' parts?' And I said, 'Yes, anything.' And so I had Prince Hal, Ferdinand, Lancelot, Gobbo, Feste, and a whole lot of them.

You said that acting was a way of discovering people, that you find all these people in yourself. Now you started finding the male principal in yourself.

Yes, I know. When you're an actor you cease to be male or female, you're a person, and you're a person with all the other persons inside you. That was a really thrilling thing to find out.

It was at the Old Vic that you first played the great Shakespearian tragic parts, Lady Macbeth for instance.

You see, I'd never played Lady Macbeth and Ben Greet wanted me to do it. I was reading it through and remembered about Mrs Siddons. When she had read it, she went to her husband and said, 'I can't play this, this is so awful.' And I felt the same thing. You know I'd played about with it with amateurs, and with Russell, but this was the first time I'd seen it in a mature way, and I thought, 'This is so awful, I can't, I haven't got anything in me like that woman.' And I said to Lilian Baylis, 'I don't think I can play it, I don't know the beginnings of this foulness.' She said, 'Don't be nonsensical. You love your husband, don't you?' I said, 'Yes.' 'Well', she said, 'she loved her husband. She was only doing it for him, so there you are.' And that started me off right. And I thought of it through him, and through doing things for the children, and being willing to do any awful thing, so long as they were all right. It was very clever of her to twig it like that. She had a great insight into things, although she was, in many ways, an ignorant woman. She always said she got it from prayer and she did; she was extraordinary in that way.

But, do you know, I don't really believe she ever saw one play all the way through. I don't think she ever did. She used to sit in that box, see little bits, and then run away again and cook the steak at the side of the stage, that she was going to have between shows. Always in the last act of *As You Like It* you could smell steak and chips. Always.

It must have been a hard life doing all these plays and working at the Vic under wartime conditions; and by this time you had a family.

Oh yes, I had another baby after I'd been a year at the Vic. But it was so funny, and typical of Miss Baylis. I had the baby, and she was about three weeks late. I was only allowed off for a very short time. And the moment she was born Lilian Baylis hopped into my room and said, 'What about rehearsing Ophelia?' and I said, 'Well, I've only just this minute had the baby, I can't come just at once.' 'Well,' she said, 'I can't put off my show, you know.' I was there very shortly. It was torture, I tell you.

It must have been nearly as hard work as touring America with Ben Greet?

Even harder in a way, because we were very poor, you see. I was getting separation

plate 43b

allowance from Lewis, but it didn't make it very much better. I did have two darling girls from father's village who came and worked for me. I couldn't always pay them, because I didn't have enough money. We were paid ten shillings a show, at the beginning at the Old Vic, so you can imagine; three pounds ten a week it came to, and that was pretty stiff with a family of four children.

And how did you stand up to the strain physically?

I stood up to it extraordinarily well, because I was very healthy and very strong; but I did go and get some help from Elsie Fogerty.

So you had voice trouble again?

Yes, I did have a bit of voice trouble. I was overworking, rushing back and forth, and I couldn't take taxis because I didn't have the money. I was using my voice wrongly, over-straining it, trying to push too hard. If you strain, then you do something to your vocal cords, and Fogerty got me through difficult times. I never had to be off at all. She went through the whole thing of breathing; and relaxing was one of the first things she taught me. She had a wonderful way of focusing the voice and helping you to get all the notes. She said, 'You must have your three octaves.' Well, I did have my three octaves until I was over eighty and now I've only lost two notes. She had a wonderful technical knowledge of the voice. She was often extremely tiresome and we could have blown her head off; but she knew what she was up to. I've never known anybody quite like her. She taught me a great deal.

Were you able to use all she taught you when you were acting, without being conscious of the method?

Oh yes, because if you're conscious of the method, that again is a strain. You've got to have the voice so poised that you don't have to think about anything technical. Of course, you have to know where you're going to take your breaths. But knowing what you've got to say, in a way, gives you the correct breathing, and then if you are trained technically, your tummy muscles hold you up.

Your life has always been full of contrasts, because after several years of this astonishing experience at the Old Vic you were off into the West End with Cochran.

Yes, with Cochran. You see, every Christmas at the Old Vic we did a revue. Russell wrote them, sometimes collaborating with somebody else, and I had to compose the music. I had no originality, so I took all the hymn tunes I knew and all the psalm tunes, and bits of oratorios, and turned them into dances and songs. 'We plough the fields and scatter' was one of our best numbers. Cochran came to see it. In the middle of the revue Russell and I did a travesty of *Ghosts*, only we called it 'Spooks' and we played it in a foreign language, which no one understood; I mean gibberish, you know. Cochran sent for me to come and see him the next day. Well, I went to see him, looking the old dowd as I usually did, and he looked at me and said, 'Were you the girl who played in "Spooks"?' And I said, 'Yes.' 'Very nice, very clever, thank you so much', and off I went, not a word more. But a week or two later he and Seymour Hicks came down to see me as Lady Teazle in *School for Scandal*, and after that he offered me a job right away in a revue at the London Pavilion. I played the leading part in a short play with Leon Morton, the clown – oh, what an actor! But it was a change going to Cochran and mixing with an entirely different sort of actor. It was great fun and a very great education for me, in lots of ways, where I'd been extremely green before.

So you became a West End actress and you had your own management with Lewis. The culmination of that period really was Saint Joan, the part with which you're everlastingly associated.

That was the biggest thing that could happen to anybody. To play a great play like that for the first time.

Had you thought of 'Saint Joan' before Shaw came along?

Yes indeed, but didn't you know about it? We commissioned dear Laurence Binyon to write a play for us. I'd always wanted to play St Joan, because I adored her. Then we suddenly saw in the newspaper that Shaw was writing one too. So Lewis wrote to him and said, 'Here, Laurence Binyon's going to write the play for Sybil and me', and he said 'Nonsense', on a postcard, 'Nonsense, Sybil is playing my Joan, let so-and-so play Binyon's.'

plate 44b, c

Was he writing it for you from the start?

Yes, that's the exciting part, which I never knew anything about. You see, Shaw had seen me in *The Cenci*. Now in *The Cenci* there is this wonderful trial scene, and he went back to his wife Charlotte and said, 'I'll write the play now; I've found the woman who can play it.'

It must have been a tremendous moment when the script arrived.

That was one of the most exciting things that ever happened in my life. We went down with Bronson Albery and Cherry Garrard, the South Pole man, and we sat in Shaw's little room and he read it to us. I thought I'd die. I thought I'd *die*. It was that first scene; I thought, 'God in heaven, you've given me something which I never dreamed that I was ever going to be asked to play.' He read the first three scenes and then he came to the Tent Scene. Just before he read that he said, 'Now the play really begins, the rest is all flapdoodle.' But Shaw himself was a perfect Saint Joan; he could have played it far better than any of us.

And when you started to study it, I don't imagine that you really had to think about it a great deal. It was all there, wasn't it?

Shaw said to me, 'Have you read all the histories?' I said, 'Every single one of them.' So he said, 'Forget them. I'll tell you what to say.' And when he read us his play I knew they were all the things I passionately wanted to say. And to prove it, that's the only time, on a first night, that I haven't had one nerve. I was exalted. God was there and I didn't care a hoot for anything, except getting over what Shaw had written. Oh, what a wonderful man. I must tell you, he gave me a book, my book that I'd been rehearsing with, and he wrote in the beginning of it, 'To Saint Sybil Thorndike from Saint Bernard Shaw.'

What about the rehearsals? Lewis directed them really, didn't he?

Well, Shaw always took the morning rehearsals, and he said that Lewis undid everything that he had done in the mornings, when he rehearsed in the afternoons. Lewis translated Shaw to us in terms of technique. But Shaw knew every tune of every sentence. I could go through Saint Joan now like an orchestral score. And when I see other people playing it and they don't do it the same way, I say, 'You know, that's not the right intonation.'

59

The conception of the character – the peasant girl with the Lancashire accent – did that come from Shaw's text?

It was easy for me not to be London English. And Shaw said, 'Lancashire', but it was only mildly Lancashire; it was slightly northern.

So really those rehearsals could never have had any problem?

The main things were always there. And Shaw was so polite and so charming. He was quite fierce with me, but there was no ding-dong between us, because you see I worshipped him, and I would have done anything – crawled on my hands and knees to do what he wanted. Shaw and Gilbert Murray are the two men – not counting Lewis – that have been the guiding lights in my life.

There was something God-like about Murray, and it's so funny because the two men who are the biggest Christians I have known were neither of them professed Christians. Isn't it extraordinary? But Murray gave you something tremendous. I met him first in Manchester, when we were doing the *Hippolytus*, and Lewis was producing. I was playing a goddess and I thought, 'Well, this is child's play, anybody can play these old goddesses.' At a rehearsal I went up on to the stage and I knew I could do the whole thing, and when I'd finished I thought, 'Well, there.' I mean, this is what comes of long experience as an amateur, I can do it. Gilbert Murray came up to me and said, 'Charming, my dear young lady, charming. Now what I want is opalescent dawn.' I thought to myself, 'My God, what's opalescent dawn?' But you see, I was knocked right flat to the bottom, and had to build up again.

Opalescent dawn needed a certain detached clarity of tone, I imagine.

plate 48b

Yes. A clarity of tone and a thing which is beyond innocence, which was knowledge – a knowledge of truth. And then, of course, later on I was mad to do the *Trojan Women* and *Medea*, which we did under our own management, first in 1919 for matinées at the Old Vic and the following year for matinées at the Holborn Empire. They are tremendous plays and you know, when there's big emotion as there is in the Greek plays, you've got to have something very large in imagination to carry it off. That's where purely realistic plays don't always satisfy you, as an actor, in the same way.

It's only recently, I think, that people are beginning to feel that they want big tragedy. We seem to be getting more of it now, don't we?

It's coming back, yes.

But during the Second World War, I remember, you and Lewis did these plays all over the country.

plate 48d

Yes, we did. We took them to the mining towns. And I remember the authorities saying, 'Oh, are you taking tragedies down to the poor miners?' Lewis said, 'I know the Welsh people, I am a Welshman, they like a tragedy.' And do you know, we were playing in one little place, and the audience was electric. They were sitting on the edge of their seats, playing the parts themselves. And one miner came round after *Medea*, which is a bit of a pill, and he said, 'This is the play for us. It kindles a fire.' And what more do you want to do in the theatre but kindle a fire?

I think it really must have been during the twentieth century, and particularly the twenties and thirties, that the idea grew up that the only respectable theatrical world for a distinguished actor or actress was London; and that it was a great condescension when one went and played in the provinces.

60

We have always found that in the country you get a different atmosphere, and that is the thrill. You find yourself at oneness with such different people; it was the same on our big tours in Africa, Australia, Egypt, all over the place. That's why the theatre is so desperately important in the world.

It's an astounding life – sixty-two years as an actress. What do you think are the most important things you've got out of it, and what would you like to feel you've given to it?

I like to think that I've helped to make living people feel, in themselves, that they are working towards some better existence. I've had a very full, very rich life, with exciting work to do, all the time, and a lovely happy life in the home, and if I've made people understand more about human beings by what I've done in the theatre, then that will give me satisfaction. In fact, as the old miner said of *Medea*, 'I would like to feel that I've kindled a fire.'

RALPH
RICHARDSON

Ralph Richardson talked to Derek Hart at his London home and in a television studio. Derek Hart is a television journalist and broadcaster. His comments are in italic.

The whole of my early life was a complete disaster, a most frightful muddle. And it all started when I was at school, or when I was not at school, because I was at school, perhaps, only a couple of days in the week.

Why was that?

Because I was ill. It was the fashion to be ill in those days. Whether I was really ill or whether I only pretended to be ill so as not to go to school, which I didn't like, I've never been able to decide. However, like many other children in those days, I caught all the diseases. I had diphtheria, scarlet fever; and I was in hospital half the time. By the end of my schooldays I'd learnt nothing. What's more important, I had absolutely no discipline of mind at all; in fact, I was in a disastrous muddle. And then, in 1917 when I was only about sixteen or seventeen, I went into the office of the Liverpool and Victoria Insurance Company, at Brighton where I lived, as an office-boy at 10s. a week. I felt myself a millionaire. I put away 7s. 6d. in the Post Office every week and kept a half-crown for my pocket money, it seemed like gold. And there in this office I enjoyed myself very much for the first time in my life. I didn't like school because people weren't very kind to me; perhaps I wasn't very kind to them; we didn't like each other. But in the office people were extraordinarily kind. It was the first time I'd met real kindness in the world outside my own home. I lived with my mother, and she was extremely kind to me. I'm not saying I had a chip on the shoulder, but if I ever had one it was certainly removed when I went to the insurance office. As I say, I was a disaster, I was a muddle, it was terrible.

I had to take care of the post. You see, money was received through the collectors and it was sent out by them; big cheques, £200 or £300 or more. It was my business to enter them up in the book, stick them in envelopes, and send them out. But it was a disaster. I put the wrong cheques in the wrong envelopes and a chap instead of getting, 'Dear Sir, unless . . .' received a letter which began, 'We are delighted to send you a cheque for £400'! Well, of course, you can imagine that to squeeze the money out of a chap who received this took a bit of tact. At the office they called me all the names under the sun when these things happened, but they were awfully kind to me.

How did you come to leave them?

I received an enormous fortune, it was the beginning of my colossal chain of good luck, through the death of my grandmother; I suppose it shouldn't be called good luck, exactly. But this dear old lady, having heard that I had had such a poor time, one way and another, provided that the sum of £500 be left in her will, for Ralph's education. We lived in rather simple circumstances and this fortune was staggering. I remember that Mr Barry was the manager of the branch, a very nice man, and I waited to tell him this great news. I had talked it over with my mother and we decided that my education should start and that

62

I should not go back to school, which I probably ought to have done, but instead I should go to the Art School and try to become a painter. My father was a painter, and it was the thing that I felt I really wanted to do. And so I went on Monday morning and knocking on the door I said, 'Mr Barry, may I speak to you, Sir?' and he said, 'Yes', and I closed the door behind me, to make the scene more solemn, and he said, 'What is it, Richardson?' I said, 'I have bad news for you, I'm afraid, Mr Barry', and he stared at me manfully and said, 'What is it, Richardson?' I knew that he was perfectly certain that I had posted another even more valuable cheque to the wrong destination. So I said, 'Mr Barry', looking at him very straightly, 'I have to give you two weeks' notice. I am leaving your employment and I am going to the Brighton Art School.' 'Oh, thank God, Richardson', he said, 'I was going to give you the sack at the end of the week, but I was putting it off as long as possible. Good luck, Richardson. Good luck, my dear boy.' Then I did go to the Art School at Brighton, and there again it was a disaster, the whole thing was a chain of disasters.

After I'd spent some months there, hopefully, it began to dawn on me that I was not ever going to make a painter after all. I had no real talent, not enough to carry me through to earn my living. And this was sad, to be given the chance of doing what I really wanted to do and then to find it fizzling out. As my little sum of money was about half gone, I still had the other half, and I thought I had better make up my mind quickly what I would do. Would I be a chemist? That was a thing that rather struck me; perhaps it was going into a chemist's shop and seeing people dressed up in white coats, or mixing things in bottles. I thought a chemist was a hell of a guy who says, 'Take this three times a day'; I mean, that rather appealed to me. So I went to a chemist and I said, 'Do you think I could become a chemist?' And he told me how long a study it was, how much Latin you had to learn, and I thought, I don't know, I don't know whether I'd be a very good chemist after all. I think I'd look all right in the coat, but that's as far as I could get; I'll try something else.

I thought maybe I'd be a journalist, this attracted me very much. I went down to the office of the *Brighton Herald* and talked to them about it and I said, 'Do you think it would be possible that I could ever be a journalist?' They were awfully nice and I said, 'Would you take me on as an apprentice here at the *Brighton Herald* for instance?' They said, 'Well, we might, we might. What examinations have you passed?' So I said, 'I haven't passed any examinations at all.' 'Well,' they said, 'how's your shorthand and typing?' I said, 'What?' They said, 'How's your shorthand?' I said, 'Shorthand?' 'Yes, I mean what speed have you?' 'Well,' I said, 'it's not – I must – where do I learn it?' So they said, 'It's quite simple, you buy a book.' I said, 'How long does it take to . . .?' 'Well, you go and have a try.' So I thought this is easy, and I went and bought Pitman's *Shorthand Instructor* and I worked at this pretty hard, but it was absolutely awful, I couldn't get anywhere. I couldn't concentrate, you see, so it didn't seem that it was possible for me to join the office of the *Brighton Herald*.

Did you go to the theatre a lot in those days at Brighton?

Oh yes, I went to the theatre a great deal when I was a boy at Brighton, and a very rich and marvellous theatreland it was. There was the Theatre Royal, the Grand Theatre, the Hippodrome, the West Pier and the Palace Pier, changing their bill every week. I saw the most wonderful shows at the Hippodrome, all the great heroes of my time: Little Tich, Harry Tate, George Robey, Marie Lloyd; every week I was up in the gallery seeing these marvellous performers.

63

When did you begin to have thoughts about being an actor yourself?

As a matter of fact, I'd always, vaguely, thought about being an actor. I had no actors in my family. They were a Quaker family and, by tradition, rather disapproved of anything to do with the theatre; I'd never even met an actor. But I did perhaps prolong the period in my life, which every child goes through, the sort of dressing up period. I had the most wonderful scarlet jacket that my Aunt Maud brought back from Turkey, it had brass buttons all the way down the front, it had epaulettes, and I used to wear this jacket a great deal when I was a little boy of nine or ten; I used to practise deaths. I used to fall off groynes into the shingle and lie asprawl, pierced with assagais, or shot with arrows, torn to pieces by wild Indians. I enjoyed this very much. It was a great consolation to me in my very lonely youth. This dressing up period was rather stronger, in me, than it is in most children, and it lasted a long time. Perhaps, after all, acting is something to do with dressing up. I often think that actors are the only people who have preserved, in some way, this childish nonsense of liking to put on some tremendous helmet or something. They'll do it still, it's awful, but it's part of the business of acting.

I remember how the desire to act did really click, just in one moment; I can remember it vividly. I went to the Theatre Royal at Brighton and I saw Sir Frank Benson playing *Hamlet*. Even as a boy I read a great deal of Shakespeare, and so I knew the play fairly well. I'll always remember when the ghost appeared and he said, 'Remember me', and Benson took his sword and he scratched it on the stage, there was a terrible noise, the sword moving across the floor of the stage – it was a wonderful, weird effect. 'Remember me', the ghost said. It sounded like Vengeance, it sounded like Hell, where the ghost came from. It absolutely mesmerized me. 'My God', I thought, 'if I could do that. That's the job for me, sheer magic. Oh, goodness, if I could touch something like that', and my heart was really beating quite wildly. 'Oh, oh,' I thought, 'if only I could be an actor, if only I could have a sword and scratch it on the floor, I wouldn't ever want to do anything else.'

I did then make enquiries as to how I could possibly enter the acting profession. There was a little company, half amateur, at Brighton, performing in a small theatre made out of a disused bacon factory near the station. It was run by a fellow called Growcott. I found great difficulty in getting his address, but I did find it somehow, and I cycled up there frantically one Sunday morning. I remember knocking on the door and Growcott coming out and standing in the doorway and he said, 'What do you want?' So I said, 'Well, my name's Richardson and I would very much like to be an actor.' He said, 'What?' I said, 'I would very much like to be an actor if I could. I mean, you've got an acting company, could I join your company?' 'Well,' he said, 'what acting have you done?' 'Well', I said, 'I haven't done any acting at all. Never.' Well, he was sort of playing with the door. He was having his breakfast or something. I was so eager at that time I didn't care what time it was. So he said, 'What's all this about? I mean you say you want to be an actor, you've never done any acting. I mean, look here. What did you say your name was?' I said, 'Richardson.' He said, 'Look here, Richardson, why fiddle about with this?' I said – I was very disappointed – 'I couldn't possibly be with you then?' 'Well,' he said, 'I don't know about that.' I said, 'Look, Mr Growcott, a short while ago I came into some money, and I've still got a little of it left. I mean if I could come to you in any way as an apprentice I could pay a little premium, you know, Mr Growcott.' 'Well,' he said, 'what was the name?' I said, 'Richardson'. He said, 'Come inside, Richardson.' And so, when I did go in, I really did enter that first portal – it was Porthall Road as a matter of fact, that's where he lived at Brighton.

That was my entrance into the theatre world. Then we fixed up the terms, and although I'd only had little experience in the office, I had picked up something of business ways. When we discussed it upstairs, over his breakfast, I said, 'Well, I think it would be fair if I paid you ten bob a week for twenty weeks, and, if you kept me on after that, you paid me ten bob a week, until we've sort of equalled the thing out, then we can think again, eh?' He was rather struck, he was no business man at all; I was sharper than he was. So he said, 'Well, that's all right. Come and recite something to me tomorrow, at the theatre. But learn something and let me listen to your voice, let me get some idea if I could employ you as an actor at all.' So I did. I learnt a speech from Falstaff. Why, I don't know, but I studied a speech from *The Merry Wives of Windsor* and I delivered this to him. 'Oh,' he said, 'that's absolutely awful.' So I said, 'It's the first acting I've ever done.' So he said, 'It's frightful, Richardson. I mean you don't even know the goddam thing. It's unbelievable, I can't think why you chose the piece – you could never be any good as Falstaff.' Oh, I was so disappointed. I had the first ten bob stuck in the book as a bookmark – I think he'd noticed that. So he said, 'Don't let's despair, Richardson. Don't let's despair. No doubt we can do something with you. I mean you're handy with the brush, aren't you, I mean, you could fix up the lights, eh? Sweep the floor, and that sort of thing. Of course, you'll have to start at the bottom Richardson, you know, you'll have to start at the bottom.' I said I quite realized that. Anyway he took the ten bob. The first thing I learnt was how to fix the lights. In fact, he taught me to do everything. He worked like a dog, we were rehearsing all day, he was acting at night, and then after that we'd stay on, he and I, we would sit up half the night painting the scenery. My first job was mixing the black. Mixing the black, I tell you, was terrible. I don't know how it was, it floated, and there was nothing on earth that I could do to get it to mix in with the water; the weary hours I spent mixing the black.

How much acting did you do with the company?

I didn't do very much at the start. The very first part I played was walking on as a gendarme in *The Emperor's Candlesticks* and to my great satisfaction they found me a scarlet coat to wear; and so, remembering the scarlet coat of my youth, I felt rather more at home in my first appearance on the boards than I had expected to be. In fact I rather enjoyed it. I started by playing very small parts with Growcott and I ended up by playing pretty well all of them. In *Macbeth* I played both Macduff and Banquo, which is an unparalleled double; he was rather short of actors. Oh yes, and I played Malvolio in *Twelfth Night* – I got my first press notice for it. I'm not ashamed to say that I do keep press cuttings in books and I have found them a very useful record over the years. I stayed with him for about a year and I became, really, his leading man. But it was, as I say, a half amateur company, we weren't allowed to charge money, we had to rely on a collection, you know, people putting money in the box, because we weren't licensed.

So you left him?

Yes, I did, There was a chap that used to come to Brighton once a year, Charles Doran, and in those days he had quite a famous company, the Charles Doran Shakespeare Company. And as the Shakespeare plays that we did very much interested me, I wrote to him, told him what I was doing, asked him if he would give me an interview with the idea of my getting a job with him. I got a reply, he was very good in that way, and he asked me to go over and see him at Eastbourne, after the matinée of *The Merchant of Venice* the following Wednesday. 'Oh, my goodness,' I thought, 'what a wonderful thing.'

I got out my bicycle and gave it an extra clean – I had the cleanest bicycle, it was so clean that if there was only a spot of rain I never dared take it out, I'd walk. I put on my cycle clips and away over the downs I went and I saw part of the show. I was as nervous as a cat, I'd never really been behind the scenes of a professional theatre before. It was the Devonshire Park at Eastbourne. However, Doran came off the stage as Shylock and his dresser said, 'Come in, the Guv'nor'll see you.' He was taking his make-up off, and he hardly looked at me. He could just see me in the mirror and he said, 'Oh yes, Richardson, let's hear you spout something to get an idea what kind of voice you've got.' I'd thought this was probably coming, so I had learnt – pretty carefully this time – Mark Antony's funeral oration from *Julius Caesar*. 'Yes,' said Doran, 'stand over there will you, just over there so that I can get a look at you.' So I stood over at the back where his street clothes were hanging and he was watching me in the mirror. So he said, 'Go on, start away.' I said, 'Friends, Romans, countrymen, lend me your ears. I come to bury Caesar, not to praise him', and I went on with the speech, 'Remember on the feast of Lupercal', becoming then, quite dramatic, and he said, 'Stop, stop, pack it up'. So I said, 'Isn't it any good, Mr Doran? Isn't it any good, don't you like it?' And he said, 'It's fine, it's fine, but you're standing on my trousers.' His trousers had been hanging on a peg behind me and, in my excitement, down went the trousers and I was plunging on them, feeling that they might serve as Caesar's mantle or something like that. However, it was all right. He said, 'I liked that, I liked that, Richardson, that's fine. Would you like to join my company?' I said, 'Of course, it's been the ambition of my life.' So he said, 'We might fix that up. How much do you want?' Well, my business acumen came very much to the fore. I looked at him challengingly, and I said, 'Mr Doran, I'm getting thirty shillings a week at the moment.' I might say that Growcott owed me thirty shillings a week, which was true enough. 'Oh,' he said, 'you are, are you? I'll give you three pounds a week. That's the Equity minimum salary; but you'll have to give me a pound a week back.' It was ten bob more than I'd ever dreamt of, and on those lines, like several others of his students and pupils at that time, I joined up and a very good company it was. He had some very fine actors.

And you stayed there for several years?

I stayed with him three years. I did A.S.M. to begin with, you know, looking after the props, packing them up at night. I played the smallest parts in the repertory, always very, very old men – I was only in my teens. But it was the tradition in those days, the younger you were, the older you played. We had ten plays in the repertory, all Shakespeare of course, so I was playing ten parts at once which was a terrific training. In the end I played all his leading parts: Mark Antony, Orlando, and Macduff, all the best parts after Doran; he was the boss, he always played the leading part.

plate 73c

Then after this time with him, I thought that I should get some training playing in modern clothes. On my twenty-first birthday I threw myself on the mercy of the world, and went up to London and took a little room in Bernard Street next to the tube station at Russell Square, very nice digs they were, and I went round the agents to try to get a job. In those days, there were about sixty companies on tour, no talking pictures, and every play that was a success in London was copied by the number one, the number two, and the number three touring companies; and so there were a tremendous number of actors wanted. I'd had some experience by then, but none in modern clothes. However I did get a job in the tour of a play that was running very successfully in London and we copied the West End production and the actors. They were very good actors indeed, the great school of du Maurier. I toured for a few years and then I got married to my first

66

wife, who most sadly died but is certainly in heaven, and we got a job together in the Birmingham Repertory Company: the tour of *The Farmer's Wife*, and we got a joint contract under the generous management of Barry Jackson. He employed us altogether for nearly ten years. After *The Farmer's Wife* we went back to the Birmingham Repertory Theatre together, and we played in a host of plays under the direction of H. K. Ayliff, a marvellous director of his time.

At what point did you first appear in London?

We had been in London for two weeks in 1925 with *The Farmer's Wife*. Then Barry Jackson bought a play called *Yellow Sands* which was a follower-up of *The Farmer's Wife* by Eden Phillpotts, and he invited me and my wife, and Cedric Hardwicke and Frank Vosper, to be in the company, and he took us to London. We opened at the Haymarket Theatre in 1926, and it was an enormous success. For the first time in my life – I suppose I must have been about twenty-three or twenty-four – I was a London actor and in *Yellow Sands*. I had a very small part indeed and I was on the stage for a very, very long time. And this was the making of me as an actor, such as I am, because, as I've told you before, I was a very undisciplined, tangled, muddled, disaster of a chap. We played for well over a year and we had three matinées a week; and I had to sit there on the stage, listening, for instance, to this tremendously long reading of the will, in the second act, in which I think I only had two or three words to speak. And this was what I didn't know that I needed, but I did most desperately need – discipline. There I had to sit, day after day, performance after performance; to do this was torture, but I had to do it. And it gave me the beginnings of the sinews, which every actor must know is necessary, this discipline. I'd played perhaps a hundred parts before that, but never under the iron discipline, night after night, whether you feel like it, whether it's sunny, whether you want to get out and play cricket, whether you want to go to the cinema, of having to give a performance of the same part.

One of the high spots in your theatrical career, as indeed it was a high spot in contemporary theatre history, was the Old Vic season of 1930–1.

Yes. Harcourt Williams did invite me to go to the Old Vic for that season, and I started there a friendship with John Gielgud which has lasted for a very long time. His *Hamlet* at the Old Vic had been the toast of the town. It was a great performance of its time and it had drawn all the fashionable people across Waterloo Bridge; it was really the foundations of the popularity of the Old Vic. Gielgud was about to leave the company and they asked me to join him, in his last season, as partner, sharing the parts. The idea was that, if it was any kind of success, when he was gone, God help me, I was going to be the leading man. And this, of course, was a very attractive proposition to me. So I went down there and I worked with John Gielgud; and it was a curious thing, I didn't really like him at all. We played in *Henry IV* together – he played Hotspur, I played Prince Hal. Then the next production was *The Tempest* and I played Caliban; I had very great difficulty with the part, I'd never played it before. One day at rehearsal Gielgud said to me, 'It seems to bother you a bit, doesn't it, this scene', and I said, 'It bothers me dreadfully' in rather a disagreeable way and then he said, 'Would you like, after rehearsal, just to run this scene with me? Maybe we could go through it together and see what happens.' I didn't like the idea very much. Anyway, I said, 'Oh yes, all right.' When everybody was gone he said, 'Now, come on. let's do our Caliban scene together.' So I started. And then he said, 'Stop.' And he said, 'You know, there's something about Caliban, he's much more un-

67

happy than this, he's much more twisted. Try it this way.' And I tried it that way, and he said, 'But don't you understand, this is so liberating for Caliban. I think if you come up the stairs this way and come round here it would help you, you'd immediately be in the key position for your first line. Why not try it like that?' The scales fell off my eyes. I thought, 'This chap I don't like is a very great craftsman, he's a wonderful fellow, he knows an awful lot about his job.' And from admiration for him, as a professional, came friendship and admiration for him as a man, because he's a wonderful chap and a great director; we've worked together many times since.

Harcourt Williams, of course, was the director?

Harcourt Williams was our director and our mentor; everybody who worked with Harcourt Williams remembers him with great affection. Somehow he had the faculty for getting the best out of everybody. How he did it, I don't know. It was a kind of secret magnetism. He never bullied, he never worried you, he found out what you could do best and brought the two bests together. He himself was a terrible bundle of nerves. He was always eating Bemax in the stalls and rushing up and down and pulling his hair; but he made us calm, he took all the calmness out of himself. A very unselfish and delightful fellow.

During that season you played, for the first time, in Bernard Shaw's 'Arms and the Man'.

plate 78e Yes, we did *Arms and the Man*, John Gielgud was Sergius and I played Bluntschli. Shaw came a good deal to rehearsal and he helped me very much indeed. As you remember, when Bluntschli comes on at the beginning of the play, he has escaped from the enemy, and climbed up a drainpipe and in through a window in a terrible state of exhaustion. I tried to act the exhaustion and to show how utterly tired and shot to hell he was. We rehearsed this for a time, and I thought it was rather a good effect, and that I was rather good in it. Then Shaw came to me and he said, 'You know, Richardson, I'd like to have a word with you about your Bluntschli. It's going to be a very fine Bluntschli, I'm sure.' He was a wonderfully courteous, wonderfully polite man, I think perhaps the most polite man I've ever met in my life, especially sensitive to actors. You know, he'd take you aside and talk to you very quietly, very gently, very encouragingly. 'But,' he said, 'you know there's one thing the matter with your Bluntschli. When you come in, you show that you're very upset, you spend a long time with your gasps and your pauses and your lack of breath and your dizziness and your tiredness; it's very well done, it's very well done indeed, but it doesn't suit my play. It's no good for me, it's no good for Bernard Shaw.' He said, 'You've got to go from line to line, quickly and swiftly, never stop the flow of the lines, never stop. It's one joke after another, it's a firecracker. Always reserve the acting for underneath the spoken word. It's a musical play, a knockabout musical comedy.' That taught me a lot about playing in his plays.

When you undertake a new role for the first time, do you have a particular way of going about it?

Well, yes, we all have, we've all got different methods of working. Mine's very pedestrian, I'll tell you that, because I write my parts out before I go to rehearsal. I find this the easiest way to get a glimpse of the works of the speech, as it were; sometimes I write them out on odd bits of paper, sometimes in sketch books – it's dreary work, I can tell you.

You copy out the whole of the part, every single line?

No, no, not every line, just the key speeches. For instance, I have sketch books here filled

68

with hundreds of random bits and pieces. Sometimes I want to write them out big, some-times in very small writing; at other times, for a change, to make it look different, to see it in another way, I do it in blue or green ink. If I were to sit down like a Hindu and try to concentrate on the beauty of the speech, I couldn't concentrate on it at all, because I'd go to sleep or bore myself to death; and so I make myself, just as an exercise, write the thing out. It might take two hours to do a speech, but during the time that it takes to write it out, I have in fact made myself concentrate for that time on a bit of the work.

And it contains no more surprises for you?

Oh yes, it does. I find the most extraordinary things which if I'd just read the speech I'd never see at all. This is only a preliminary study. I do this work before I go to the first rehearsal and then, of course, it's changed again because when you start to speak the part and move in the part, to work with the other people, it's very often changed out of all recognition.

And you approach every part that you play in this way? The Falstaff that we all remember so well from the 1945 Vic season?

Oh, yes, yes. Falstaff must have taken quite a lot of paper, because, as you know, it's quite a complicated part.

Many people think that your Falstaff was, in many ways, one of your more successful Shakespearian ventures. Would you agree with that?

Yes, it did seem to go very luckily; I will admit that. It's a big part to tackle and I didn't think I could do it all. But my partner at that time, who was Laurence Olivier, said, 'Nonsense, all parts are difficult. Don't be so coy, don't be so silly. Just have a go at it.' So I did, and we did both Parts of *Henry IV*. My costume was wonderful, it was Alex Stone who designed it. She created a complete anatomy for me in padding, I had two or three stomachs, two or three chests, and two huge arms. And over this she put a very light, revealing flannel material, so that you could see the anatomy of the creature; in other words, he wasn't a puffed-up football, as he has often been. This was entirely Miss Stone's work and it helped me a great deal.

plate 75a, b

Do you think, on balance, that you've had greater success with characters like Falstaff, Bottom, Caliban, Toby Belch rather than the Iagos, the Othellos, and the Macbeths?

Yes, Perhaps I've done better in comedy than in the heroic Shakespearian parts. Iago wasn't too bad, but Othello and Macbeth were disasters.

plates 76, 77

Why do you think they were?

I don't know. They are parts that I would wish to play more than any other. And in the bathroom I'm rather good. I don't know what it is. I found, when I came to play Macbeth – 'Is this a dagger that I see before me?' – I just damn well didn't see the dagger and neither did anybody else. Perhaps I haven't the necessary emotional imagination. An actor's got to believe that he's all right in himself, otherwise he can't convince others; and I never believed that I was right, myself, in those parts. They attract me more than anything; I mean, I'd give half my life to be able to play Othello perfectly.

What about the semi-classic roles like Peer Gynt?

They're comparatively easy. They don't carry such a titanic voltage of poetry as the two parts I've mentioned. Peer Gynt is one of my favourite parts, I have a great liking for the character; the shape and structure of the plot also appeals to me.

You were talking about the enormous help it was, in playing Falstaff, to have the physical accoutrements sculpted for you, because, in effect, it gave you a springboard into the role. Now if you're playing in a contemporary play, you haven't got this kind of machinery. Does this worry you?

Oh, no. I mean, you're not waving swords and strange hats and things; but you're wearing the suit, the collar, the tie, and the make-up that you've chosen to express that man. You've got less material to work on, but the problems are the same.

You've played, with success, in a number of plays by J. B. Priestley.

plate 78b

I've always been tremendously attracted to Priestley's prose writing; it has considerable music, to my mind. I'm very devoted to Priestley and I find great beauty in his particular form of simplicity. The best of the shorter parts I have ever had was in *Eden End*; there I was given wonderful jokes all set to music.

Does he write specifically for you?

plate 78d

Yes, I think he did have me in mind when he wrote *Johnson over Jordan*.

What are your recollections of that, when you first played it?

I think I managed to find my feet in the part fairly well. It's a very simple part, it's a very simple play.

plates 80, 160b

By the time you were acting in 'Johnson over Jordan', you were already a well-established film actor. Over the years, which films have given you the most satisfaction?

It's hard to answer that. I don't think films give an actor very much satisfaction, when he's making them; but if they go well and they're successful, well, then he's very happy and lucky.

You rather imply that films don't give you the same kind of satisfaction as theatre work does?

In films the work is really never carried very far. It's never carried much further than an early rehearsal would be in a theatre part. You're unable to strike the deeper thoughts that you might have about the part, because they only appear after one has rehearsed for three or four weeks, tried it out for three or four weeks, and then perhaps played it a hundred times. It's only then that you're able to express what you really would like to get out of the part; and no film actor can do that.

You had a very long association with Alexander Korda, didn't you?

Yes, I did. I had a contract with him from 1935 to 1956, when he died, twenty-one years altogether.

Could you speak a little about that?

Anyone who has worked with Korda, actors and most directors, feel that they have worked with a prince, not only because of his generosity in business terms but because of his personal magnetism, interest, and sympathy.

Did he affect your acting very much?

No, I don't think he did, you know. One of his charms was that he left actors alone. He

70

didn't let directors alone because he'd once been a director himself; he didn't let the cameramen alone, he was a devil with them, because he'd been a cameraman himself. But he'd never been an actor, he never wanted to be an actor, and so he had this marvellous trick of encouraging them without trying to teach them. It may sound conceited, you know, but actors don't really like, finally, to be told how to do things.

Is it reasonable to infer from this, then, that in the theatre you have quite a different relationship with the director?

No theatre director, who really knows his business, ever gives an actor an important direction within two or three days of the final dress rehearsal. He's passing the work over to the actors, for them to take charge, for them to fly out of the nest, for them to be the masters, when he will unselfishly retire. But it's quite different in the film studio; there the director is simply collecting his material from the actors, till the moment when they've gone and he's going to take over and use all these little pieces of acting that are lying about in the laboratories and put them together. Then he will make the performance; the actors will not make the final performance at all.

How easily do you find you are able to establish a relationship with your audience in the theatre?

The actor feels the temper of the audience very swiftly, almost the moment he steps on to the stage. And, of course, it is his business to control that temper. But I don't think actors really love their audience; they are more in the nature of a lion-tamer. Perhaps the lion-tamer loves the lions, I'm not certain about that; but the actor must dominate the mood of the audience.

How far do you identify yourself with the character that you're playing? Do you have to believe in this person absolutely? Is he based entirely upon your own resources, or on your observation of other people? How do you set about it?

When you've decided to take a part, you think of all the people like that character that you've ever met; it's surprising then how vividly you remember people in your past, that you think you've completely forgotten – some old schoolmaster, or somebody who ran a shop – memories come crowding back. You change their costume, make them up differently, in your mind, till you get nearer and nearer to the identikit as the police say, don't they, if you recognize someone – and so you try to form the identity of the person that you're seeking to portray. You never really get very far until you start to rehearse, to concentrate on the one subject; and then, gradually, if you're lucky, the image of this person comes to you, and you try to make yourself as like him as you can.

Once you've created a character to your own satisfaction, during the course of a performance, how far are you aware of yourself in relation to the character that you've created? In other words, are you fully inhabiting the character, or are you stepping aside and having a look at him from the outside?

Part of it is stepping aside and controlling it, that's the first thing. You're really driving four horses, as it were, first going through, in great detail, the exact movements which have been decided upon. You're also listening to the audience, as I say, keeping, if you can, very great control over them. You're also slightly creating the part, in so far as you're consciously refining the movements and, perhaps, inventing tiny other experiments with new ones. At the same time you are really living, in one part of your mind, what is happening. Acting is to some extent a controlled dream. In one part of your consciousness it really and truly is happening. But, of course, to make it true to the audience, all the time, the actor must, at any rate some of the time, believe himself that it is really true. But in my experience this layer of absolute reality is a comparatively small one. The rest of it is technique, as I say, of being very careful that the thing is completely accurate, completely clear, completely as laid down beforehand. In every performance you're trying to find a better way to do it, and what you're reshaping, the little experiments, may be very small indeed, and quite unnoticed by your fellow actors; but they are working all the time. Therefore three or four layers of consciousness are at work during the time an actor is giving a performance.

A 1914 Aged 12

B 1925 Richard Coaker, *The Farmer's Wife*, with Primrose Morgan (Sibley Sweetland)

C 1923 Mark Antony, *Julius Caesar*

D 1928 Ben Hawley, *Aren't Women Wonderful?*, with Dorothy Turner

F

A 1944 Peer, *Peer Gynt*, with Sybil Thorndike (Aase)   B 1944 Peer, *Peer Gynt*

C 1946 Cyrano, *Cyrano de Bergerac*

A 1945 Falstaff, *2 Henry IV*,
with Laurence Olivier (Shallow)

B 1945 Falstaff, *1 and 2 Henry IV*

C 1944 Richmond, *Richard III*

D 1947 Face, *The Alchemist*

A 1931 Henry V

B 1952 Prospero, *The Tempest*

C 1952 Volpone, with Anthony Quayle (Mosca)

D 1956 Timon, *Timon of Athens*

A 1967 Anthony Absolute, *The Rivals*

B 1962 Sir Peter Teazle, *School for Scandal*, with Anna Massey (Lady Teazle)

C 1938 Othello

D 1946 Cyrano, *Cyrano de Bergerac*

E 1964 Shylock, *The Merchant of Venice*

A 1932 Sergeant Fielding,
Too True to be Good

B 1934 Charles Appleby, *Eden End*

C 1953 Dr Farley, *A Day by the Sea*

D 1939 Johnson, *Johnson over Jordan*

E 1944 Captain Bluntschli, *Arms and the Man*

A 1957 Cherry, *Flowering Cherry*

B 1949 Dr Sloper, *The Heiress*, with Peggy Ashcroft (Catherine Sloper)

C 1959 Victor Rhodes, *The Complaisant Lover*,
with Phyllis Calvert (Mary Rhodes)

D 1966 Waiter, *You Never Can Tell*

A 1962 James Tyrone, *Long Day's Journey into Night* (film)   B 1948 Karenin, *Anna Karenina* (film)

C 1948 Baines, *The Fallen Idol*, with Bobby Henrey (film)

A 1913 Aged 5

B 1929 Naemi, *Jew Süss*

C 1930 Desdemona, *Othello*, with Paul Robeson (Othello)

A 1933 Portia, *The Merchant of Venice*

B 1933 Perdita, *The Winter's Tale*

C 1935 Juliet, *Romeo and Juliet*

D 1935
Juliet, *Romeo and Juliet*, with
Laurence Olivier
(Romeo)

82

A 1944 Ophelia, *Hamlet*   B 1950 Viola, *Twelfth Night*   C 1950 Beatrice, *Much Ado about Nothing*

D 1950
Cordelia, *King
Lear*, with John
Gielgud (Lear)

A 1953 Cleopatra, *Antony and Cleopatra*,
with Michael Redgrave (Antony)

B 1951 Mistress Page,
Merry Wives of Windsor

C 1944 Titania, *A Midsummer Night's Dream*, with John Gielgud (Oberon)

D 1953 Portia, *The Merchant of Venice*

E 1957 Imogen, *Cymbeline*

F 1960 Katharina, *The Taming of the Shrew*

A 1963 Queen Margaret, *Richard III*

B 1961 The Duchess, *The Duchess of Malfi*

C 1963 Queen Margaret, *Edward IV*

D 1963 Queen Margaret, *Henry VI*, with William Squire (Suffolk)

A 1937 Irina, *Three Sisters*, with Michael Redgrave (Tusenbach)

B 1961 Madame Ranevsky, *The Cherry Orchard*, with John Gielgud (Gayev)

1964 Madame Arkadina, *The Seagull*, with Peter Finch (Trigorin)

C 1936 Nina, *The Seagull*, with Stephen Haggard (Konstantin Treplev)

A 1951 Electra, with Pauline Jameson

B 1954 Hedda, *Hedda Gabler*,
with Micheál MacLiammoír (Brack)

C 1949 Catherine Sloper, *The Heiress*,
with James Donald (Morris Townsend)

D 1959 Rebecca West, *Rosmersholm*

A – C 1947 Evelyn Holt, *Edward, My Son*

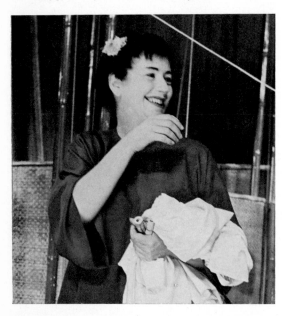

D & E 1956 Shen Teh/Shui Ta,
The Good Woman of Setzuan

F 1966 The Mother, *Days in the Trees*, with Brian Badcoe (Dede)

PEGGY
ASHCROFT

Peggy Ashcroft talked to David Jones on the stage of the Aldwych Theatre, London, and in a television studio. David Jones is a theatre and television director, and is Artistic Controller of the Royal Shakespeare Theatre Company. His comments are in italic.

I'd like to say that I think this title, Great Acting, is misleading, because it means different things to different people. You *could* say that great acting is something that happens just perhaps for a moment in one performance, if you're lucky. Perhaps not at all at another performance. Or other people might apply it to a whole performance.

Do you think you're sunk if you ever think about great acting?

Yes, absolutely.

Have you ever done that? Said, 'I'm going to give a great performance'?

No, never.

Have you ever thought about other actors, then, as you've watched their performances and said, 'That's great acting'?

If one thought it *during* a performance, it wouldn't be great acting! Afterwards – yes, I have said 'That is a great performance', like Laurence Olivier's Othello – that was great acting.

plates 38c, 39c

Have you ever got thoroughly fed up with the whole business of acting?

Oh, yes. I've thought I'd like to do something else. I think the point about it is that you can be awfully bored and fed up with your own acting, the business of having to do it all the time, you know; but the thing that you don't get fed up and bored with is the theatre.

Yes. Tell me one thing. Komisarjevsky in his autobiography gets very cross with people who said of his sister Vera that she went on the stage to get away from life. Now do you get cross when people suggest that acting is an escapist profession?

I don't get cross because I expect there is an element of truth in it. Perhaps it is sometimes an escape from life or it can be an enlargement of life. I think, too, many people say that you have to live in order to be able to act, and that what you put into your performance is what you've learned from life. But I have a theory that you can learn about life from acting, because an author's creations of character can teach you a great deal about psychology.

What was your first impulse towards acting? Was it a socially acceptable thing, that everyone did at school, was it a psychological need in yourself, or was it more of an instinct?

I think it happened when I came to love Shakespeare – at school. This is supposed to be very unusual! But I was fortunate at my school because we were encouraged to *act* Shakespeare and not just 'study' him.

Was it the thought of speaking marvellous speeches or becoming different people that attracted you?

Originally Shakespeare excited me because of the words, but then it became the excitement of character and drama; the fascination of a character living apart from you, and you becoming that character, or involving yourself in it; finding out how to make the character alive.

Did you have some magical marvellous teacher?

We had a very exciting 'elocution mistress', as she was called in those days, Gwen Lally, who had been a Shakespearian actress herself. Once a year at school she produced a full-length Shakespeare play which she directed; and that was very stimulating.

At what age did you seriously think that this was something you could do for the whole of your life, that you could become an actress professionally?

I think when I was about fourteen.

And there was a battle for this? Was it regarded as an okay thing to be an actress?

No. I was told that I was never going to be an actress, but when I was sixteen I put up a big fight, and I was allowed to leave school. It wasn't perhaps an advisable thing but I did get taken on at the Central School when I was sixteen, with a proviso, on my mother's side, that I should take the Teachers' Course and become a teacher. But fortunately dear Elsie Fogerty weighed in and I did the straight acting course, which in those days was shorter than it is now – and so I started work in the theatre at eighteen.

When you first went into the theatre and you were finding your first job and holding it down, when you were young and inexperienced, was it a very tough atmosphere to move in? Did you have to steel yourself to start off?

The difficult thing was getting one job after another, and the first break was the difficult one. I started in a very gentle way because I went into a theatre called Playroom Six which all took place in quite a small room. But I had had one experience in a theatre before that when I played Margaret in *Dear Brutus* for the Birmingham Rep., when I was still at the Central School.

Did you find the leading actors at that time helpful when you came into a company as a young actress or was it a question of survival of the fittest?

In *Dear Brutus* I played with Ralph Richardson who was then a young man; I already considered him a great actor, because I'd seen him when I was at school play in many Shakespeare parts which had impressed me enormously. But I was much too frightened of him to learn anything and I knew I was completely inadequate. Anyway it was only for a week. But I expected when I went into the theatre to learn, to be taught, by directors that I came into contact with much more than I found was the case. It wasn't really until I had the good fortune to play in a production that Granville Barker directed that one suddenly met somebody who really knew all about it, and whom you knew could teach you something that you desperately wanted to learn.

Did it seem unsatisfactory to you right from the beginning that, as an actress, you were at the mercy of a series of individual plays, set up under the star system to make money, or did you accept this as how the theatre was in England?

Well, of course, at first, the excitement is that you're going from part to part and trying to get one job after another; whatever you are asked to do – whether you like the play or not – you must do it. Sometimes I longed to walk out because I thought it was nonsense, or rubbish, or I couldn't do it, or something like that; but fortunately I never did. And then gradually, I think, I did have this feeling that it was a disordered profession; I wasn't slowly building from one thing to another.

As early as 1929 Komisarjevsky had outlined everything that was wrong with the English commercial theatre, and he spread the news of the Russian system, which was something quite alien to England, with a permanent company performing in repertory. Was it from him that you got your idea of what the theatre might be, or did a certain amount of it come from working at the Old Vic in 1932–3?

I certainly learned a great deal from Komis about acting and the theatre in general and I had worked with him before I went to the Vic. The Vic, in those days, was run on a three-weekly repertory system and had little in common with the repertoire system as we know it now. We were mostly young actors and I don't think we had much time to think about anything except learning our lines and getting the play on in time. It was a fairly testing time for me as I had never done any repertory before, and twelve major parts in nine months seemed an enormous burden. I think it's very good for actors to stretch themselves beyond their capabilities up to a point, but not to go on doing it too long, because finally it's discouraging to find you can never achieve what you know should be done.

When did the company idea first get planted in you?

I think I realized the true value of a permanent company when I began to work with John Gielgud at the New Theatre; he had also worked with Komis. John became, in a sense, the first actor-manager of my generation, and he wished to surround himself with actors all of a certain calibre. He never wanted to be the star of the company, he wanted an ensemble of acting, which he managed to achieve: first at the New Theatre, and then later at the Queen's Theatre – I was in seven of these productions – directed by John himself, Komisarjevsky, Tyrone Guthrie, and Michel Saint-Denis, and it was by far the most formative part of my acting experience.

I suppose the production which, in a way got the whole ball rolling on this idea of a first-rate company of players was John Gielgud's production of 'Romeo and Juliet' at the New Theatre in 1935, in which you played Juliet. When you came to tackle that part, you had already done it before and with Gielgud. Did you find this was a help or a hindrance?

plates 34a, b, 82c, d, 147a, b

An enormous help. I think it is a tremendous help to be able to play any of the great Shakespeare parts more than once; the younger you are the more that applies.

Do you think it's true about Juliet, that you can only play the part either when you're Juliet's age, or when you're old enough to be totally distant and detached about it?

I think you probably play Juliet better when you're in your late twenties than you can when you're twenty, because you've got to have a lot of technical experience to encompass such a very long and elaborate part; but the essence of it is that she is a girl of fourteen, and, as long as you can convey that, you are not too old to play it. Look at Ulanova and Fonteyn.

Were you satisfied with that Juliet you did in 1935?

No one is ever satisfied with a performance, I don't think, but I was much more satisfied. I mean, I felt far nearer to it than I ever did in either of the other two productions.

What about Cleopatra? With a part as difficult as this, where do you find you really begin. What was the starting point, what was the first thing you did when you knew you were going to play the part?

plate 84a
I wanted to play her as a Greek, which she was historically, and not as an Egyptian, because I think this makes a great difference to one's interpretation.

Did you start from that character idea first, and then go back to the text and find out whether it was legitimate?

No, one begins with the text because it's the text that leads you to the character. Then you inquire more about Cleopatra and you find out this or that fact about her, and finally one is entirely in the hands of the text.

Was the idea of Cleopatra being Greek something that appealed to you because it was historically true, or was it something you felt you could use in your approach to the part?

The Greek tradition of cunning and bravery and trickery and seductiveness was something that one could read and understand in her character in Shakespeare's play. I think that an Egyptian would be more Sphinx-like and veiled than the woman Shakespeare drew.

Of all the parts you've played is Cleopatra the one that you've found most rewarding and exciting?

Yes, I think so.

Now, to go on to something quite different. When you were playing Chekhov in the thirties, did you find that your approach to characterization was different from your approach to the characterization in a Shakespeare play?

The problem in Chekhov is quite different because it's such a tremendously detailed study of a character, and the lines you speak are never telling the story because that in a way is immaterial – mood and atmosphere are more important. What is said is, of course, important – but what is unsaid, what we call the sub-text, is more important. The characters reveal themselves indirectly, but they are completely *there* to be revealed – layer by layer like Peer Gynt's onion! And one's trust in Chekhov can be complete, for there is not a pause or a comma which is irrelevant to his intention.

When you were in those Chekhov parts in the thirties you worked for two very remarkable directors, first for Komisarjevsky and then for Saint-Denis. In general, have you found directors a help to you?

With those particular directors, an immeasurable help – but there are very few directors who can give actors inspiration or directors to whom actors will completely entrust themselves. Of course, the most brilliant directors always make the actors feel that they're really doing it themselves!

I like a director who works very systematically. I don't really like the director who says, 'Let's do it this way', and then tomorrow says, 'Oh, let's try it quite another way', because I think that, on the whole, actors like to dig their roots in and build their characters slowly and develop them, rather than be constantly uprooted and have to do it another way. This is particularly so the younger you are. As you get older you can probably adapt yourself to think, 'Well, I can just wait and I shall get back to the roots, even if I have to branch out and do something quite different.' Now, I think I can work happily with both methods.

I love working with Peter Hall; to me he is one of the most exciting directors I've worked with. 'The Wars of the Roses' really came to life, because of his and John Barton's conception of the historic pattern of the whole thing. They knew just how they wanted to present them.

In that 1936 'Seagull' you played Nina, Edith Evans played Arkadina, and John Gielgud played Trigorin. Twenty-five years after that you appeared in 'The Seagull' again and this time you played Arkadina, Vanessa Redgrave played your old part of Nina, Peter Finch was Trigorin. When you started on that new production, did you find you were able to start completely from scratch or were you in any way haunted by the ghost of the old production?

plates 86c, 126a, 150c

plate 86d

Certainly I remembered the old production fairly completely, but fortunately I was playing another part.

Take Arkadina herself; I suppose one of the qualities you've been most praised for in your acting, always, is emotional sincerity. Here was a woman, one of whose hallmarks was emotional insincerity.

I don't think a quality you may have been praised for must always be used! Perhaps she is an insincere woman and a shallow one, but her feelings are real, although she shows them in a terribly over-emphatic and actressy way.

I remember that the audience laughed at the end of your appeal to Trigorin to go away with you. Do you mind that?

Oh no, no, that's what one wants.

In a way that's really what I was trying to get at, I think, when I talked about her being emotionally insincere. As an actress, what you do with that part is to me, in the best sense, a satirical portrayal; and although you are completely the woman, you are also showing the audience the elements of that woman which can be laughed with and laughed at, at the same time.

Yes, the scene you mention illustrates exactly what I meant about her sincerity and in-sincerity – her fear of losing Trigonin is absolutely genuine. The means she uses to try to keep him are artificial and ludicrous, and the interplay of these two factors makes the scene both tragic and comic.

You were saying just now that the process of discovering a Chekhov character was like having to reveal, layer by layer as with Peer Gynt's onion, the character that is underneath it. Is it the same process in discovering an Ibsen character?

No, I don't think so. In one sense all acting is the same process, but nothing could be more different, could it, than the styles of Chekhov and Ibsen? And it seems to me that the process you go through follows in a way the difference in the character of the writing. Chekhov is instinctive, poetical, impressionistic, and therefore one finds a Chekhov character in a much more intuitive way than in Ibsen. Ibsen's plays are more like mar-vellous pieces of architecture that he has constructed subtly, carefully. There is a plot, there is a definition of character, and there is a story and a theme, a social criticism or a disclosure of something he feels about society and about people. And though of course I know he is a poet too, I think he's a much more intellectual writer than Chekhov. So one's processes in finding how to play an Ibsen character are on a more conscious rather than a subconscious level.

What is it about Hedda Gabler that attracts you? Why do you want to play that kind of character in the theatre?

plate 87b

What exactly do you mean by 'that kind of character'?

She's very unsympathetic, larger than life; she's a monster in many ways, and you've got to make her a real person.

Well, I think she *is* a very real person. What first interested me about Hedda Gabler and made me want to play her was – I think it was in an Archer preface when he said, 'Hedda is the sort of woman whom you take down to dinner every night.' Hedda is an ordinary woman. There are many people like Hedda. And I think one of the fascinations about Ibsen is what he himself said, 'I write about ordinary men and women.' But he showed in the ordinary person their extraordinariness. And after all we live in an age when the anti-hero is the popular character in the play. People are not particularly interested in heroes any more, or what was heroic. The conflicts in a character are what Ibsen examines and discloses. Certainly Hedda is one side a monster; one side she was a marvellous human being, but she was spoiled by circumstances – by the narrowness of society that didn't allow a girl of ambition to work her own way out. She was the victim, if you like of society at that time. She was the victim of having a father complex. She was the victim of snobbery. She *was* all those things. But I think one not only hates Hedda but one loves her too and one pities her. It's very interesting.

When I played her in Norway, I felt that the audience there loved Hedda. They don't condemn her as we condemn her. And in playing her I think I intended to underline the satiric, the comedic side of her, because I think that Ibsen deliberately put it there. Certainly she is a tragic character in the sense that tragic figures are the victims of their own natures rather than, or as well as, circumstance. The play is a tragedy but it is also satirical and sardonically comic at times, I think. But it is the marvellous mixture of all the things in it that makes it so fascinating to play, and to try to discover where the balances are.

Would you agree with one of the critics when he said that it's an odious play, clumsily constructed, coarse-textured, a melodrama without a single, sympathetic character?

No, no I wouldn't agree at all.

It's strange, isn't it, that most of the critics in this century have criticized this play for being of that nature?

I think Tesman is a very sympathetic character. Brack is a sinister, malevolent person. Thea is sympathetic, touching – and I certainly don't think the play is coarse-textured, I think it's fine and acute to a degree.

Archer, of course, and Agate thought it was a wonderful play.

Well, there are two critics who would agree with us that this is a very fine play. After all, when Ibsen was writing most of the critics were against him because he was an innovator.

Do you think that Rebecca West in 'Rosmersholm' has any similarity with Hedda Gabler?

plate 87d

I think she has similarity in that she also, if you like, is an anti-heroine, and perhaps what is so particularly fascinating in Ibsen's characters, and particularly the women (and certainly he excels in drawing women), is, again like Hedda, the ambivalence: Rebecca is partly noble, partly ignoble. She had been what she called a free women, a new woman, the sort of woman that Ibsen was writing about in his time, and she becomes as she says ennobled by Rosmer and her love for Rosmer, but she also becomes subjugated to laws which she had defied before. But I think there will always be a question mark at the end of *Rosmersholm* as to exactly why she was ready to go into the mill race.

94

Is the symbolism in Ibsen difficult to work into the general pattern of the play?

It's something that, in a way, isn't the actor's problem. Ibsen has put it there. The actor has to portray the character in the realistic, the deepest sense that he can find, and since the symbolism is part of the texture of the writing, it will come out. But I don't think one has to be too aware of it, or troubled by it, any more than you should *show* that you are aware of speaking verse when you are playing Shakespeare. You *are* speaking verse; it is a poetic play; but you, as an actor, are embodying the character in the form in which the author wrote it. So with Ibsen's symbolism the same thing applies.

When you played Ibsen in Scandinavia, did you find that the audience reacted differently from the way they do in England?

I've only played one Ibsen play in Oslo and that was *Hedda Gabler*, and as I said, I felt the audience's love and understanding of this character. Perhaps that sounds rather exaggerated, but they understood her nature in a way that we don't, or we find it more difficult.

Do you think that, now women all have a vocation, it makes a difference to the acceptance of the plays?

Yes, I do. Their problems – or some of them – are no longer ours. And I think that one has to be very much aware of their milieu and the difficulties under which they lived.

We have talked about the approach to Chekhov and Ibsen characters. What about playing Brecht? Are the problems similar or are they very different?

Well, we must go back to my answer about Chekhov, that the approach to acting all parts is basically the same, and this still applies to Brecht. Of course, we all know about the big question mark of alienation. When we did the production of *The Good Woman of Setzuan*, we were lucky enough to have Helène Weigel at some of the rehearsals and I asked her what her attitude to alienation was, because it seemed to me, when I had seen a Brecht play in Germany, that it is Brecht himself in the writing of the plays who performs this act of alienation. The actor has, as we say, to realize the character that he plays just as fully as in any other dramatist. But Brecht was not interested in psychological investigations of character, and so the actor has to make his effect with great economy of means, but the realization must be complete. I was rather relieved to find that Helène Weigel agreed with this and I am sure that some of the intensive exercise and concentration of the Ensemble – the Berliner Ensemble – is the economy of means with which they present a character. I know it is said now, for instance, that at Stratford there was a Brechtian approach to the 'Wars of the Roses'. Well, this is true, because we were covering an enormous canvas of history. It was important that we should all represent and *be* the characters that were taking part in this story as it unfolded; there was not time for development and ornamentation of character – what one might call, as an actor, indulging in the character. It was the action of the play which mattered to the spectator, and the impact of the play was from the story and the theme rather than the depth and detail of character.

plate 88d, c

Was the playing of two different characters in 'The Good Woman' a problem?

Oh yes, but it was a good fun problem for an actor. One moment to be this little prostitute whom Brecht paradoxically makes the one Good (with a capital G) character in the play; and then being transformed into the cruel, bestial male cousin. We all found it intensely difficult to arrive at the proper style in which to play, and I think we all felt that we only

95

began to discover it at the end of the run. It's always simplification and that's what actors are not used to here, and why one would probably only find exactly what this simplification had to be if one played Brecht for a very long time and in many of the plays.

What about playing in a mask?

Well, that was an enormous help. I rather fought the idea at the beginning. I wanted to be able to transform myself into the man without a mask. But we had the mask made – it was only a half mask – and I realized, when I put it on, how enormously it helped, because there was the external character created for me, and as each transformation only lasted for such a short time, I needed as much physical clarification of the change of character as possible.

You had to make direct asides to the audience, didn't you? Did you find these were difficult?

I don't think that it's any more difficult than playing an aside in Shakespeare, and most of Shakespeare's asides were meant to be addressed to the audience!

plate 85
Finally, I'd like to ask you about Queen Margaret, the part that won the 'Evening Standard' Award for you in 1965. When you were first asked to do the 'Wars of the Roses', were you at all worried by the melodramatic element?

No, I don't think so. One of the things that fascinated me about the part was that I was actually going to walk on to the stage holding somebody's head, and that seemed to me a tremendous challenge, something I looked forward to very much. And also to wipe blood all over somebody's face. Those are the things that excite you about a part. I mean, they seem so melodramatic that you say to yourself, 'Well, how can you possibly get away with that, make it believable?', and then you want to try.

It was the challenge of bringing the head on and not getting a laugh that appealed to you?

Sometimes, of course, it did get a laugh!

When you came to tackle young Margaret in the first part of the trilogy, did you find you used your experience of all the other Shakespearian ladies you'd played in getting to grips with her?

No, not really, because I think she's quite different. She's almost the only young Shakespearian heroine, apart from Cressida, a part I've never played, who isn't a heroine, who is black. She's not a sympathetic character right from the start, although she's a very intriguing one.

Was it a technical problem for you to get the extreme youth at the beginning? How did you set about doing that?

I don't think you have to think about that. You just have to try to feel that you're young and then trust to God and the make-up; the excuse that you have to play Margaret up to the time when she's an old hag-ridden witch justifies the fact that you have to play the young girl. So you don't worry about whether you can do it physically or not.

With the middle-aged Margaret you really got into your stride; the blooding of York must have been a fantastic scene to play. It had all the horror coming out of it as well as a tremendous depth of human emotion. Is it a scene that plays itself or are their great problems involved?

It is so good that in one sense it plays itself. But I would heave a great sigh, purely of physical relief, when it was over, because it's a very taxing thing to keep up the pressure, and it's very long. But it's a scene that creates such a world of horror of its own that it takes you with it.

Do you find that there's a difficult balance between the vehemence of what she was doing and the controlled violence of it all? Isn't that much more effective for being held in?

I think the bigger danger is to have it too controlled, because she is a woman in a state of absolute hysteria, on the edge almost of madness, of blood-lust. In order to play the scene that has to be apparent; so that if it's too controlled, then I think it's unbelievable. I kept in my mind the memory of having been sent my lover's head by his murderers, and the York murder seemed to me a psychological result of that. Not a justification, but an explanation.

One of the most effective things about the scene is the way in which York doesn't really break under this treatment.

The audience must see that she has lost by the end; as she, of course, loses the entire way through. She's forced to stay on as an old woman at the court of Richard III, when the only weapons left to her are her mocking hatred of Richard and her curses – she becomes the embodiment of the curse which is one of the main themes of the play.

The part of Margaret benefits more than any other by the trilogy, because if you see 'Richard III' on its own, you think, 'Who is this old bird who keeps coming on?'

Yes, I'd always thought I would never want to play that old queen in *Richard III*!

Exactly. And yet if you've seen everything she's gone through, the effect of this old ghost in the court is fantastic. From a playing point of view is it as rewarding to play as the other two stages of the character?

It illustrates what I mean about the farther a character goes in a certain direction the more rewarding it is to play. She certainly goes about as far into madness and decay as any character.

Were you aware of it as a totally rounded character right from the beginning, or did that only begin to happen when you played all three parts together?

We rehearsed the first two plays together as though it were one play, and we opened with them in one day, matinée and evening; so that part of it was one sweep, one development, the two climaxes of the part being the death of Suffolk in the first play and the murder of York in the second. Margaret in *Richard III* is the final climax of the whole character. Although *Richard III* was produced later, we had studied the three plays as one whole.

And do you think that it was this production more than anything that finally cemented the company feeling of the Royal Shakespeare?

Certainly such a production would not have been possible without a solidly founded company. I think that the season before showed clearly how much the company was coming together, how it had grown over the four years; the 'Wars of the Roses' was the culminating point.

Looking at the Royal Shakespeare Company now, do you think there is something different about its feeling of a company from what you began to achieve in the 1930's?

Oh yes, I think so. It's a larger company than we ever had in the 1930's. It's a wonderfully young company, on the whole – and that, of course, from an older person's point of view is partly the excitement of playing with it. The Royal Shakespeare Company has produced real leading players coming up from the company. This in itself is a very exciting thing. If I were young I should count myself very lucky to be starting at Stratford and the Aldwych. And when one thinks that there is the National Theatre as well, where actors can begin and develop their careers, it seems to me the theatre has come a long way since my early days!

MICHAEL
REDGRAVE

Michael Redgrave talked to Richard Findlater on the stage of the Yvonne Arnaud Theatre, Guildford, and in a television studio. Richard Findlater is a writer and journalist. He is an Assistant Editor of *The Observer*. His comments are in italic.

The Yvonne Arnaud Theatre is the theatre that we and the people of Guildford have been dreaming of for some years now; we were afraid we might not get it ready in time but we have. It's a pretty good theatre.

It's a wonderful thing to have done and an exhilarating experience for you, opening the theatre with your own production of 'A Month in the Country'. Returning to Guildford, in that way, must have been like coming full circle, because it's just about thirty years ago that you first started acting here, before you became a professional actor. I believe you were acting then as a schoolmaster at Cranleigh, nearby, and with the local amateur rep.

plate 116d

I like the phrase, 'acting as a schoolmaster', that was about what I was. I don't think I was a very good one, but I did do six productions in eight terms, which was rather stretching the school's dramatic capacities. I also did four productions with the then semi-amateur Guildford Rep. So I led a fairly theatrical life at the same time as I was teaching.

You seem to have been acting from your early schooldays. I know that your mother and father were actors; both sides of the family tree, way back, there were actors, uncles and aunts and grandparents. It seems to have been in your bloodstream.

Yes, I was always acting which, I suppose, meant that I had a definite urge. But it wasn't until I retired from being a schoolmaster that I determined to be a professional actor.

Although your mother was an actress, she didn't start you off as an actor?

No, on the contrary. Of course, being with her, and seeing her in plays, and seeing my uncles and aunts in plays, must have stimulated my interest enormously; but in fact it was my mother who *put me off* going into the theatre. She said – she had a very good phrase for it – 'too many people go into the theatre for what they can get out of it, and not enough go for what they can put into it', which is, I'm afraid, true. And I didn't think I had enough to give at that time. She also told me, bluntly, that I was 'too tall'.

Then when you went to Cambridge you acted a good deal with the A.D.C. Did that experience give you a kind of basic training which you found useful later, when you went on the professional stage?

Yes, it did. It wasn't only the A.D.C. I acted with, but mainly with the Marlowe Society which, as you know, has a very high reputation, especially for verse speaking. My friend George Rylands, who did most of the productions, is one of the best teachers of how to speak verse. He speaks it wonderfully himself, and he has got several generations of young undergraduates to speak it and understand it.

What about the bad habits? Were there any that you had to unlearn later on, when you went into the professional theatre?

I think I'm a little less conceited than I was then, but that wouldn't be difficult. I was very highly conceited: I thought I could do anything.

You were a star of your generation at Cambridge, according to my recollections.

I played the leading parts. . .

But not only in the theatre. You were a literary figure, a poet and a critic, a journalist; a Cambridge character, I imagine.

Yes, I was dramatic critic of the *Review*, and film critic of *Granta*. I started a paper of my own and I was editor of the *Cambridge Review*. Yes, I fancied then that I was going to be a writer.

So that's one reason why, when you left Cambridge, you didn't go on the stage?

Yes. That, and my mother's discouragement. Also my stepfather didn't want me to go on the stage.

Why did you choose schoolteaching?

There was little choice. I came down from Cambridge at the time of the slump, the depression; and the only commercial asset I had was a university degree. As I wanted to earn my own living I took a temporary job as a schoolmaster, and stayed nearly three years.

The extraordinary good fortune about that spell at Cranleigh was that you were able to do those productions; I mean that you played absolutely mammoth parts and you directed.

plate 113b, d I chose all the best parts, I must say – Hamlet, Prospero, King Lear, and Samson Agonistes.

Any special influences when you started on your Hamlet?

I was influenced by other actors of course. When I was a boy, Henry Ainley, Ion Swinley, Ernest Milton, and Godfrey Tearle were all my heroes.

You were as interested in producing then, as in acting, I imagine?

Yes, I was more interested in directing because I had this feeling that perhaps I *was* too tall, and not good enough as an actor. It was while I was there that I took a French class up to London to see the Compagnie des Quinze – Michel Saint-Denis's company – acting a play by André Obey; and I suddenly became fired with what it means to be a director and to have an ensemble company that really does express a point of view. And I dreamed that I could do something of the sort. To be a director – in the British theatre – you usually have to start by being an actor.

What was it about the Compagnie des Quinze that impressed you?

It was a near-perfection of style, the like of which you didn't often see in the English theatre, especially at that time.

How did you make the break?

In the Easter holidays, having given a term's notice as a schoolmaster, I went and gave an audition to Lilian Baylis at the Old Vic. She was not very encouraging; she said,

'Well, you'll hear from us.' Well, I didn't hear, the summer term started, and I thought 'I shan't hear anything. I must spread my nets a little wider.' So I went up to Liverpool over the Whitsun weekend holiday, and on the very day that I was going there, to see William Armstrong who ran the Rep., a contract arrived from the Old Vic from Lilian Baylis, for three pounds a week. So I thought, 'Well, if the worst comes to the worst, I can go back to that.' It wasn't the worst, because I should have been very glad to go to the Vic. But William Armstrong was so impressed that I had a contract for London and that I wanted to come to a theatre in the provinces that he said, 'How much is your contract for?' and I said, like a fool, 'Three pounds a week', and he said, 'I'll give you four.' I've always thought, ever since, that if I'd said eight, he would have said nine.

At that stage of your career, coming as you did for the first time into a professional company, did you not feel that you needed some kind of particular propping?

As I told you, I thought I could do anything: I was still very, very conceited.

What was it that Armstrong did? Was it the emotional temperature he created for you and the other younger players in that company?

It was a wonderful rep., really wonderful, and he was a great encourager. I wouldn't put him in the front rank of directors, but he had a flair for finding people and a great love for the work, which he could instil into young people, and that was very fine. It may not sound the ideal set-up, but in a kind of way what he created was a very happy family. It was a very lovely theatre, and we had enthusiastic audiences: we were always packed every night, I think, for whatever play we did. They were nearly all modern successes of the West End stage; we never did anything like, say, Ibsen; once a year we did a Shakespeare, just as a touch of culture.

At Guildford and Cranleigh, of course, you played in classics almost entirely.

That was one of the reasons I was very glad to go to Liverpool. If I'd gone to the Vic, I would have been carrying a spear and playing tiny parts in Shakespeare, and I thought I'd done enough Shakespeare for the time being; I wanted to learn how to act in modern plays.

In adjusting yourself to this new life, did you find a way of making short cuts which rep. actors traditionally have to do, or did you see other people making them and pick them up?

I know what you mean but, when you've got three weeks' rehearsal and three weeks' playing time for each play, there is much more time, so that you don't have to rely on short cuts, which later develop into almost ineradicable tricks and mannerisms.

Then, after being only two years in the professional theatre, you went zoom *to the Old Vic, playing leading roles. How did that happen, that sudden jump?*

Tyrone Guthrie, on the way to Ireland, stopped off at Liverpool and saw me and my wife, Rachel Kempson, in a play of Bridie's. He offered us the juvenile leads at the Old Vic, with Laurence Olivier and Edith Evans; so our cup of happiness was full.

Before you went down to London had you overcome the feeling of being too tall?

I used to be a little self-conscious about it, I think, but various people, including Edith Evans, helped me enormously. Edith, of course, was one of the very greatest influences on me; I owe a very, very great deal to her.

You played Orlando to her Rosalind in 'As You Like It'. That must have been a wonderfully kindling experience for you.

It was the most thrilling thing that had ever happened to me. I had gone into the theatre in a somewhat idealistic way. As I said I wanted to be a director of a fine ensemble company, which I thought I could be, even if I couldn't be a leading actor; and Edith said something, once, that really changed my whole attitude towards the profession. She said, 'What sort of actor do you want to be, Michael?' and I said, 'Well, how do you mean? I'd like to play all sorts of parts.' She said, 'No, no, I don't mean that. I mean do you want to be like John, or Larry, or do you want to be like Peggy Ashcroft, or me? What sort of standards are you aiming at?' Up till then I'd just had this idea of a company at the back of my mind; but I was fascinated to see myself playing starring parts, and then all that mattered was the parts. I realized that what she meant was that you've got to make up your mind, and set yourself a certain goal, before you can get anywhere.

Did you set it after that?

With her help, yes.

Apart from the wisdom Dame Edith passed on, about the craft of acting, the approach to acting, did she give you technical pointers?

No, not lessons; I mean we didn't sit down and go into it like that, but I remember that she would casually drop a remark which would later impinge. For instance, I remember her saying to me, 'When you hear me say that line' (which was just four words, 'perfectly, perfectly, Mr Horner' in *The Country Wife*) 'put your hand on my diaphragm,' and I did, and she said, 'Perfectly, perfectly, Mr Horner,' but so that you could hear it through the whole house. And she said, 'Do you realize I'm using more strength of voice just to say those whispered words, than I need for when I'm speaking loud.' That was a subtle way, I think, of telling me that I was occasionally dropping my voice, and that when I wanted to talk quietly I had to use more force and not less.

You worked with Sir Tyrone Guthrie in that season, of course. Was that a kindling experience in a different way?

A very different way, yes. And though I owe him my chance of having gone to that season at the beginning of my career, which was very valuable to me, as a director he made me very nervous. Somehow the thought that I was sure was in his mind conveyed itself to me; namely that he'd made a mistake in choosing me. At least, I think that's what he thought. I wasn't as good as he'd hoped I would be. And I wasn't either.

Wasn't one particular difficulty that season the way you had to play Mr Horner in 'The Country Wife', against what you thought was the grain of the part?

Yes it was, and that perhaps was one of the reasons why Guthrie and I weren't quite at one that season. He wanted this part, which is essentially a rather dirty-minded man, played as a fresh young man, to take the nastiness out of the play, because he thought he wouldn't get it past Lilian Baylis and the board of governors at the Old Vic. And so he, as it were, cleaned the play up. I kept wanting to leer, and make all sorts of noises that sounded lascivious and all the rest of it, because it is a very lascivious part, and he would say, 'No, no, I don't want any of that, just say it straight.' And that was very frustrating.

You were playing against your instincts?

I was playing against the text.

I think it is time we talked about some of the Shakespeare productions you have been in. Can you give us some idea of the way in which your imagination goes to work on different Shakespearian characters? Let's start off with the Chorus to 'Henry V'.

That's rather difficult. The only thing one thinks about the Chorus is that he is the personification of England and how much Shakespeare loved England.

A vocal instrument as it were, a voice.

That happened to be the way I played it. There are other ways, and very good ones too. I've heard it done as a sort of compère, quite quietly and with touches of humour and warmth, and a feeling of 'Now, I want you to understand how it was when King Henry V went to war': that works extremely well. I've seen Roger Livesey do it like that and give a very good performance. I don't think the way I did it is the only way by any means; it just happened to suit me and the kind of production we were doing. Remember also that the Memorial Theatre at Stratford-on-Avon is quite a big theatre to fill.

The problem of tackling a part like Antony in 'Antony and Cleopatra' must be very different. It's been avoided, as a role, by so many actors in the past. Why is that? I mean, Garrick tried it and wasn't successful.

It's a very curious leading part because it has all the appearances of nobility and strength, when in fact Antony is a weak man; and, except for what Enobarbus says about him, he's not a very noble man, at least you never see him doing anything noble. You have to create, convincingly, the image of a man who held part of the world in thrall, and you have very little to do it with; all you have is his voluptuousness. And what's more he dies at the end of the fourth act.

It must be difficult to sustain, when the part is so relatively fragmented. There aren't any big anthology chunks in Antony. I think I'm right in saying that your success in the part was quite a surprise to you?

plate 118a

Yes, I think it was. I had great difficulty, for the first time, in learning the text; it's an extremely difficult text to master, partly because it's chopped up, short sentences, short phrases.

Did you feel you learned something particular from the fact that it was such a success?

Oh, yes. I had, in fact, turned down the part at one time, with my same triumphant Cleopatra, Peggy Ashcroft. At that time I didn't think I could do it. And then I was persuaded, and so I was enormously relieved, as well as surprised, when it was such a success. It has occurred to me that I like attempting parts of men, as it were, in invisible chains.

Then there was Harry Hotspur – with a very good accent, I remember. Why did you choose it?

Because Hotspur is described sometime during the play as having a thickness of speech, and that is usually got round by the actor attempting a stammer. It works, as you remember, very well for the last line of his part, where he has a broken sentence. Antony Quayle suggested that perhaps the thickness of speech might be due to the Northumbrian country accent, and I don't mean the Geordie, but the country accent. So I went up to Northumberland with a tape-recorder and made inquiries and found people who could help me; especially one called Jack Armstrong, who has the title of the Duke's Piper, a splendid fellow. He took me all over the place visiting crofters and pubs, needless to say; the Duke himself was very kind, and I saw Alnwick Castle where part of the play takes place. And then I found a Northumbrian in London who worked with me on my recordings. It was never meant to be a perfect Northumbrian accent, it was an approximation, a selection, adapted for the theatre; I don't think anybody but a Northumbrian audience would have understood the full Northumbrian accent. But it was an enormous help to this rather braggart of a character, very boastful.

Of course, you were de-romanticizing Hotspur in that production.

Yes. I was trying not to make him the hero of the play but leaving that to Prince Hal, who was Richard Burton.

You didn't find this accent inhibiting in performance?

plate 119d

No. Of course, it must be worked on, and if you have time to work on it, that's fine. I must confess that last year, when I was at the National, one of my parts was in *Hobson's Choice*, as the Lancashire boot-maker. Lancashire doesn't come easily to me, nor to my shape of mouth; but because I was playing two other parts in the repertoire there was no time for me to go up to Lancashire with a tape-recorder and work on it. There were friends in the company who had good Lancashire accents, with whom I worked, but I didn't work hard enough. The result was that I didn't satisfy myself, and I didn't satisfy anybody else.

Getting down to the craft of acting, the technique of acting – every actor has to learn his business as he goes along, or at drama school, or wherever it is; did you start out, at an early age, consciously to learn the techniques?

No, I didn't. I had heard people talk about the art or the craft of acting, but it just seemed to me to be something you either had or you hadn't. It wasn't until much later that I started to think consciously about the craft of acting.

Was that because you felt that you were, sometimes, marooned without some kind of technique?

I think I became concerned about it when I got into longer runs, and there was time to think about it and how to preserve a performance; or indeed, how much you may vary a performance. I do vary a great deal, deliberately. I try to keep the same spirit but I use a lot of different details.

For your own refreshment, apart from the audience's, you mean?

And also for the other actors. I think if you can give a line a feeling of freshness, you get a better response. Of course, you mustn't be wild and erratic. At worst, I think I have been erratic at times, but at other times I hope not.

Going back to the learning of technique, and the immensely important question of voice, was it a technical process, this, apart from an attitude of mind towards your own equipment?

plate 114c

I was lucky enough to be born with what is called a well-placed voice: it is in the right place. But I was enormously helped by the singing coach at Glyndebourne. When I came to do *The Beggar's Opera*, Rudolf Bing, who then ran Glyndebourne, said that I could sing it all right, but he wanted me to be taught breathing, because he thought that I might, in a long run, lose my voice singing quite a lot of numbers.

You have said you were naturally endowed with a voice which worked for speech, but with this training for singing, didn't you find that it inhibited you, at the time?

No, no. The very fact of playing long, big strenuous parts, fairly constantly, in a sense limbers you up. You can't do a rehearsal of *King Lear*, or for that matter *Uncle Vanya*, or anything, without adding a sufficient timbre to your voice and increasing your stamina. I think Shaw was right when he said that if anyone would sing for half-an-hour each day they'd be in much better health; I'm sure he was right.

Have you found during the past ten years or so that your voice is always at your command? That it will respond to your will?

Yes, on the whole I think it does. I go on working at it a bit. I still sing a certain amount, but I think once you've got a voice, unless you're very self-destructive with it, you keep it.

There is often a strong attachment to naturalism in the theatre today, and the feeling that it is fake to project, in case a performance might lose its sense of reality.

Yes, and there is a more insidious trend at the moment that, unless you have some form of dialect, you can't be very real. People produce a number of quite phoney dialects to try and roughen their voices. This, I think, is a temporary fashion and won't, I hope, last very long. There is nothing more real about a dialect than there is about good speech, but people tend to think there is, and are encouraged to think so.

Right from the beginning, you had the ability to tackle these huge emotional parts. I wonder when you first realized that you could do this, work yourself up into a passion, and give this enormous demonstration of an assumed emotion and make it real?

I've always found it very easy to 'switch on' emotion, and that sounds as if it's phoney, but to me, at the time, it is real; and if it is real to me, then the chances are that it will be real to the people watching. I suspect it has something to do with the glands. Perhaps the adrenalin gland – I hope I'm right in saying that – is the one that tends to cause anger. There must be other glands that produce, more readily in some people than in others, emotions of different kinds – anger, love, misery, or whatever they may be. I am quite aware that some emotions come more readily to me than others; the torrential anger needed for Lear, for instance, is something that does not come easily to me.

It must be a matter of constant study and thought to know how to control the jet, the stream of emotion?

I think the best description of how that is controlled is the one by Joseph Jefferson, the American actor of many years ago, who, when he was asked his opinion about the so-called Coquelin controversy (Coquelin believing that an actor shouldn't feel anything at all, and Irving believing that the actor should appear to be feeling the very things he's talking about), said very meekly, 'As for me, I find that I act best when my heart is warm and my head is cool.' Even if it's only a metaphor, I think it's as near as anybody can get to explaining the state of mind and being that you are in, when you want to control something that could easily become excessive. If you cry too much you offend the audience – I have known that happen to me sometimes.

You can measure how much?

There's a little man inside my head, knocking and saying, 'Now steady, don't enjoy yourself too much.'

On the really big evenings of your life, when the god descends and you yourself, as an actor, feel the magic is working, does it feel as if something has taken over, or are you still in control?

It feels as if somebody has taken over, but in fact I think it is that you have complete

H

control. A conductor once told me that people frequently say to him, 'It must be wonderful to have such a feeling of power over this huge orchestra.' But, as the conductor says, that is the opposite of what you feel; unless the orchestra is responding perfectly and playing brilliantly you feel frustration rather than power. On the other hand, if they're playing extraordinarily well, it all becomes extremely easy. And it's roughly speaking the same with the actor: when you're working well, everything's ticking over, the glands are working right, and then, of course, it's easy, it feels as if a god were guiding you. But when it's not one of those evenings, then you have to be more careful.

Do the evenings when you feel at your best coincide with those evenings when the professional critics think you're at your best?

It's very difficult for me to know. I'm very seldom at my best on a first night. In fact I would almost say never at my best, and to me it's one of the sad things about our theatre in England that its history is largely a history of first nights. In other countries, the critics are allowed, even encouraged, to come later, when the actors have had time to play themselves in; the theatre is not regarded as news. It is in England.

How do you take criticism?

Actors and also creative artists instinctively resent criticism of any kind; they really like lots and lots of praise; but that's only part of it. I have noticed, looking back at the reviews of plays that I thought had been rather unfairly attacked, that on the whole I have agreed with the consensus of critical opinion.

plate 117c   *What about your 'Macbeth', which the critics didn't like in 1947?*

Well, that goes back to this first night thing, I'm afraid. I wasn't, perhaps, very good on the first night, but I'm not in the least ashamed of some of my later performances. I think I was very good when I was at my best. I thought the first night in London went quite well, and so did those concerned with it. In fact we triumphantly celebrated with a party, we thought we had a winner. It may have been that, because I had been making films for a number of years, in Hollywood and London, the critics thought it was rather presumptuous of me to play a leading Shakespearian role, which I had hardly done. I mean not of the size of Macbeth. It may have been that. It may have been that we were all wrong and I was just not very good. But we did run for our three months, and we did make money with it in London.

Will you come back to it?

Yes, but with a certain amount of dread. There is something about Macbeth which rather appals me. There are some parts of the play which are very, very hard work for the actor. There is only one scene, the scene in England, where the chief actor gets a rest, otherwise it's going the whole time.

Taking a rough division of the parts you've played during the last thirty years, they could be pigeon-holed into the haunted, tormented introverts, and the rather extravagant, social extroverts. Do you find one easier to play than the other?

However hard an actor tries it's difficult not to become typed to a certain extent. I have tried to make as great a variety in my parts as I was able. But evidently it is the sort of character (haunted you called them) that comes most easily, or more easily to me, and I may succeed in them a little bit better than I do in the others. I think that I have a natural

106

sympathy with ineffectual people like Tusenbach and Uncle Vanya and Uncle Harry – in fact, a whole series of Uncles; on the other hand, that doesn't deter me from trying the King Lears and Mark Antonys and so on.

It's something that satisfies you in playing both these kinds of parts, for different reasons?

I've only played one neurotic murderer for as long as a year and that was Uncle Harry. At the end of the year I had to leave the play, it was getting me down. It was not only the effort of doing it, night after night, but the strain that such emotions put on you. In simulating hysteria, you're bound to experience it a little yourself, I think.

plate 116a

There's one big influence on your work I'd like you to say something about – the writings of Stanislavsky. I wonder whether, because of his codification of the experience of acting, he supplied a kind of body of feeling, which gave you an extra something that you needed, coming into the professional theatre?

Yes, when I first came across Stanislavsky (because nobody told me about him) I misused what I read in much the same way as the later disciples of what is now called The Method have misused it; that is to say, I thought it permitted me to do anything that came into my head, regardless of whether it was right for the play. Very shortly after I first started reading him, for instance, I was acting in a naturalistic play which took place in a very untidy room. I was only playing a supporting part, a doctor. Intoxicated as I was at that moment by Stanislavsky, I thought a doctor would probably be rather a neat, tidy person, and I began to use the untidiness of the room, by picking up threads, tucking things away in a drawer. It wasn't my room, I was just visiting. I hadn't warned any of the other actors I was going to do these things, they thought I had gone quite mad, and in a way I had gone mad. That is an example of the way people do misuse Stanislavsky's teachings, especially in the phase which is now called The Method. But this doesn't get across to the audience, and it just throws the actors, unless it's been rehearsed. After all, a visiting doctor wouldn't tidy up other people's rooms for them, unless he thought something was going to be trodden on – it's as simple as that.

What brought you to a halt?

I don't remember. My great love affair with Stanislavsky's works slowed down, though I still have great admiration for him as a figure. What I value him for now is something that comes through all his writings – his enormous respect for his craft and for the art of the theatre.

The writings of Stanislavsky must have been helpful when you first came to play Chekhov, when you played Tusenbach in Michel Saint-Denis's production of 'Three Sisters'.

*plates 86a, 114f, 115c,
153b*

It was a good thing that I'd read Stanislavsky; I should have floundered a lot if I hadn't. But really Michel Saint-Denis was the greatest possible help. For instance, when I came to a big speech of Tusenbach's, which starts, 'Cranes, and migratory birds', and I started to spout it off, Michel said, 'No, no, no – this man is a bore, and he has no personality. You are playing this as if you had personality and were trying to make sense of this speech.' And I said, rather aggrieved, 'Well, isn't it the actor's job to try and make sense of the speech?' and he said, 'In this case, no.' I was rather upset, especially as it was in front of the whole company, and I felt I'd made a fool of myself, and so I said, 'Well, all right, let's try again. "Cranes, and migratory birds", for instance?' and went on for a few lines, and he said, 'Ah! You *hear*? That is *it*. One should not listen to him.' And I said,

'Well, if that's what you want, it's easy.' And from that moment on my performance started to grow, I had something to work on, the fact that I was playing a bore, which is one of the most difficult things to play and make interesting.

As a director Saint-Denis must have had a particularly stimulating influence.

Oh yes. He has very definite ideas of what he wants, sometimes up to a point that is a little frustrating, because you want to explore another avenue and he brings you back again and says, 'No, no, no, that's not the way to go, and this is.' And you say, 'I want to try', and he'll say, 'Well, all right, but you're wrong.' And he convinces you because he is a brilliant man.

Co-operative but, on the other hand, getting his own way?

This is how it should be with a director.

That he should have autocratic authority in the end?

In the last resort, yes.

What other advice did he give you?

plate 115c

It was with the details of the performance. For instance, I had invented, during re-hearsals, a bit of business where I went to sleep on a bolster, with my mouth open and breathing heavily; and this seemed to get a pleasing reaction from the audience. I re-member him coming round after we'd been playing for about a week. And he said, 'Do you know that moment when you do that? When you first did it, it was perfect. Now you are aware that you are moving the audience. Whenever you underline anything, which is what you are doing now, it is wrong. Anything that is underlined is bad art.' That is true.

One of your great performances in Chekhov was in 'Uncle Vanya' at Chichester and at the National Theatre. I believe you had wanted to play the part for some considerable time?

Yes, I had. Before the war I had been asked to go to the Old Vic and do, amongst other things, a Chekhov play. I chose *Uncle Vanya* because I could see certain things that re-minded me of Tusenbach. I thought that if I could do Tusenbach I could certainly do Uncle Vanya; and it was agreed that we should do it. So I decided to go across to Paris, to see a retired Russian actress who had been a great help to Michel Saint-Denis with his production of *Three Sisters*; and this woman, I was told, was very thrilled to know that I was coming. I had brought an interpreter with me and we went into her room, but she took one look at me and said, 'Non, non, non, no Vanya! no Vanya! Astrov! Astrov!' That put me off for quite a time. Anyway she said 'non' all the time. She wanted me to play the part of the doctor, Astrov, because of my size, 6 feet 2½ inches. And so I was delighted when Olivier rang me up, two or three years ago, for the Chichester Festival,

plate 119b, c

and asked if I would play Vanya; by then I had got over the feeling of being too tall.

It must have been of particular technical interest for you, playing on the open stage at Chichester and then coming to the proscenium stage at the Old Vic. Did it make a great deal of difference in projec-tion, from your point of view?

It didn't make too much difference. I took to the open stage quite well. The technical problems had been worked out very carefully by Olivier, keeping the action moving, allowing first one part of the audience and then another to see you and not turning away from any part for too long; those sorts of things he had worked out brilliantly, and it wasn't difficult to follow his instructions. But Vanya was written for a proscenium stage and it was, to my mind, much easier to play it in a proscenium theatre. Acoustically, moreover, the Old Vic is rather better than Chichester was at the beginning.

You played Vanya for the second year running at Chichester; did you find the character thickening, gaining spiritual density, from one season to the next?

No, I don't think my performance varied that much. As I told you I vary from performance to performance, partly deliberately and partly because I find it quite impossible to give an exact replica of a performance. Many actors can do it and do it well, though I frequently distrust that approach myself.

You've had a very successful film career. Some actors who have moved from the theatre to the cinema, backwards and forwards, rather endure *the cinema. Ralph Richardson, I recall, said that the actor didn't get anything out of the cinema, as an artist, because in filming he felt one never got beyond the stage of a first rehearsal in the theatre. Do you feel like that about it?*

No, I don't. I think the two media are different in this respect. At rehearsals in the theatre you can find things spontaneously, which you then have to work to make seem spontaneous when they no longer are and cannot be by the nature of things, because repetition makes that impossible. In the cinema, in some of the early takes, or in rehearsal, you will find something that is absolutely spontaneous and not modelled; and the camera can go right in and read your thoughts.

Even though, by the nature of filming, you're filming in little fragments rather than having a flow of acting as you are in a theatre?

Yes, I don't mind that now. When I first started in films, it worried me extremely.

When you first went in, I believe it was against your better judgement?

Yes. I had a great dislike of English films. In 1936 very few good films were being made, and English films generally were at their nadir. At that time Edith Evans had never filmed, Peggy Ashcroft hardly ever, John Gielgud not much; Laurence Olivier, it's true, did; they had quite a struggle to persuade me to do films. When I eventually did, I was persuaded into signing a long-term contract. But I made it part of my contract that I should have six months of the year free to do stage work, whatever happened; that was the deadline. The film-makers didn't like that at all; but I kept to it.

You don't feel that your films interrupt the development of your stage work, because you've kept the two in play, as it were, for a number of years?

No, I don't think it interrupted anything, and it allowed me to do some plays I wanted to do which I didn't think would make very much money.

Would you say that great acting is possible on the cinema screen, without an audience?

I have seen some screen performances that are as great – to use a word I don't really like using – as any that I've seen on the stage.

You once said that you wouldn't recommend the cinema as the place for a young actor to learn to act. You should learn in the theatre?

Yes, I wouldn't recommend the cinema to a young actor. Ralph Richardson said to me once, 'You sell to the cinema what you've learnt in the theatre.' There is some truth in that. But I do think there are some things you can learn from both. From Carol Reed I learnt a great deal about the craft of film-making as apart from film acting. I learnt a good *plate 120a* deal from Cavalcanti during *Dead of Night*, the ventriloquist film; there are several others, Joe Mankiewicz for one. Fritz Lang taught me quite a lot in a very bad film. There isn't time to establish a really close personal contact with a film director; he's wanted all the time. You're very lucky if you can say to him, 'Can I have twenty minutes to talk to you about something?', very lucky.

plate 120b   *I remember you did Terence Rattigan's 'The Browning Version' which Anthony Asquith directed.*

There's a man who's taught me a very great deal and I really loved working with him each time. I think we've done three films together. He has complete sympathy for the needs of the artist and he understands those needs very well. He knows what he wants, and yet he is very flexible. If you say you would rather do it here, or you would rather do the whole thing in long shot, he'll listen and perhaps he'll agree. So many directors, the coming directors, develop a *persona* of absolute authority which must never be contradicted over anything, and that, I think, is a pity. Asquith with all his gentleness and humility knows what he wants, but he is quite susceptible to other ideas.

Coming back to Guildford, this was the third time you had played Rakitin in 'A Month in the Country' – what is it about this character that has drawn you back?

plate 116d   Quite frankly it isn't so much Rakitin as the play; I think it is an enchanting play. Although I was young enough when we first did it, I could still, perhaps, have played the tutor. I certainly couldn't now. I'm getting a bit old for Rakitin, for that matter.

Each time, I imagine, you found new corners, new depths, new directions in the play?

I thought for a moment you were going to say new things to add. On the contrary, one finds things to subtract. And I think that's true of all parts, of any content; you don't think 'What more can I do?' but 'How can I achieve the same effect by doing less?'

Looking back, would you say conditions are better for a young actor going into the profession now, compared with 1934, 1936?

Oh yes, I would indeed, especially in terms of tackling these great parts that we have been talking about and which I think it is essential for young actors to be able to do, as they progress. Then there was only the Old Vic – and a very different Old Vic, too – and the Memorial Theatre at Stratford, working in very, very difficult circumstances; at Stratford they had about twelve rehearsals per play, at most. Nowadays, apart from that, there is more available employment. Television and films have made it much easier for them to earn a living. But also they have the National Theatre and the Royal Shakespeare Company as solid achievements, which set a standard and an aim, and will set an even higher standard and aim. I would wish to see this reflected all round the country in different municipal areas, Manchester, Edinburgh, Cardiff, and so on, and I'm happy to say most people think the same.

EDITH
EVANS

Edith Evans talked to Michael Elliott at her London home and in a television studio. She also spoke to students at the Central School of Speech and Drama. Michael Elliott has directed plays for the Royal Shakespeare Theatre Company and the National Theatre, and was the last Artistic Director of the Old Vic company; he also directed Edith Evans in a television production of Anouilh's *Time Remembered*. His comments are in italic.

My mother and father had nothing to do with the theatre. My father was a minor civil servant, in the Post Office, in quite a position of authority. And then my mother had a great deal of energy and skill – she was not very happy at doing nothing – so he took a house in Ebury Street, as an apartment house, mainly for her; it was actually next door to Noël Coward whose parents were doing more or less the same thing.

I love this picture of you when you were five, standing with your hoop. Did you have a happy childhood? *plate 121a*

Oh, I think I did. I can't remember anything except that I was very naughty, but I didn't mean to be naughty; that's the only thing I can say in my favour. There was too much of me altogether, you know, I nearly drove them crazy.

Did you go to the theatre when you were a child? Or think of the theatre?

No, no, hardly at all.

Did you start as an actress as soon as you left school?

No, I was apprenticed to millinery, two years up and down, to Mr Blackaller in the Buckingham Palace Road. The shop's gone now, but it was this side of Gorringes, a very respectable sort of draper, with Mr Blackaller in charge.

Did you enjoy making hats?

I enjoyed being with people, and I liked touching lovely materials and things like that, but I could never make two hats exactly the same.

What made you go to night school?

It was a Shakespeare class, where I met other boys and girls – I was an only child and a very lively one, and so I always wanted to be where there were other people. Then the class was run by a friend, Nell Massey; she's still alive, a most wonderful woman, over ninety. She's very well known amongst a lot of professional actors and actresses who started working with her as amateurs.

Was it with her that you played Beatrice in 'Much Ado About Nothing'?

Yes. At the Streatham Town Hall. William Poel, the famous old Elizabethan specialist, came. He was responsible for all the continuous work that the Players do now; in those days they always stopped dead at the end of every scene and did a lot of back-slapping; but he got all that tidied up. He saw me play Beatrice and he thought I'd be just right for

Troilus and Cressida, and I played Cressida for him. I stepped in where angels fear to tread, because I didn't know anything about him or Cressida or anybody.

They were all professionals?

Yes. And I was an amateur; I just did what I was told. Then George Moore came to see the play and made a tremendous fuss of this milliner; he couldn't get over it.

Do you remember what William Poel said to you?

Yes, a lot of things. He is really the reason that I've had any success that I have had, because he made it so clear that you must have the life in a part. You must find the truth and the real life in the person. And that was what I needed, I'm sure, because it's been my maxim ever since – to make the people true people, then put them in their time, in their period; that was the great thing with him.

And George Moore became a fan of yours?

He couldn't make me out at all, it was very peculiar. I've got some letters from him somewhere. In one letter he said, 'You take yourself as a sculptor takes marble.' I went to dinner with him, and wore that black velvet dress which I made myself.

You were in a play of George Moore's, weren't you?

Yes. He wanted me to play the leading part, but the Stage Society said they couldn't have a milliner playing the leading part and they gave me a small part of a housekeeper. She was apparently amusing and I got my first contract from that.

And after you'd given this performance as Cressida with William Poel, you felt you couldn't go back to making hats?

I couldn't; I knew this was where I really belonged. When I got into the theatre, I knew that was all right. Two pounds ten a week I think I got.

And after that you went on to play many parts in the West End, always in London I think, and very often parts much older than yourself.

Always much older. Much older and more peculiar than I am; frightened little ladies, big fat ones, everything. It was extraordinary because I was always years too young for the character parts and years too old for the others. But that was marvellous because there was a good deal of vitality there – a great deal too much. And these character parts taught me to hold it.

Did you have any difficulty in finding confidence in yourself as an actress?

I don't think I've ever been confident. I've always been tremendously interested and, when I'm doing it properly, I don't remember myself. I mean that I don't remember me if I'm right in my part because she's doing it. And if I'm sure of my words and that sort of thing I don't feel any sense of self-consciousness or anything like that.

Most actors now either spend three years training in a drama school or a number of years out of London in repertory. This you never did, and it seems to have been right for you, doesn't it?

I should have caught all the tricks – the bad tricks of the provincial theatre of those days. I'd have picked them up quicker than anybody. I was very imitative indeed. And the Almighty saw fit to start me off with some of the best actors in London.

A 1912 Aged 4

B 1933 Hamlet, Cranleigh School

C 1935 Richard Newton-Clare,
Flowers of the Forest, with Rachel Kempson

D 1933 Prospero, *The Tempest*, Cranleigh School

A 1936 Orlando, *As You Like It*, with Edith Evans (Rosalind)

B 1936 Mr Horner, *The Country Wife*

C 1940 Macheath, *Beggar's Opera*, with Audrey Mildmay

D 1937 Charles Surface, *School for Scandal*, with John Gielgud (Joseph Surface) and Peggy Ashcroft (Lady Teazle)

E 1937 Laertes, *Hamlet*

F 1937 Baron Tusenbach, *Three Sisters*

A 1937 Bolingbroke, *Richard II*,
with Leon Quartermaine (John of Gaunt)

B 1938 Sir Andrew Aguecheek, *Twelfth Night*

C 1937 Baron Tusenbach,
Three Sisters, with Frederick Lloyd
(Chebutykin), Peggy Ashcroft
(Irina), John Gielgud
(Vershinin), and Leon
Quartermaine (Kulygin)

A 1944 Harry, *Uncle Harry*   B 1942 Gribaud, *The Duke in Darkness*   C 1949 Young Marlow, *She Stoops to Conquer*

D 1965 Rakitin, *A Month in the Country*, with Ingrid Bergman (Anna Petrovna)

116

A 1950 Hamlet

B 1953 Shylock, *The Merchant of Venice*

C 1947 Macbeth

D 1949 Berowne, *Love's Labour's Lost*

A 1953 Antony, *Antony and Cleopatra*

B 1951 Prospero, *The Tempest*

C 1951 Richard II

D 1953 King Lear

A 1948 The Captain, *The Father*

B 1962 Vanya, *Uncle Vanya*, with Laurence Olivier (Astrov)

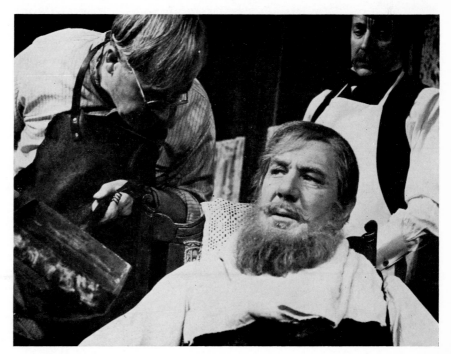

C 1962 Vanya, *Uncle Vanya*

D 1964 Hobson, *Hobson's Choice*

A 1945 Maxwell Frere, *Dead of Night* (film)

B 1951 Andrew Crocker-Harris, *The Browning Version* (film)

C 1952 Orin Mannon, *Mourning Becomes Electra*, with Rosalind Russell (Lavinia) (film)

EDITH EVANS

B 1913 Aged 25

C 1912 Cressida, *Troilus and Cressida*

A 1925 Portia, *The Merchant of Venice*

B 1934 The Nurse, *Romeo and Juliet*

C 1937 Katharina, *The Taming of the Shrew*, with Leslie Banks (Petruchio)

D 1936 Rosalind, *As You Like It*

E 1946 Cleopatra, *Antony and Cleopatra*

F 1961 Queen Margaret, *Richard III*

122

A 1959 Countess of Rousillon, *All's Well That Ends Well*, with Zoë Caldwell (Helena)
B 1958 Queen Katherine, *Henry VIII*, with John Gielgud (Wolsey)

C 1959 Volumnia, *Coriolanus*

C 1943 Hesione Hushabye, *Heartbreak House*

D 1928 She-Ancient, *Back to Methuselah*, Part 5

A 1924 Mrs Millamant, *The Way of the World*

B 1930 Mrs Sullen, *The Beaux Stratagem*, with Helen Cane

C 1936 Lady Fidget, *The Country Wife*,
    with Michael Redgrave (Mr Horner)

D 1948 Lady Wishfort, *The Way of the World*

A 1936 Madame Arkadina, *The Seagull*   B 1946 Katerina Ivanovna, *Crime and Punishment*
C 1948 Madame Ranevsky, *The Cherry Orchard*, with Robert Eddison (Trofimov)

A 1954 Countess Rosmarin Ostenburg,
The Dark is Light Enough

B 1949 Lady Pitts, *Daphne Laureola*, with Peter Finch (Ernest Paise)

D 1951 Helen Lancaster, *Waters of the Moon*,
with Sybil Thorndike (Mrs Whyte)

C 1956 Mrs St Maugham, *The Chalk Garden*,
with Peggy Ashcroft (Miss Madrigal)

127

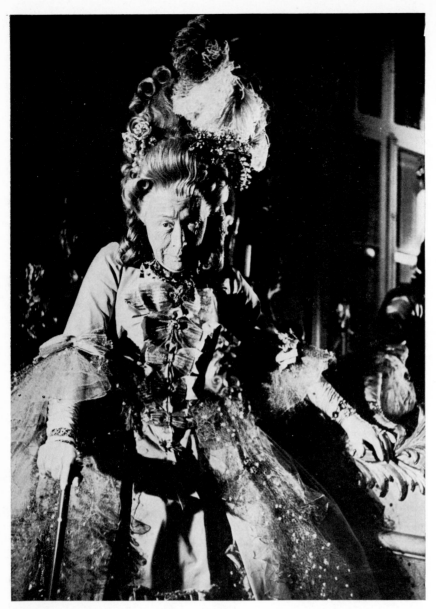

A 1948 Countess Ranevskaya, *The Queen of Spades* (film)

B 1951 Lady Bracknell,
The Importance of Being Earnest (film)

C 1963 Miss Western, *Tom Jones* (film)

D 1959 Mrs Porter, *Look Back in Anger* (film)

Well, quite romantically really. We were at home at Claverton Street and a brougham drove up and a bell rang and down I went and there was a lady and she said, 'Will you come and speak to my sister?' And I went out and it was Ellen Terry. And she asked me if I would come and play Mistress Ford to her Mistress Page on the halls. Then I went to see Ellen at her house in the Kings Road and she said to me, 'Well, now what wages, child?' And I said – I like my answer as much as I like her question – I said to her, 'I've never had more than five pounds a week, Miss Terry.' Imagine anybody saying that to-day! And she said, 'I shall give you fifteen and take it off the man.'

Did you learn anything from her?

I learned a great deal. Whenever she moved, she was lovely to look at, and whenever she stopped, she was always pictorial; it was so natural to her, she didn't pose to be pictorial. I've tried without any self-consciousness to do the same because I love movement.

And then you made a very important and difficult decision because, rather than take a part in the West End, you decided to go to Birmingham.

That was very hard because it was a wonderful play in the West End, *Our Betters* by Somerset Maugham, and I was going to be given thirty-five pounds a week. And then Barry Jackson asked me to go to Birmingham to play in Bernard Shaw's *Back to Methuselah*, which is a great play, for eight pounds a week. I decided on the eight pounds, but I must say, I'm glad they didn't run after me and ask me again, because I don't think I could have stood out. It was wonderful because, as a result of playing the She-Ancient in *Back to Methuselah*, Nigel Playfair asked me to play Millament in *The Way of the World* at the Lyric Theatre, Hammersmith. It's very odd you know, but it did follow. And then Millament, of course, is the most wonderful part – anybody who touches that touches the height of comedy.

plate 124d

plate 125a

Were you aware that you were creating something for the first time in your life?

No, no, not the faintest notion I was doing it. I just did what my old master told me to do – find the life in the part.

The next eleven questions were put by students of the Central School.

Dame Edith, you had an enormous success playing the part of Millament but, when you came to rehearse it, did you find a lot of the character in yourself, or did you do it by observation?

Oh no, not by observation. Almost all the parts you play, if they are well written and if you are suitable to them, you find them, bits of them, in yourself. Millament was a very real woman, you see, a very real, feminine woman. But I had to be checked a bit. I had an extremely good friend who was watching me one day and I'd got the sort of larkiness of the part you know, and I was doing all sorts of things and he said, 'Here, that won't do. None of that.' And so I said, 'What do you mean?' And he said, 'You must remember one word and one word only, a very good word – superb.'

When you tackle a part like Mrs Millament, do you concentrate first of all on the style of the character, in this case Restoration, or the reality?

No, I concentrate always on the life in a part. That is what my old master, William Poel, taught me and it was most valuable advice. I don't think too much about being great but I think an awful lot about being true in a part. It depends on your approach. I've never had an intellectual approach, but a lot of people have. I don't say it's wrong to have it or not to have it – but you've got to understand it yourself. You can't make the audience understand it if *you* don't understand it. I used to have a rule: whenever I didn't understand anything I always said it as if it were improper.

Costume must make a difference. Do you discuss your costume with your designer?

Oh yes, of course; you must be comfortable. I've never had any real trouble, they're always very co-operative. But you must be comfortable. And you must have all the right underclothes, corsets and things, otherwise you can't feel as they felt. After all, our clothes today are for the way we behave and the way we walk and sit and everything. Theirs were just the same for the way they behaved.

I know one doesn't put on the actual clothes until fairly near the performance, but they are probably making them in the wardrobe. Does this not throw you?

No, because I always have rehearsal clothes, as near as I can get to what I am going to wear. If you don't rehearse in long skirts, and if possible some form of restriction, corset or something, you can't feel right.

Before playing in Restoration plays did you study the rather flamboyant deportment?

No. That's a mistake people sometimes make when they're playing Restoration comedy with fans and things. I once said, and I really mean it, that the only thing you don't do with a fan is fan yourself. You poke the fire with it, you hit someone, you do every sort of thing, but you never fan yourself. If you've got a fan and you want to convey something and you know how to use the thing, you can quite easily talk behind it, or above it, or round about it; or slowly wave it if you want to think about something else while you're pretending to talk to someone over there, do you see.

Does it help with the asides?

Yes, but they're gorgeous. Sometimes, in some plays, the asides must be spoken straight out to the audience. That's quite different from talking out, not seeing the audience. They are two quite different things.

Is the audience always able to accept the direct aside?

I've mostly found that they do. Then you must govern them, you see. This is one of my hobby horses. You must govern the audience, you must never let the audience run away with the play. Don't be delighted when they scream at you and think it's awfully funny; you should be upset because they've no business to scream. They should laugh but only if you want them to laugh. When they start getting out of hand you must calm them down.

Can you sense the temper of the audience immediately you go on?

Oh, immediately. I always listen at the side for quite a while before I go on, to know what they're up to. You know by the way the lines are going whether they want a little gingering up or calming down. When I was young – I don't know if your mothers said it to you – 'you'll be crying tonight, you're so lively this morning.' But that's what the audiences are. If they start laughing like mad at the beginning, they won't have any strength left to laugh at the end.

Well, of course it does. That's why you've got to be strong if you're going to be actors. You must be very strong, You must have a lot of breath, a lot of physical strength, because you've got to manage a lot of human beings. They've got to be held, brought up and set down, every sort of thing. And you've got to do it. It's no good being tired; and don't come off saying, 'They're awfully good tonight, aren't they?' I got my lesson over that many years ago. I was in a play with two very well-known actors and I was doing what all the other actors did. I was very young and I said something about 'they weren't very good tonight,' and the actors said to me, 'I wonder, have you ever thought how good we are?' I never needed to be told twice. If they're not so very good tonight, have a look at yourself, perhaps you're not so good. After all, they've paid to see you, you haven't paid to see them – to put it at its lowest.

Do you have a strict routine of preparation before a performance?

No, except quiet, you know. I never go to cocktail parties or tea parties or anything like that. Never. After about half-past three or four I keep pretty quiet. I'm a person that gets put off very quickly, so I have to concentrate very hard.

You had a great success playing in Restoration plays at the Lyric, Hammersmith, a small intimate theatre. Do you find it very different or more difficult to play in big theatres?

I'm not very fond of large theatres, unless you have a lot of spectacle, because I think, quite often, the actors are not heard, and you have to use much too much voice and breath where you could get more variety, more nuance, if you were playing in a smaller theatre. The ordinary, nicely-average theatres are the size I like.

Dame Edith, I wish everybody in the theatre could be in that class to hear you say that comedy is always real and that comedy characters are always real. The other thing that strikes me about your performance in Restoration comedy is your astonishing vocal technique. It must be something that you worked at very hard.

I think it's just that my voice runs up and down more or less naturally, and I let it.

Did you have difficulty with your voice at any stage in your life?

Yes, always, because it's a funny voice, I believe. It has a very big range but it has to be like a singer's voice. It's got to be smooth all the way through. It was entirely due to Elsie Fogerty, the founder of the Central School, that I have the voice control that I have today. It's better than it was in that way.

Now, if I may take you from comedy to Shakespeare. This is a very different style from Restoration. Do you find it presents special problems?

Shakespeare has this wonderful rhythm which, as my old master taught me, was either for speed or slowness. You learn to go from emphatic word to emphatic word like springboards, and then if you want to slow up you lean on them a bit. Once you know about that, it's ordinary talk really, it's life, it's the way we talk. After all, we don't emphasize every word when we talk, do we?

One of the parts you played was Rosalind in 'As You Like It'.

Yes. That was a bit of great good luck because I was about thirty years too old for it. But there was a Rosalind in me somewhere. I got myself very slim, so that I didn't look ridiculous, and it was the first time I'd ever had my hair cut short, and it was a battle that I won. As Shaw says, Rosalind is at the loveliest time of any woman's life, when she's just falling in love and she knows that she's welcome.

You played Rosalind for the first time at the Old Vic in the great days under Lilian Baylis. Was she a hard task-mistress?

Well, it's awfully difficult to say. Lilian was a very one-track-minded person. I know when I worked out my expenses so that I could say to her, 'Well, I can live on so much, Lilian,' she said I could have it; and then out of that I paid my own dresser, because they didn't have dressers then. Later on I found out that the leading man had got two pounds more than I did. She was like that.

One of the things I find most interesting is the range of characters that you've played. Not only have you played great aristocratic parts and comedy parts, but you've played a number of very important and highly successful 'earthy' or demonic parts, especially in films. You played Jimmy Porter's mother in 'Look Back in Anger'. There you were working with theatre people – Tony Richardson who directed the film and John Osborne who wrote the play. Were you in sympathy with their ideas?

Yes, perfectly. We got on splendidly. We had a lot of fun together and a good deal of discussion. The part was originally written in North Country, but we both got down to it and made it into Cockney, we got it true with lots of good things in it. For instance a woman of Mrs Porter's years when she had a drink would raise her glass and say 'another kind love'. They never say that today. They say 'Mud in your eye'.

Then something quite different, the Mother Superior in 'The Nun's Story'; were you influenced by your own personal convictions?

Yes, I was. I am not a Catholic, and so I had to translate what I believe into what she believed; it was quite a test. We had two priests and two nuns with us, all the time, keeping us right, they were awfully sweet and said they would have believed I was a Mother Superior, they thought it was very convincing. I was very flattered. I had to try to keep the tremendous serenity and power that comes from absolute dedication to the work she was doing. She was sure of her reasons for her love of God, her love of Christ, and I adored doing it.

Before that you played a rustic Welsh woman in the film 'The Last Days of Dolwyn'. You are not Welsh?

No, I have a Welsh name but I am not Welsh. My father was a Londoner, my mother was Surrey – my grandparents also came from Surrey. I was the only English person in the cast, everyone else was Welsh.

Did this worry you?

No, it didn't. I felt and understood the atmosphere; Emlyn Williams came and read Welsh to me. You see, a Welshwoman speaking English is speaking a foreign language. He used to read Welsh to me and that was how I got the Welsh intonation. It was like a Yorkshireman trying to speak a dialect. Emyln Williams also used to speak Gaelic, and that again helped to get the Welsh into me. She was a very simple woman, very sincere; it was a lovely part.

How is it that you have managed to play so many different kinds of part?

I don't really know, except that I seemed to have an awful lot of people inside me. Do you know what I mean? If I understand them I feel terribly like them when I'd doing them.

I think it was Herbert Farjeon who said about you, 'She has the great power to become what she thinks she is.'

Yes, yes, by thinking you turn into the person, if you think it strongly enough. It's quite odd sometimes, you know. You are it, for quite a bit, and then you're not. It's what I call bridges.

During rehearsal?

Yes, you can't find the bridge to be that woman. Maybe it's a little fault in the writing, maybe it's a fault in you. Then I have to work very hard to make the woman that I can know join up to the one that I can't know.

Does this mean, then, that all the time behind the speeches there is a continuous secret life in your own mind?

Oh, but I rehearse my thoughts. I think my thoughts when I'm playing a play that matters, because then I am that woman all the time through. Now and again, I expect, one thinks about the housekeeping, but mostly I don't. That makes it interesting to me, otherwise I think if you haven't some quality like that it's a terribly boring profession, I do really. I'm not a bit stage-struck, you know. Not a bit. I love it. I really love it, but I'm not stage-struck.

When you come to rehearse a part, do you learn it all before you start rehearsing?

No, oh no. I try to break the back of the longish speeches, because obviously they're going to be said without interruption, and they don't depend on movement and other people; but that's the battle I'm having today, because a lot of the younger ones are all being told they've got to learn it. I think it's terrible. I don't like it at all.

So you learn it in rehearsal?

As I'm rehearsing, yes. I go home at night and do the swotting.

Until it is alive to you, it can't be learnt and shouldn't be learnt.

No, I can't believe it, you see. I can't believe it. The person I talk to and where I am, when I say what I say, tell me what I'm talking about, do you see?

As you rehearse, do you find the part becomes simpler or more complicated?

I work, and other actors do too, on a thing I call a process of deletion. I like to get it clearer and simpler until it's just bare bones.

And what do you expect of a director, Dame Edith?

I like a director to direct. I don't like him to show me how to say things until I make my mistakes, and then when I've made my mistakes I say to him, 'I don't know, come on,

133

come and help me.' I always ask for help, because I like to be helped, but I don't like to be helped before I want help, if you know what I mean.

Yes, absolutely. But you like a director to be firm?

Oh yes, indeed, and to have discipline and do his homework too. I like him to have done his share at home so that we aren't all messing about waiting for him to have ideas. He should have done that before.

Perhaps never again will there be a generation of actors who have, as you have, spent nearly every night of their lives in front of an audience. Don't you think there's a loss in that?

I think there is masses of talent about. But young actors don't have our discipline and our training. From the point of view of discipline they can make very serious mistakes. After all, there are basic rules, however much you play the Method or any other thing, there are basic rules – and they're not even taught them.

Could you give an example?

Well, yes. When an actor is about to say something which the author has intended to be noticed, such as a laugh – good authors write so that you get laughs on certain lines – and another actor makes a very swift movement or something at the same time, well, goodbye to the laugh. He's created a diversion, you see.

Do you find the other media as rewarding? Do you enjoy working in films, for instance?

When I have a sensitive director – and up to now I have had very sensitive directors – I like it very much.

Do you enjoy television?

Yes again, when I have a sensitive director, and I have been very fortunate up till now. The only trouble I have is my stage technique of never masking anybody. You know, in the theatre you always very politely back so that they can be seen, whereas you don't have to do that in television because they can, of course, take the camera round you. The audience isn't static, you see. I had to learn, in fact I still have to learn that.

But the cameras don't worry you?

Oh, not a bit. I like them because they're so expert. I feel it's like a delicious person; and I always try to get on good terms with the camera-man. Well, then they're kind to you, do you know? They help you.

Do you enjoy playing with young actors?

Yes, I don't mind as long as they're not – what's the word? – I don't mean conceited, but if they don't know it all.

Don't you think it's very dangerous, the kind of immediate success that some young actors have today?

Yes, we didn't have that. I had to work like a black from two pounds ten up. I didn't mind. I thought it was a lot of money in those days.

You said once, a long time ago, that you wanted to be an actress because you wanted a job without end.

Well, it's not quite true. It was when I was a little girl, somebody asked me what I wanted to be and I said, very ungrammatically, 'I want a job that I can't see the end of.'

Yes, *The Chinese Prime Minister* by Enid Bagnold. It's a very modern play, very interesting indeed. The part I played was an actress, a very successful actress, who was getting awfully tired of the routine of it and rather wanted to get out. There is a scene which says something that I rather approve of. She is interviewing her prospective daughter-in-law, who is seventeen, and she says this, that and the other, and then she says, 'And there's another thing.' And Alice says, 'What other thing?' 'I don't want to seem ridiculous. In your eyes no doubt. . . But my private life isn't run on age. It may surprise you, Alice, but men still fall in love with me.' 'I should think so,' says Alice. 'Yes, there's a glamour hangs about a woman of power and success. But that's not exactly what I mean, what I want. What I'm trying to say is that my life is still full of surprises. I have an extra vitality and extra expectations. I can't imagine living on when there are no more expectations.' And that's me.

JOHN
GIELGUD

John Gielgud talked to Derek Hart on the stage of the Phoenix Theatre, London, which was set for the first act of Chekhov's play *Ivanov*, and in a television studio. Mr Hart's comments are in italic.

Ivanov, which I am acting in now, is rather a rare play to be done. It was put on at the Arts Theatre some years ago, but the general public didn't see it. I think it fascinates people, because it has so many prophecies of what is to come in the later plays, which are so much better known.

It was, of course, in Chekhov that you first established yourself as an actor, wasn't it?

plate 153a

In the part of Trofimov in *The Cherry Orchard*. It was the first time I ever went on the stage and felt that perhaps I could really act. Before that I felt I could exhibit myself, to some extent, and I rather enjoyed the business of going to the theatre and walking about on the stage. My instincts told me that I wanted to have something to do with the theatre, but really I wanted to design scenery, have something to do with the lighting and the movement of plays: that was what I admired most when I was a boy. I think this really meant that I wanted to be a director, which I've had the luck to become as well as an actor. Acting to me is a responsibility and a great difficulty, whereas the feeling of work in the other departments of the theatre has always been the easiest and most happy part of my life.

Your attitude to the theatre and your persona *as an actor have always seemed, to many people, essentially romantic. Do you feel this to be a fair picture?*

plate 145b

I suppose it is true that I always used it as an escape. I'm a terrible escapist in life, and to go to a theatre, shut myself up in a dressing-room and come out as somebody else, and live a mimic life, does give me pleasure; I suppose it always has done. All children dress up and play games, but my brothers and sister and I were tremendously theatrically minded, in that way, in our nursery days, and even in our schooldays. I was always living in some sort of fantasy world.

Do you think the strong Terry influence in your family made it certain that you were bound to have something to do with the theatre?

I suppose it must have done. I was enormously englamoured by my family, particularly the ones who were still acting when I was a boy. My parents didn't encourage this very much, although they were naturally very proud of it too. My mother was the theatrical one because she was a Terry; but my father, who was partly Polish, had a curious, practical, middle-class English realism, mixed with a certain romantic *panache*.

How did you prepare for your stagework in the theatre?

I went to two dramatic schools. My cousin, Phyllis Neilson-Terry, gave me a job as assistant stage manager and understudy on a tour she was doing of a play she'd played in London. We did an eighteen or twenty weeks' tour of all the provincial cities. But one of the actors said, 'You ought to go to one of the dramatic schools,' and I went. Before that

136

I'd been at Lady Benson's school for about a year, and when I came back from the tour I went to the Royal Academy of Dramatic Art, and I was there for about a year. While I was still working there Nigel Playfair gave me a job in *The Insect Play*, in which I was terribly bad. But it was rather wonderful to be with men like Playfair and J. B. Fagan (whom I afterwards worked with at Oxford), because they were wonderful talent-spotters. At that time, I know, I must have been very clumsy and conceited, silly, vain, and those men made you feel that you had something, although they didn't spoil you. They didn't make you feel absolutely hopeless and wretched as a beginner.

The time you were with J. B. Fagan was at the Oxford Playhouse, wasn't it?

Yes, in repertory. I was there for about three University terms, and we did about eight plays a term. I suppose I played about sixteen parts.

After Oxford, what?

After Oxford I was very lucky. Because I played the piano a bit, by ear (a gift I inherited from my father), this got me the opportunity of understudying Noël Coward in *The Vortex*. He was very nice to me. Finally, when he was directing a revue in Manchester for Cochran, I went on and played for him one night, and did rather well, they said, so much so that, when Noël left the play, they kept it on another month and I played his part. Soon after that, in 1926, I again followed him in *The Constant Nymph*, which was an enormous commercial success. That was the first time I played a leading part in the West End except for the month in *The Vortex*.

How did you react to being in a long run in the West End?

I found it terribly irksome. The part of Lewis Dodd in *The Constant Nymph* was extremely tiring, and I had a bad time because the company didn't like me very much. They resented Noël leaving and I wasn't very happy with the direction that I got, such as it was. But the play was an enormous success and I learned the hard way, how to carry this very long and exhausting part for more than a year and afterwards for quite a long tour. It really was a strange experience because I was playing this leading part, and I felt that I was beginning to know how to act, but I got no particular credit for it. This was perhaps rather a good thing, because, after the tour was finished I thought, 'Well, I had better go back to repertory'; and soon after Harcourt Williams invited me to go to the Old Vic.

May I stop you, just for one moment. I think I remember your saying that you appeared in no fewer than nine plays during the eighteen months after 'The Constant Nymph'. Did you find it a depressing period?

I thought they were terrible plays, but I took everything that was offered to me, pretty well. I was the leading man, which was a new experience for me; I was getting good billing and a good salary; so I thought that perhaps acting was just being in work and doing whatever came along. That was what I thought, until the chance came to go to the Old Vic. I had toyed with the idea of doing Shakespeare, of course; I had walked on at the Vic in the very early days, when I was a student at Lady Benson's. It was in a production of *Henry V* that I first had a line to speak. The Vic fascinated me, I used to go there to see as many plays as I could. I read everything that was written about the actors who played the classics, and I'd always wanted to play Hamlet and Richard II. In those days the Sunday Night Societies gave young actors a tremendous chance, and the critics saw them in a lot of good parts that they weren't experienced enough to play for a run in the West End.

Experienced actors, also, like Edith Evans and Isabel Jeans, made enormous successes in plays like *The Country Wife* and *The Maid's Tragedy*. I tried to be in these Sunday Night plays as often as I could; one wasn't paid more than about two guineas for two or three weeks' work, but it was a fascinating exercise.

Were there actors at that period in your career who influenced you particularly?

Just before I went to the Old Vic I was working with Edith Evans in a play called *The Lady with the Lamp*, in a part which Leslie Banks had originally created. I was asked to come in, because he had to leave the cast three or four weeks before it ended. Gwen Ffrangcon-Davies, who had been extremely kind to me before, was also in the play and was a great friend of Dame Edith's; and so, through those two actresses, I was very happy in the play. Gwen had been my first Juliet, when I played Romeo at the Regent Theatre in 1924 and made a frightful mess of it.

Looking back, is it possible for you to decide why you made such a mess of that Romeo?

I had the most terrible clothes, to begin with, and the most wickedly unbecoming wig. I was only nineteen and I can't have been so hideous as all that, but I didn't know how to move. I think I spoke not badly; but we had a very, very drastic director; and I just wasn't ready. I didn't know how to select what I wanted to do, or put over emotion. I just enjoyed indulging in my own emotions, and imagined that that was acting. I only learnt, long afterwards, that you may indulge your emotions in imagining a part, but you mustn't allow them free rein until you have selected exactly what you want to show the audience, and how much you should show while you're doing it.

Is this something you learned with Harcourt Williams at the Vic?

I don't think I learnt it until a very few years ago, really. I remember Komisarjevsky used to tell me to relax, relax, but I thought relaxing was something that had nothing to do with acting. When I was on the stage I felt it was my duty to do something, give something, and be something. And through imagination, intense imagination, and tremendous emotional desire, I did create a certain effect, but it was always very tense. I think people found me affectedly artificial and over-strung. It was, of course, very helpful in parts like Richard II and Hamlet to have this emotional tension. But I exhausted myself most terribly, I used to be absolutely whacked playing the big classical parts and trying to live every moment of them; it didn't occur to me that there are places where you really must do nothing.

It was fascinating to me, last year, rehearsing Richard Burton in *Hamlet*, which I directed for him in New York. I said to him, 'Well this is going to be *your* Hamlet, you know, I'm not going to try and give you mine; but perhaps I can help you a bit with the technical side of it.' And he said, after the first week or two, 'The thing which I've got from you is that you've shown me where to save myself; I'm not exhausted at the end of this scene or that scene, which used to kill me when I first played the part at the Vic.' And I said, 'Well, that's all I've learned over the years.' I remember, too, Basil Dean saying to me years ago, 'You work much too hard and you don't think, you don't use your mind at all on the stage. You're so busy projecting, pushing it over.' On the other hand, *plate 152b* this had a certain value when I was first playing things like *Musical Chairs, The Constant Nymph*, and *The Vortex*, acting the neurotic young men who were so fashionable in the twenties. I came in on the crest of the wave with the sort of parts that were written for those kind of boys; they were meant to be very jumpy and highly strung. And there was enough of my own personality that went with that to allow me to give some effective performances in those days. But I think if I saw them now I would be horrified at the amount of energy and violence I wasted in them.

JOHN
GIELGUD

plates 34a, b, 147a, b

When I first worked with Laurence Olivier in *Romeo and Juliet* we alternated the parts of Mercutio and Romeo. I was directing and I bullied him a great deal about his verse-speaking, which, he admitted himself, he wasn't happy about. I was rather showy about mine, and fancied myself very much as a verse-speaker, and I became very mannered in consequence. But I was so jealous, because not only did he play Romeo with tremendous energy but he knew just how to cope with it and select. I remember Ralph Richardson saying to me, 'But you see, when Larry leans against the balcony and looks up, then you have the whole scene, immediately.' Because he has this wonderful plastique, which is absolutely unselfconscious, like a lithe young panther or something. I had been draping myself around the stage for weeks, thinking myself very romantic as Romeo, and I was rather baffled and dismayed to find that I couldn't achieve the same effect at all.

It was 'Richard II', I suppose, that became one of the great landmarks in your early career?

plate 146a

It was for me, because I loved the play. I'd seen Ernest Milton in it at the Old Vic, and then I was allowed to play it. When I first went to see Lilian Baylis – she was a canny old lady, sort of landladyish – she said, 'Oh well, there are a few parts going. We might give you Hamlet but, you see, we've got Gyles Isham in the Company, and two or three other good actors. We can't promise anything.' So I rather jumped at the parts she *had* offered, and Richard II was one of them, which really decided me to go. The extraordinary thing, looking back, is to think how quickly one gobbled up those plays. We did eight or nine plays a season, and in two seasons I played, I suppose, about fifteen big leading Shakespeare parts; I learnt them, rehearsed them, and played them, with about three weeks' rehearsal; then we gave about nine or twelve performances only. It was a marvellous bosh-shot, you know, at all these great parts; and in certain moments of Macbeth and Lear and Hamlet and Richard II, I know I played them better then than I ever played them afterwards, when I had had time to study them and really rehearse them properly. Because you sort of played it like charades, you got an idea of the character and you just buzzed on and had to do it.

Many people thought that when you first played Richard II, your interpretation was the spearhead of a new kind of acting. Do you think there was any truth in that?

No, I think it was more the result of an old kind of acting that I inherited from the Terrys and what I call the *panache* actors I admired so much in my youth: a certain gift of projection and an unreal kind of romantic acting, which I did with so much conviction for myself that I did manage to convince the audience. Richard is, after all, a very affected and elaborately romantic, attitudinizing, part. But now, when I listen to my old recordings, they sound to me very voice-conscious, and I'm rather ashamed to think that I was so contented with that kind of acting. I don't really believe it has the truth in it that I would like, except, of course, that in *Richard II* the man is meant to be studying himself and indulging in his own sorrows, so that it may have been more appropriate.

It was during that season at the Old Vic, under Harcourt Williams, that you played Hamlet for the first time. Was this a particularly arduous thing to do, for somebody who was playing in all the plays in the repertory?

plate 146d

It was arduous because we played the entirety, without any cuts at all, for several performances; then we played a cut version; then we went back to the entirety; then we moved to the Queen's Theatre and did another cut version; so that we were always learn-ing new bits. Curiously enough, I found the entirety less tiring, because the other parts are longer and Hamlet has a few more rests. The king's part, which is usually rather stringently cut, is given much more chance; and he makes, I think, a more worthy opponent to Hamlet, which I always feel he should be when his part is left longer in the play.

Did you have any conscious model for Hamlet when you were studying the part for the first time?

No, I didn't. I thought I had. I thought I would copy all the actors I'd ever seen, in turn, and by then I'd seen about a dozen or fifteen Hamlets. Of course, Irving was my god, although I'd never seen him; I'd just read about him being Ellen Terry's partner. But the whole idea of this magnetic strange man, whom I knew I could never be anything like, somehow appealed to me more than any other past actor that I'd ever read about. I didn't try to copy, I only took note of all the things he'd done and looked at the pictures of him, and so on. But when it came to the Vic, the play moved so fast and there was so much of it that I suddenly felt, 'Well, I've just got to be myself,' and I really played it absolutely straight, as far as I could. Of course, I was fortunate in that, except at Oxford, Hamlet had never been allowed to be given to a very young actor until I played it. It was the kind of prize that an actor, when he went into management at the age of forty or fifty, H. B. Irving or Baynton or whoever it was, allowed himself. I don't think anybody (except Master Betty) had ever played it under thirty-five, and it made people realize the tragedy of the beginning of the play in a way that an older man can never achieve. When I played it in 1944, at the age of forty, I was well aware that, with the help of various directors and actors with whom I'd worked over fifteen years, I knew more about the part, had better staying power, and perhaps more selectivity. But I didn't think I could contrive the open-ing of the play in the way that it had come to me when I was absolutely fresh, because I really felt it then; I was young and so I naturally put it over in the right way. But later I tried to imitate that, and I felt false. It always disturbed me that I was putting on my young voice and face and everything, for the beginning of the play.

You have produced 'Hamlet' as well as acted in it. But how far are you able, to your own satisfaction, to produce and to direct a play in which you are also playing the leading part?

That is a very moot point. People are always saying they think it's not a good plan; my most intimate friends have always counselled me against it, and thought I took on too much. There's no doubt that I did overtax my strength very often. When I directed *plate 152d* *Richard of Bordeaux* in 1932, it was the first time I had ever directed a play in the West End of London, and Gwen Ffrangcon-Davies and I, the two heads of the company, were in some ways a kind of focus between the older generation and the younger one. I've always found that this was a very good plan. In later productions I had the same kind of mixture, *plate 147c* both in *Romeo and Juliet* and in *Hamlet* in 1934 and 1935. Since then I've always found that, with the leavening of the ages and experience of the company, if you are sufficiently selective at the head of it and you have a foot in both camps (as I have, through my age and experience), you can create a team much more quickly. We've all heard about the Moscow Art Theatre taking six months to rehearse a play and so on. But if you get the right ingredients, including, if possible, some people with whom you've worked before, you do find you can very quickly establish a rapport with the company. After the play has opened, if I've only directed it, I come back every six or eight weeks to see it, and I find things have slipped and gone wrong, and I go back and see the actors and they're

very hurt. They say, 'Oh, we've been working very hard, while you were sitting at home
drawing the money, and why should you tick us off, we've made this pause and it's so
effective, and we get a big laugh on this line.' If you complain about these things they
take it rather badly and it's hard to make them rehearse well. But if you're in the play
yourself, you can, two or three times a week, send little notes down, or you can rehearse
a little bit before the play begins, or a little bit after, or you can go over something yourself, or you can talk to the person you're acting a scene with. And this influence, of doing
the work with the actors, and keeping an overall hand on the production, is of the greatest value.

JOHN
GIELGUD

Do you never feel that your own performance suffers as a result?

I think it does to begin with, but what I always do is this: when I go on the road before
we come to London, I get all the players as good as I can, and I put my own part in really
as a sketch; it's rather hard on the audience, and perhaps on the actors too. But I keep on
making my understudy walk for me, and when we've been on the road for a few weeks, I
have another rehearsal and I make the understudy walk my whole part. I remember this
worked extremely well, particularly in *The Lady's Not For Burning*, *Ivanov*, and *Much Ado*, *plates 151a, c, 152c*
and certainly in *Love for Love*; because I was able, after a few weeks, to see exactly where
my part belonged, in the pattern, and drop into it to complete the picture, like the missing
piece of a jigsaw puzzle.

*Could we go back a little to the Queen's Theatre, 1937 to 1938. Now that was a season of great
success.*

In 1937 I went into management, with Peggy Ashcroft as my leading lady, and we did
four plays: *Richard II*, *School for Scandal*, *Three Sisters*, and *The Merchant of Venice*; I played *plates 148a, b, 151b,*
in all of them. There was Michael Redgrave, Anthony Quayle, Alec Guinness, George *153b*
Devine, and Leon Quartermaine – it was a very fine company indeed. *Three Sisters* was *plate 115c*
really a remarkable production; we rehearsed eight weeks, which was very rare. Because
we were playing at night, we were able to take it very slowly, and we didn't find a moment
of it boring or too hard work; and the result was really stunning. Everybody said it was
the best Chekhovian production that has ever been done in this country, and the finest
work that Michel Saint-Denis, who directed it, had ever done.

It was, really, during the thirties that you alone brought back Shakespeare to the West End.

Shakespeare was considered box-office poison until Barrymore came, in 1925, to the
Haymarket Theatre, with an English cast surrounding him. He had a huge personal success. He brought over a most wonderful setting of *Hamlet* by Robert Edmond Jones, in
the Gordon Craig tradition; and the play, which was billed for ten weeks, ran for thirteen.
Then three years later I went to the Old Vic and played *Hamlet*, and soon after that
Bronson Albery gave me a contract for three plays. The first one was *Musical Chairs*, an *plate 152b*
excellent drama, a modern play by a young man, completely new, which we played at
the Criterion for a year. We then did *Richard of Bordeaux*; we had tried out both plays at the *plate 152d*
Arts Theatre first. *Richard* was then re-written and put on at the New Theatre, for
a run, and this was also a great success. For my third play I suggested doing *Hamlet*,
because of the other two which had made a lot of money. Albery agreed to let me do
Hamlet with a company of my own choice, and under my own direction. And that was *plate 147c*
such a success that we then did *Romeo and Juliet*, with Olivier and Peggy Ashcroft and *plates 34a, b, 82c, d,*
Edith Evans. Those two productions certainly did put Shakespeare on the map for the *122b, 147a, b*

West End. After that a lot of his other plays became successful and the Vic also immediately began to get more prestige from the carriage trade.

plates 86c, 126a, 150c

The Komisarjevsky production of 'The Seagull' occurred about this time?

That was in 1936, after *Romeo and Juliet*. But I was only able to play it for six weeks because I was going to America in *Hamlet*.

How did this production compare, do you think, with the Saint-Denis production of 'Three Sisters'.

Well, I'd been in Komisarjevsky's *Three Sisters* in 1926 at Barnes – it was one of the first things I did with him, I played Baron Tusenbach. Then in Saint-Denis's production in

plate 153b

1938, I played Vershinin, which I didn't think was very good for me, and I didn't think I was very good in either. Anyhow, I did play it, and it was all right apparently. The others were all simply wonderful in the play. But Michael Redgrave was cast for the Baron which, as I say, I'd played with side-burns and a handsome make-up at Barnes

plate 114f

twelve years before. When he came on as a pimply boy with steel spectacles and a funny straw hat, a gangling awkward creature, it was so wonderful for the play and it was obviously what Chekhov meant. I couldn't understand why Komisarjevsky, who was a Russian, should have deliberately misled me in the reading of the part when I'd done it all that time before, because I would have been very happy to have played it ugly, as I played Trofimov; it wasn't that I was too vain, but because he encouraged me.

Komisarjevsky was a perverse and strange man. He had the idea that he knew better than anybody what the English public wanted. I remember him saying to me, 'Oh, my dear, there must be a juvenile interest, you know, a romantic love story,' and I said, 'But you've cut out all the lines about the Baron being ugly, and this is the reason Chekhov gives why she won't marry him.' And he just roared with laughter. But he had a wonderful talent for helping young people all the same, and for setting the stage with his lighting and

plates 86c, 126a, 150c

scenery and movement. His *Seagull* that he did for me in 1936, with Edith Evans and Peggy Ashcroft, was sensational, it really was a most beautiful production. But curiously enough, he was at his best when he worked at Oxford with the students, or at Stratford with Randall Ayrton in *Lear*, and when he did things at Barnes, with us in 1924, for nothing. In some funny way, it is often when there's a lot of money to spend that people spread themselves too much, spend too much on the scenery and dresses, perhaps even the actors get too much, and then it isn't as good.

plates 86b, 153d

How highly would you rate the production of Michel Saint-Denis's 'Cherry Orchard' in which you played Gayev?

I had directed the play myself, at the Lyric, Hammersmith, in 1954 and so I expect I was prejudiced. I'd adored Michel so much in the days of *Noah* and *Three Sisters* at the New and the Queen's that I expected tremendous things of it. I never saw it from the front so it was hard for me to judge. It seemed to me a heavier play than I'd remembered when

plate 153a

I directed it, and before when I'd acted Trofimov under Fagan's direction; but it may have been only the passing of the years. I loved playing Gayev and working with Michel on the part because he helped me enormously with it. But somehow I felt there was something in the spirit of the production that was not as successful as in *Three Sisters*.

We've talked almost exclusively about period plays, the Classics – romantic plays, if you like – but essentially costume plays. It's difficult to resist the impression that you are happier with such plays than you are with modern authors.

Except in *Musical Chairs*, when I was playing a neurotic, consumptive young man (a part which I liked very much, and which I think I was rather good in), I've not had very fascinating parts to play in modern clothes. I have enjoyed enormously playing what I consider to be slightly boring, rather priggish characters. I used to love playing the furniture-conscious, prim husband in *The Circle*; I enjoyed *A Day by the Sea*, where I was meant to be a rather stupid, helpless man; it was a very Chekhovian play, which I loved both directing and acting in, and it was a great success, as you know. The parts that I've never cared for very much were Inigo Jollifant in *The Good Companions* and the young man in *Dear Octopus*; they really were rather dull, conventional, juvenile characters.

Do you think there's anything at all in the thought that great experience, in the theatre, can sometimes lead to an inhibiting of an actor's instinct?

Yes, I think one is inclined to turn on clichés; the old plays gave one that opportunity. I've heard one good character actor, a great friend of mine, whom I always try to have in plays if I get the chance, saying, 'Well, which of my six old men do you want this time?' I think there is that danger, if you've played too many parts. I remember various occasions when I've been playing with actors who were getting tired, or getting old, but who were magnificent actors; and I would sometimes be shocked to see that they would bring over a trick of voice or movement, or a way of getting a laugh which they'd used in another part. I think it's dangerous not to start completely fresh with a new part. Edith Evans has always said to me, 'I won't even look at the old copies of Shakespeare, I want a brand new edition to study from, I want to feel that I'm reading a new play'; or with Restoration plays; she doesn't want to hear what the old actors did.

I think, therefore, that you can perhaps lose, through skill and technique, a certain feeling of spontaneity which is still very important. One's got to keep the childlike thing one had when one first went into the theatre, of saying, 'Oh, I'll pretend to be somebody else, and I'll try and live this part,' or 'I'll dress up and pretend I'm somebody else.' And although that is only the external part of acting, for many people it leads to the internal part, too. There are many actors who say, 'Oh, I can't rehearse without a particular property in this scene, I must have my book', or 'I must have a handkerchief in that scene', or 'I wanted to have a bag – or something.' You suddenly begin to feel these things will help you to become part of the character. Once when I was rehearsing *Crime and Punishment* – it was a very hot day, I was walking through St James's Park – I saw a tramp lying down, with his head buried in the dirty grass, filthy hands and everything, and he was absolutely relaxed. I thought, 'This is the way that Rasknolnikov must lie on the bed,' and immediately it gave me a kind of line on the part.

plate 153c

I believe Harley Granville-Barker directed you in 'King Lear'?

He didn't really direct me, but he was a friend of mine in a wonderful way, over many years. I was once in a Spanish play by Quintero, at the Court Theatre, that he had translated. He came for one rehearsal and gave me the most wonderful hints, and wouldn't stop to see them; he'd gone off to lunch and never came back. I was absolutely dazzled by his brilliance over this short hour in which he showed me this part.

How did it demonstrate itself?

Well, he just got up on the stage and did the part for me in the most simple way without really acting it, but showing me just where I was wrong, the timing and everything, and I said, 'Let me write it down, let me write it down.' 'No, no, no, I have to go to lunch', and he went away. He was living in Paris. Then he used to come to see some of my pro-

143

ductions, and afterwards write me letters of criticism, most of which I've kept, I'm thankful to say; they were marvellously shrewd and constructive and interesting. He came and saw my *Hamlet* before I took it to Elsinore in 1939 just before the war; I had a whole morning with him at the Ritz, after he had seen a run through, and he went through the play with the book in his hand and told me everything that was wrong with the production. Then I went back to the theatre and rehearsed with the company all the afternoon, to put things in; it was a Sunday, the day before we opened, and the advice he had just given me was unbelievably helpful.

When war broke out, I went back to the Vic to do Lear; we collected together a wonderful company, for which Tyrone Guthrie and Lewis Casson were also responsible, and they did the preparations for the production, while Barker agreed to come over for one week. He'd never been in England without his wife, who was a very anti-theatre lady, and so we got him on our own for once. He used to come every day to the Vic and rehearse, looking like a marvellous surgeon. The company was transported. I never saw actors watch a director with such utter admiration and obedience. It was like Toscanini coming to rehearsal – very quiet, business suit, red eyebrows, and text in his hand. And I was so angry because there was nobody there to take his overcoat, or take notes for him, and he filled every moment; so much so that people didn't even go to try on their wigs, or have a bun, or anything – they just sat there. I got actors and actresses, from outside, friends of mine, to come and peek in, because I said, 'You really must see these rehearsals, they're something absolutely extraordinary'. And we would go on until quite late at night. I remember doing the death scene of Lear with him, and he began stopping me on every word, and I thought every moment he'd say, 'Now stop, don't act any more, we'll just work it out for technical effects.' Not at all, he didn't say stop, so I went on acting and crying and carrying on, and trying to take the corrections as he gave them to me. And when I looked at my watch, we had been working on this short scene for forty minutes. But it was extraordinary that he had the skill not to make you wild and not to exhaust you so much that you couldn't go on; if you had the strength to go along with him, he could give you more than any person I ever met in my life. And he seemed to know about the technical side of acting, about the quality of the actor himself, so that you knew he was trying to bring out the best in you from what he had sensed of your possibilities; it wasn't something he'd worked out at home. Saint-Denis sometimes comes with such a finished feeling for the part that you can't find your own way of doing it because it's his. But Barker made you feel he was working on you, what you did was something that was your own, but that if he could make it better he would. He was allowing for your own physical limitations, as well as wanting you to do what he knew was much cleverer than what you were doing.

How does Peter Brook compare with Barker?

It's very hard to describe Peter Brook. I've worked with him three or four times, always with success, always with love. He's a great friend of mine and he's enormous fun. Some actors find him very difficult and don't like working with him – I suppose that happens with all directors. But he's immensely imaginative and immensely patient, and I feel on equal terms with him, although he's so much younger than I am. Barker, of course, was a good deal older and so it was more the devoted pupil attitude, whereas with Peter I feel, in some way, it's a kind of collaboration, though I know he's going to do something much cleverer than I could ever dream of. I think he's very good at handling people who are experienced; he's very honest and very fearless; and he can tell me when I'm putting on

144

A 1913 Aged 9

JOHN
GIELGUD

B 1912 In fancy dress, with his sister Eleanor

C 1916 Mark Antony, *Julius Caesar*,
aged 12

A 1929 Richard II

B 1929 Macbeth

c 1924 Romeo, with Gwen Ffrangcon-Davies (Juliet)

D 1929 Hamlet, with Martita Hunt (Gertrude)

146

A 1935 Romeo, with Peggy Ashcroft (Juliet)

B 1935 Mercutio, *Romeo and Juliet*

C 1934 Hamlet

D 1939 Hamlet

A 1937 Richard II

B 1937 Shylock, *Merchant of Venice*

C 1942 Macbeth

D 1950 Angelo, *Measure for Measure*

A 1957 Prospero, *The Tempest*   B 1951 Leontes, *The Winter's Tale*   C 1961 Othello

D 1950 King Lear   E 1940 Lear, with Stephen Haggard (Fool)

A 1950 Cassius, *Julius Caesar*,
with Harry Andrews (Brutus)

B 1955 King Lear, with Claire Bloom (Cordelia)

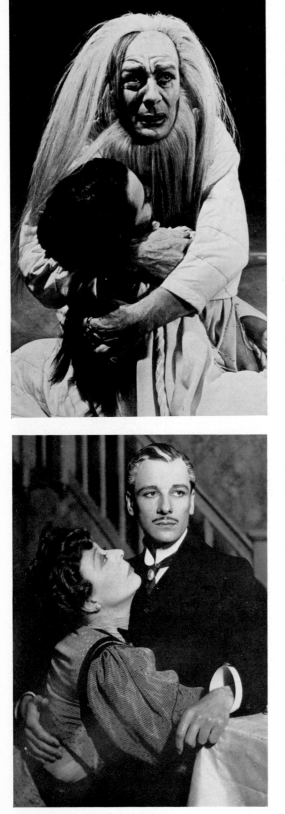

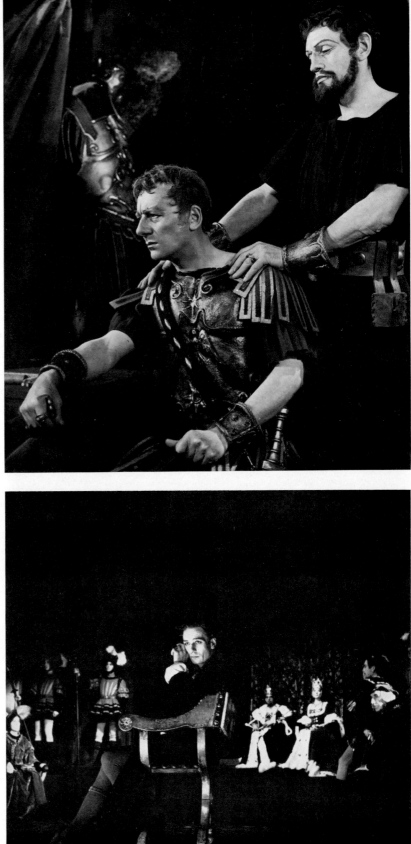

C 1936 Trigorin, *The Seagull*, with Edith Evans (Arkadina)

D 1944 Hamlet

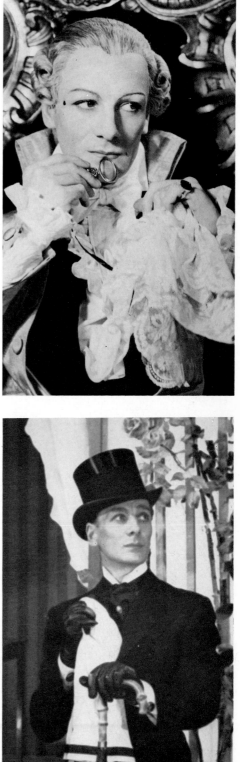

C 1952 Benedick, *Much Ado about Nothing*, with Diana Wynyard (Beatrice)

D 1942 John Worthing,
The Importance of Being Earnest

A 1923 Poet Butterfly, *The Insect Play*

B 1932 Joseph Schindler, *Musical Chairs*, with Carol Goodner

C 1949 Thomas Mendip, *The Lady's not for Burning*

D 1933 Richard of Bordeaux, with Gwen Ffrangcon-Davies (Anne of Bohemia)

E 1958 James Callifer, *The Potting Shed*, with Redmond Phillips

A 1925 Trofimov, *The Cherry Orchard*

B 1937 Vershinin, *Three Sisters*

C 1946 Raskolnikov, *Crime and Punishment*

D 1961 Gayev, *The Cherry Orchard*, with Paul Hardwick (Simeonov-Pishchik), Roy Dotrice (Firs), George Murcell (Lopakhin), Dorothy Tutin (Varya), and Peggy Ashcroft (Madame Ranevsky)

B 1904 Aged 4

C 1911 Pageboy, *The Great Name*,
with Lydia Bilbrooke
and Charles Hawtrey

A 1901 Aged 2

D 1917 Ripley Guildford, *The Saving Grace*,
with Emily Brooke

E 1921 Clay Collins, *Polly with a Past*,
with Edith Evans and Edna Best

A 1924 Nicky Lancaster, *The Vortex*, with Lilian Braithwaite

B 1926 Lewis Dodd, *The Constant Nymph*

C 1926 Lewis Dodd, *The Constant Nymph*, with Cathleen Nesbitt

A 1930 Elyot Chase, *Private Lives*, with Laurence Olivier

B 1936 *Tonight at 8.30*: *Red Peppers*, with Gertrude Lawrence

C 1930 Elyot Chase, *Private Lives*, with Gertrude Lawrence

A 1933 Leo, *Design for Living*, with Lynn Fontanne and Alfred Lunt

B 1933 Leo, *Design for Living*,
with Lynn Fontanne and Alfred Lunt

C 1943 Garry Essendine, *Present Laughter*, with Judy Campbell

A 1953 King Magnus, *The Apple Cart*, with Margaret Rawlings (left) and Laurence Naismith (third from right)

B 1943 Frank Gibbons, *This Happy Breed*

C 1953 King Magnus, *The Apple Cart*

A 1925 *Hay Fever*: Marie Tempest (Judith Bliss) and
W. Graham Browne (David Bliss)

B 1965 *Hay Fever*: Edith Evans (Judith Bliss) and
Derek Jacobi (Simon Bliss)

C 1966 *Suite in Three Keys*: George Hilgay,
Shadows of the Evening

D 1966 *Suite in Three Keys*: Verner Conklin,
Come into the Garden Maud

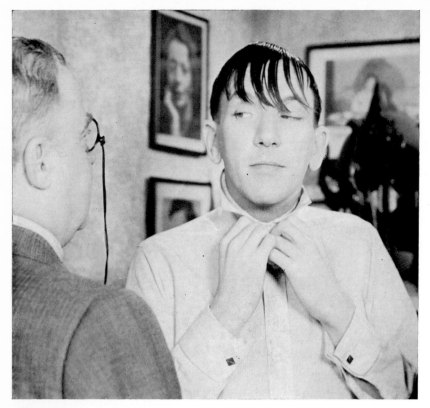

A 1935 Anthony Mallare, *The Scoundrel* (film)

B 1960 Hawthorne, *Our Man in Havana*, with Ralph Richardson (film)

C 1942 *In Which We Serve*: Noël Coward as Captain 'D' saying farewell to his crew (film)

my face or my voice or my sort of mannered things, which are affected and untrue, in a kind and frank way which doesn't upset me. That's very important, because if you have a director who attacks your personal mannerisms brutally, it can make you very self-conscious and you can't go on. I'm fairly thick-skinned and I don't really mind being told when I'm terrible because I know it only too well myself; but Peter can do it in a tactful, sensible, and direct way which wastes no time. Then I feel we can go on from there, and I remember to cut out the things he has warned me about the next time I come to rehearse.

Barker never talked much about mannerisms, but he used to make one aware that one could only do a certain amount and not to try to do more. He got Lear within my orbit. From the very beginning, which was extraordinary, he said to me, 'Lear should be an oak, you're an ash; now we've got to do something about that.' Barker (like Brook) had this extraordinary gift for seeing what the actor playing Lear could do, as indeed you have to with any actor tackling Hamlet or Macbeth. With those great plays, you've got in some ways to gear the production to suit the principal actor. The old actors like Irving starred themselves in those parts, and then geared the whole production round them, in a kind of old-fashioned way in which they immediately became the top of every scene. But Barker had this real honesty for the text. Brook is in his element making plays like *Titus Andronicus* or *Measure for Measure* or *Venice Preserv'd* (which are not the greatest plays in the world), into thrilling plays in which everybody has the right balance and the right orchestration.

You've made two very successful appearances in films of Shakespeare, as Clarence and as Cassius. How did you respond to playing Shakespeare for the cinema?

I loved it because I like knowing the parts so well beforehand. All the same I've never found in films that I've enjoyed very much doing a stage part, because I feel I am still bound by the conventions of the stage, and I have created my performance with those conventions in mind. I had never played Clarence on the stage, so that was new to me; but I had a conception of how I thought he should be played. It was interesting with Cassius because I had to cut down on everything I'd done on the stage; I couldn't make the faces or give the shouts, and it was quite a different feeling. But I was much more in control of the part because I knew the whole line of it, each scene, even if there were cuts or scenes shot out of sequence. Actually with that film we did rehearse for three weeks in empty studios, with marks for the furniture, like a play; and we did do the film pretty well in sequence. But of course one knows that the best things in films are nearly always done by the director. Somebody told me the other day that in Orson Welles's film *The Chimes at Midnight*, in which I play Henry IV, one of the most effective moments is one after Hotspur's death in which I look at Falstaff, at Hotspur's body, and then at Prince Hal; but we never did the scene at all. On the last day Orson said, 'There's a close-up I have to do of you, just look down there, that's Hotspur's body, now look up at me.' I never even saw Orson made up as Falstaff, but it appears that, because of the clever cutting, this scene of glances between four people is enormously effective. That shows how much you owe to the cutter and the director when it comes to the screen, you can't really control your own performance at all.

Are you happy that your performance of Cassius, in the film of Julius Caesar, *should be a record for all time of the way you play Shakespeare?*

I do think it was fairly successful. I arrived in Hollywood rather frightened because I thought they'd all think, coming from London, that I would be trying to teach them how to play Shakespeare. So I kept very quiet, as far as I could. I was a bit frightened of Brando but we had very little together, and he was extremely nice to me. I was afraid people would be either too respectful, or else think I was very grand and snobbish. I got on extremely well both with Mankiewicz and with James Mason, whom I'd known slightly in the old days; he was most generous and we got on extremely well in my scenes, which were nearly all with him; he gave me the stage whenever I seemed to need it.

Was the Marlon Brando performance of Mark Antony successful?

Well, I thought it was very striking. I saw the picture again, last year, in Canada, and I think that Marlon's difficulty was that he didn't really know the whole play. But he was very quick, because one day he asked me to help him with a certain speech, and I talked to him for a couple of hours, and the next morning he came down to work, and he'd put in everything that I'd suggested, and executed it most skilfully. He made a great success in the big soliloquy, in which I thought he copied Olivier rather, but not with great success. I wasn't in any other scenes with him and the director never asked me to interfere again, and Marlon didn't ask me, so I didn't like to press myself. I don't know whether I could have helped him.

Can we talk a little about the playing of comedy?

plate 151a, b

I've always enjoyed it very much, particularly in period parts, like Joseph Surface in *School for Scandal* and Valentine in *Love for Love*. They are wonderfully showy, romantic parts in the tradition of my uncle, Fred Terry and the old actors who, I think, have bequeathed to me a certain *panache*. I enjoyed doing Benedick very much, to my great surprise. I had loved Tony Quayle in the part when I directed him, and I hadn't really thought of playing it myself. I mean, I didn't resent him playing it, and not me, when I was directing the play. But of course having directed it and seen the whole production,

plates 83b, 151c

from the front, I went into it the following year, with Peggy Ashcroft as Beatrice, who played it quite differently from Diana Wynyard (who had done it with Quayle and later played it with me for a time); and later again in America, I played it with Margaret Leighton. So I've played Benedick with three Beatrices, all equally different and equally attractive, and equally wonderful as partners. Benedick is a wonderful sort of partner part, rather like the parts that Michael Somes and Robert Helpmann play in ballet with Margot Fonteyn; if you support the leading lady correctly, then you're playing the part as it should be done. Ellen Terry always said that Irving was much too slow for her, and she couldn't be at her best as Beatrice, because of the way he played Benedick, and it was the same with his Shylock. It's extraordinary that those two great actors, who were partners for so many years, rather imply that they didn't find each other's styles very accommodating. Thank God in my career I've always found the leading ladies that I've worked with to be extraordinarily sympathetic in acting in the way that I've been best able to work with them.

Do you feel that today there is far less glamour for the general public about the whole world of 'the theatre' than there used to be, say, thirty years ago?

I wonder. I don't know. I'm rather dismayed to read in magazines that so many of the public, when they're asked general questions about their lives, all say, 'We don't go to the theatre any more, we occasionally see a television play.' So I think an enormous public has been lost through the invention of television and through the movies; therefore one needs to find the attitude of young people in a new way to make them interested in 'live theatre'. There's a huge public of older people who are still fond of some of us who made successes twenty or thirty years ago. But there's also a new generation for whom you have to make a different impression. If you can retain vitality and keep your balance between the old and the new, then you can still go on being of some use to your art and your craft. But if not, I think you ought to stop, probably. Now I'd be quite prepared to play less important parts in the next ten or fifteen years, provided I could find things that I really thought I could do, in my own way, perhaps better than anybody else; that's what I'd like to do.

Is there anything that you've not accomplished, in your life in the theatre, that you would most dearly like to have done?

I would love to have done something with *Othello*. That was a great disaster and a great sorrow to me. But I don't think I'd ever dare risk it again, especially after the enormous success and the wonderful performance of Olivier last year. Also, his *Macbeth* was so good (it was a part I rather fancied and had thought perhaps to play again one day), but I feel he was too good for me to compete. There's been talk of my playing Malvolio, which I'm not awfully keen about. I did play Henry IV in the 'Falstaff' thing for Orson Welles on the screen; so I feel I've done that, and won't have to do it in the theatre. There aren't many other parts that I really lust after. I would always love to play Prospero or Lear, because I think they're beautiful parts: fortunately, they are parts that you can still play when you're an old man. So I feel those are put away in reserve, perhaps for another day.

plate 149c

plates 149a, d, 150b

How about the field of directing?

Directing I love, and I will always do it if I really like the play. I've always longed to direct a successful musical, not only because it's very profitable, but because it must be great fun, if you get the right thing. I know, from all one sees and hears, what an arduous and difficult job it is, and unless I could find exactly the script that I felt I could do justice to, I wouldn't take it on.

Do you have any thoughts about having your own permanent company any more?

Not really, no. If I've got another ten or fifteen years of career left to me, I would like to feel I could play sometimes in London, sometimes in New York; perhaps do a film in Hollywood or on location in Europe somewhere; perhaps do the Shakespeare recital a few times in countries where I haven't done it, like Japan and Turkey and Greece; be free to travel and enjoy a certain amount of spare time. One's pioneering days have been so full, I've done so many things for so long; and I've been lucky, both in the people I've worked with and in the work I've done, so that I don't really feel I want to fling myself into violent action again, to that extent; I don't think I should be able to live up to it. And so, without any feeling that I want to retire or slacken off too much, I would just like to think I was going to have a varied and interesting time and be, as Ellen Terry used to say, a useful actor for the rest of my career.

NOËL
COWARD
A POSTSCRIPT

plate 158a, c

Noël Coward talked to Michael MacOwan in a television studio. Among the many plays Michael MacOwan has directed was a revival of Bernard Shaw's *The Apple Cart* at the Haymarket Theatre, London, in 1952 with Noël Coward playing King Magnus. Mr MacOwan's comments are in italic.

Well, Michael, I gather we're going to have a little discussion about comedy acting. A fairly comprehensive subject.

Indeed yes. You started your career when you were still a boy, didn't you? How old were you?

Eleven, I think. I started in ballet school when I was younger, about ten, but I really made my first appearance when I was just eleven. It was a children's play called *The Goldfish*. Micheál MacLiammóir, June, and I opened the proceedings with a merry little trio, which was really over-bright.

And then you came under the influence of the great naturalistic comedian of the time, Charles Hawtrey, didn't you?

plate 154c

It was immediately after that. I was engaged by an agent, Bellew & Stock, to go down and play the tiny part of a pageboy in the last act of a play, and I only got there in time for the dress rehearsal. I pushed all the furniture back at home and my mother rehearsed me. I came on and electrified Charles Hawtrey, who'd never seen me before. I gave a sort of full-out, grand performance, forgetting that I was supposed to be a little pageboy.

And it delighted Charles Hawtrey?

I heard him say to his stage manager, after I'd walked off, 'Tarver, never let me see that boy again.' He was wonderful. He came to me afterwards, having relented rather, and said, 'Now listen. I want you to understand something if you're going to be an actor, and that is, that though you have a very nice speaking voice, you must remember you're playing a common little boy, and so I think it would be better if you could play it in a cockney accent. Do you think you can?' And I said, 'Oh yes, I'm sure I can', and so instead of doing it with these tremendous periods, I gabbled it in cockney and as a reward he gave me an extra entrance.

You played with him a lot after that?

Then he put me into *Where the Rainbow Ends*, another pageboy part, but a better part. He was extremely kind to me as a little boy. I can't think why, I drove him mad. He used to say, 'Keep away from me, boy,' I was always chattering at him. He signed an autograph book which I had, with sweet peas on the cover, seventeen times, then he gave up; and I was not allowed to stand in the wings, because I once made him miss an entrance by chattering to him.

164

You've often said that he's had a tremendous influence on your acting.

He was a perfectly brilliant comedian and one of the most sensitive directors. I honestly think that I've learnt practically everything I know about comedy playing from him, not only from what he actually taught me, but from his example.

Can you give examples?

Oh yes. He used to watch me very carefully when I was rehearsing and he never bullied me. I was very precocious and I think quite a lot of other directors would have said, 'Oh, shut up!' but I was eager to learn and he knew it. I used to stand at the side of the stage, watching him, and he used to teach me – he taught me how to laugh. I remember him standing over me at rehearsal, in front of the whole company, and saying, 'Now, boy, you've got to laugh. Now start with this. Ho, ha, ha, ha, ha, ha. But put your breath right.' And he stood over me till I did it. He said, 'Now smile with it a bit', and I'd go, 'Ha, ha, ha.' And he said, 'Now give way', and I'd go, 'Ha, ha, ha, ha.' That was entirely technical and, of course, it was an enormous help; he could laugh on the stage indefinitely. He taught me also to use my hands and my arms and swing them without looking as though I were acting at all.

He was completely at home on the stage.

That was his great trick and it always used to infuriate me, even when I was quite young, because certain critics at the time, and certain members of the public, said, 'Oh, Hawtrey's always exactly the same', implying that he wasn't acting. But every time he went on to the stage he raised his voice half a tone to pitch. He looked perfectly natural and relaxed, but he wasn't in the least natural and relaxed. One can never be natural and relaxed if one's a good comedian; there are too many things to think about.

Alert from what's coming from the other actors and alert for what's coming from the audience?

Yes. I think you've got to have your mind working on several different levels. You've got first of all to remember the character you've learned and studied and know about; you've got to remember your voice pitch, which has got to reach the back of the gallery, without shouting; you've got to remember your other actors – vitally important to get their eye, speak to them, not to the audience, to them. Then you've got to listen to the audience's reaction, because audiences, as you know, vary at every performance. Sometimes you have an equal number of people, one night they're a lot of cods' heads, the next night they're marvellous; and you have to know how to handle them. If they are dull, then you've got to go a little quicker; if they're warm and very responsive, you've got to watch yourself, otherwise they'll lead you astray and make you overplay. In fact, I believe that all acting is a question of control, the control of the actor of himself, and through himself of the audience.

You said you've got to be thinking about a great many different things, on different levels. People often think of this in the wrong way, don't they? They imagine you're thinking now this, now that, now the other, but in fact you're thinking about them all simultaneously, aren't you?

Yes. Always. It must be. Like reflexes in driving a car, it becomes so automatic that it isn't even conscious thought. But after three or four weeks of rehearsal, when you know exactly what you're going to say, you have time to listen for that tell-tale cough, which means that you're losing attention or that somebody's got a cough, but it's got to be silenced.

But while you're taking action to silence that cough, you're not ceasing to be that character, in that situation, in that play.

Ah, no. But by that time it is so embedded in you that you can afford to. I think the most dangerous theory advanced in modern days is that you have to feel what you do for eight performances a week. It's out of the question. And also, acting is not a state of being. Acting is acting.

It's doing something, taking an action.

It's giving an impression of feeling. If it's real feeling, then you're very liable to lose your performance and lose the attention of the audience, because if you lose yourself, you're liable to lose them.

In fact, if you get out of control, everything's gone?

The most dangerous thing which happens to so many actors, and has certainly happened to me in my time, is when, if you are playing a high comedy part and you've got a wonderful audience, you begin to enjoy it a little bit too much. And the winks come and the face begins to react and you're having a ball; and it isn't until later that somebody tells you, pray God that they do, that you were overplaying.

On this question of control and of feeling, how much one feels and how often one feels, it would be interesting to talk about 'The Vortex', because there is a tremendously emotional part. I remember something Agate said in his notice of the play: 'It was magnificently acted, particularly by Mr Coward who lived every moment of it with his nerves and was so lifelike that one was in the same room with him.'

plate 155a

As a matter of fact, Agate saw me give the opening performance at the Everyman Theatre when I did do a *tour de force* of nervous acting – I got away with it. But from my point of view it was not a good performance. I'd had a lot of cast changes, darling Lilian Braithwaite had only rehearsed for a week, and I'd been so busy getting the play on, that I had not paid enough attention to my own performance. Fortunately, I think my talent saved me, and I did do it, I think, very well, otherwise I wouldn't have made the success I made. But about two weeks later I was playing it properly, when I could turn it on at will and not feel it.

You knew that character well, because you'd written it and obviously you'd used a good many aspects of yourself in creating the character of Nicky, so that it was always there for you the whole time without effort.

Yes, without thinking. But you see, I've got a theory which I've proved over and over again about emotional acting as opposed to comedy. If you're playing a very strong scene, a moving scene, there is a moment at rehearsal when your words are clear, when you know it very well and it's beginning to flow, there is a moment when you really feel it. This is a very important moment. You cry, you overplay, but you have genuinely felt it. From then onwards until the opening night you have to begin to eliminate, because you cannot afford really to feel, when you're playing eight performances a week, and you're going to give the public their money's worth. Also it is not acting. This was proved to me many years ago, in the early 1930's when I was in Singapore: I was asked by the local company, which included Johnny Mills, to play Stanhope in *Journey's End*. I'd always longed to play Stanhope because I thought it was a wonderful play, and I did it as one of those, you know, gestures. I had two days in which to learn it. I learnt the words perfectly, and I came on and gave, I suppose, the worst performance I've ever given, because I'd not had the time to reach that point in rehearsal when the author's emotion got me. It got me on the stage and instead of playing Stanhope as a tight-lipped, controlled military man, I played him as a sobbing neurotic. I cried steadily throughout the play and completely ruined it. The only thing that saved me was that, at the end of the play, when I was carrying Johnny Mills, dying, and laid him tenderly on the cot, tears streaming down my face, my tin hat fell off and hit him in the stomach.

Did you play it several times after that?

Yes, and by the third performance I began to be good. If I'd had three weeks' rehearsal and a week or so performing, I should have been very good as Stanhope, but I wasn't; because the emotion caught me unawares. I know this is dead against the modern trend, you have to be in the mood, and feel it and all that sort of thing. I think it's very good, sometimes, for actors to believe that, as long as they don't really do it.

It is sometimes necessary to say that to actors who are weak on their feelings and have to be stimulated rather than controlled; but, of course, if they don't know what they're doing, then they're lost.

In the theatre the basis is always the author. If you're giving a true representation, and the author is strong, it's up to you, as an actor, to adapt to the author and then decide, calculatingly, what you're going to do; because you cannot play a big scene properly more than three or four times a week, I think – performances vary even if you give your all.

Then instead of the actor being his own instrument, which is himself, the instrument is playing him instead of his playing the instrument.

Lose yourself, lose the audience.

Another very emotional part that you played at a fairly early stage in your career was Lewis Dodd in 'The Constant Nymph'. You've often said that you weren't happy in that one; it would be nice to know the reason why.

Well, I wasn't happy in it for extremely trivial reasons. Basil Dean was an excellent director and very meticulous, I was young and I'd had a lot of success, and he wanted, perfectly rightly, to rob me of Noël Coward mannerisms. I was not allowed to smoke a cigarette because I would smoke it like Noël Coward smoked it. He made me grow my hair very long and I don't like long hair and I never put any grease on it. Then he made me smoke a pipe, so that every time I lit it, I set fire to my hair and a lot of burning went on. Added to which it was an extremely difficult part; I had to express in the first few minutes of the play that I was a musical genius. I had some very charming music by Eugene Goossens to play on the piano, which was lovely, but it didn't absolutely establish me as Paderewski. Technically the play was constructed so that I had a series of ghastly thirty-second changes; I was in tails, in ordinary clothes, back to tails, so that when I wasn't actually on the stage, which I was for most of the play, I was gasping away at the side, putting on my shoes or something. Then the only really emotional scene came at the end of the play, when Tessa, gloriously played by Edna Best, reached for the window, if you remember, and had a heart-attack. I used to lift her on to the bed, gasping rather, she was quite heavy, and then the last line of the play was so touching. I used to fling up the window and say, 'Tessa's got away; she's safe; she's dead.' Tears, curtain. Unfortunately on the third performance the window-cord broke and the window came down onto

plate 155b, c

167

my hands, and so what I said was, 'Tessa's got away; she's safe; she's ow!' Whereupon the dead Tessa looked up and, of course, the curtain fell in roars of laughter.

Do you think that, if an actor starts on a performance from the point of view of 'not' something, it never goes right?

No, I don't, because in later years when I'd become a more experienced and a better actor it was essential, with certain parts that I've played, that I shouldn't be like me. You see, I've been a personality actor all my life. I'd established, in my early years, the sophisticated urbane type, which is in tune with my own personality. But if, for instance, I play something which looks like me, but isn't like me at all, then I have to reconstruct in my mind, at rehearsals, my gestures so that I'm no longer like Noël Coward. But again you come up against this thing of the image you create of yourself in the public mind. When I was a little boy and a young man I always longed to be a big star and a great success. In those days I wouldn't have cared to put on too much nose paste and that sort of thing, because I was too occupied with somebody asking me for an autograph in a bus.

But later on it has become the character that you're playing that is important?

I've become a more experienced and a better actor. And also, acting a character is far more interesting than anything else, it's lovely to do. I would say that to do my own sort of dialogue, flibberty-gibbet, witty, quick, and all that, is another sort of technique. But I loved playing *Fumed Oak* for instance, with that terrible moustache. I've loved all the little bits of character acting I've done in my life.

Do you feel the difference very strongly, when you're playing something that you've written, or when you're playing something that somebody else has written?

I always forget, when I'm playing in my own plays, that I'm the author.

Do you?

Yes. Now I come to think of it, yes. Not at rehearsals when I'm after the others. But when I'm actually doing it, I can't remember thinking, 'I've written the play.' I think, of the two, I really prefer playing other people's plays to my own.

Of the parts you've played in your own plays the one I suppose you're most identified with, in the minds of the public, is 'Private Lives', which must have been one of the happiest experiences.

plate 156c Yes, it certainly was. It was a wonderful experience. You see Gertrude Lawrence at her best, and with me she was usually at her best, was the most brilliant comedienne to play with. She was so swift and her eyes were so true; it was an enchantment to work with her. Her use of voice was instinctive. Gertie was not a thinking reed, but her talent gave it all to her. She was intuitive and accurate, when she did not occasionally go overboard, which she was inclined to do. Incidentally, when we made the record of *Private Lives*, we did it in an hour, and we were opening that night at Southsea; this was before the play opened in London. When they sent the test to us on Wednesday, I hated me in it and thought she was wonderful, and she hated her and thought I was wonderful. We really were quite serious, we didn't want it to be put out; and it turned out to be a very successful record.

It's enormously moving besides being delightfully amusing.

Yes, it's a nice play, *Private Lives*, I'm very fond of it. Of course, the thing about the play

168

which went unobserved at the time is that it is the lightest of light comedies, based on a
serious situation which is two people who love each other too much. I wouldn't say it's a
tragedy, but there's a sadness below it. You see, there was Adrianne Allen, Laurence
Olivier, Gertrude Lawrence, and me. I hit Laurence Olivier on the head to make him
play Victor, because it isn't really a very good part; but I wanted not to have him cast as
an ordinary 'ho, ho, ho' stuffed-shirt. I said, 'I must have somebody who's physically
very attractive, otherwise Amanda would never have married him.' He must have something to give, he hasn't got much in the dialogue way, and poor Larry never really enjoyed playing it very much. I think he enjoyed acting with me, we had great fun, and,
curiously enough, it did him a lot of good.

*Throughout the time you were playing in 'Private Lives', could you see what was coming for him in
the future?*

I knew him to be a beautiful actor, a very good actor. He was playing this pompous prig
and the only thing was, he was a terrible giggler and I had to stop him; it's all very fine to
have a little actor's joke, but it's not very fair on the audience. If I did anything in the
part which was at all impromptu and funny, I looked across the stage to see Larry in fits
of laughter, when he was supposed to be very cross. So I said, 'From now onwards, I'm
going to try to make you laugh, and every time you do it, I'll kill you.' He got so angry
with himself for falling for it; I ruined several of his performances by doing this, but it
was worth it.

*Earlier on we were talking about 'The Constant Nymph'. Gielgud succeeded you in the part; you've
had a good many contacts with him.*

Yes, I'm proud to say in an earlier stage of his career, Johnny was my understudy. He
understudied me in *The Vortex* when he was an eager young actor and rich with talent.
He also covered for me in *The Constant Nymph* and succeeded me in the part of Lewis Dodd.
Many years later he played in *Nude with Violin* which he directed. I went to see it about
two days after it opened in Dublin, and he had directed it with such loving care for my
play, that he had rather forgotten his own performance, so I said, 'Now, you've got to be
a beautiful actor, let me help you with that.' To work with he was absolutely extraordinary. A most generous, genuinely modest big actor. There's nothing fake about him,
he is absolutely true; he was so charming to work with, we thoroughly enjoyed ourselves.
I've always loved working with Johnny in the theatre, I think he's wonderful.

*One always associates John Gielgud with Shakespeare and the classics. You have never played
Shakespeare, have you? That's still to come.*

I think I've left it a bit late. I might play the nurse in *Romeo and Juliet*. I've played in one
or two classics. I played in a rather tedious play by Beaumont and Fletcher called *The
Knight of the Burning Pestle* of which I did not understand one word. I was not very good.

*While Gielgud is in many ways a very different actor in very different kinds of plays, you and he had
this very happy relationship as soon as you worked together.*

Always, because I've never yet found a really fine actor difficult to work with. Never.
Occasionally those who hadn't quite succeeded had to have their feathers smoothed
down, you had to listen to arguments about which dressing room they had; but not the
big ones. I've directed Larry much more than Johnny; I've directed Larry three times.

Don't you think that all the big people have a certain quality, artistic humility without which you can't be really big?

Yes. And if they have a director whom they're fond of and respect it ceases to be a dreadful chore. There are very often high words and terrific arguments, but I never had any with Larry.

Do you yourself sometimes introduce something new into a performance?

Oh yes, yes. But only when I'm playing with experts. It's awfully unfair on small-part actors who haven't got the assurance. I try not to do it then. But when I'm playing a run of a play I will think of something and do it, provided it's within the framework of the character.

You could teach small-part actors a lot, in that way, because if they learned to respond to you doing that, it would raise their level of performance.

Some of the poor beasts have had to respond whether they liked it or not.

It's very good for them. They were lucky, I think, to have the experience.

Well, it keeps them on their toes, but you know Hawtrey used to do that. Hawtrey would never play in exactly the same position every night. He would think of a new way of playing a line, or not even think of it, he would do it. And whoever was playing with him, played along with him. The sign of a bad actor is if he goes away too far, and gets a good laugh by doing something out of character. It's so easy to get laughs and so difficult to control them. And that's the essence of comedy, not to get the laughs, but to control – throw them away when you don't want them. Don't let the audience rule you. Rule them.

Two of the greatest experts that you've played with are Alfred Lunt and Lynn Fontanne.

plate 157a, b

We were old friends, and when we were young together, many years ago, we planned that, when we were all three stars in our own right, I would write a play for the three of us. Eight years later it came true, and we did *Design for Living*. To play with those two is quite, quite unlike playing with anybody else; quite, quite different. Lynn, of the two, has a slightly slower-moving technique, but can play it more swiftly and more mercurially than anybody I've ever seen, once she gets it. She takes a little longer to learn it. Alfred, on the other hand, is tremendously quick. But the mixture of the three of us – the whole of America was waiting for us to have dreadful rows. Well, we had one row, at rehearsal, which lasted for two days. Exactly the opposite from what you'd think, because in the theatre, where we were going to play, there was underground – below the stage floor – a big star dressing room and a little one immediately opposite. Obvious, I thought for the Lunts. So I said, 'I'll dress upstairs.' 'No,' they said, 'you are the author, you have both the dressing rooms downstairs, and we. . .' I said, 'I'm not going to have people coming round and seeing . . .' and this became very tough. Finally, I had to go to Macy's and buy a whole lot of drapes, chaise-longue, and telephone, and make the chorus room upstairs look so glamorous that they gave in.

And another thing that the Lunts did. There are many tricks in the theatre that the comedian – not first-rate comedians, but quite excellent comedians – use. They like up-staging, which is one of the most archaic forms of acting, and quite nonsense, and they do little tricks to spoil somebody else's lines, not realizing that by doing so they are destroying themselves and the play. Now the Lunts are the exact opposite. They would spend minutes to enable me to get a laugh when I stubbed a cigarette out, and I would do the same for them. But, of course, we could experiment on stage after we'd played for a few weeks or whatever it was. Suddenly Lynn would decide, maybe, to play by the fireplace instead of by the window, and I would be delighted because it would give me a new approach. Then Alfred would come on and find us both in completely different places and it wouldn't faze him at all; we could play any way we liked. There are certain actors who like to have everything absolutely dead set. I do not think that those actors are tremendously inspired. I think that, particularly in playing comedy, so much depends on whether your audience is with you that night. If you've got a lovely audience who are on to everything, you can take a little time off. The great thing is that you, as a comedian, must enjoy what you're doing. I hate this new solemnity in the theatre. If anybody says to me, 'She's a dedicated actress', I'd like to strangle her. What is she dedicated about?

Sounds a bit miserable, doesn't it?

It sounds wretched, and all this gloomy searching for motives. Acting must be a pleasure even if you're playing something immensely tragic and dramatic; that's a sort of pleasure too.

The audience still hope they're going to enjoy themselves however tragic the play may be. Isn't this true?

I absolutely agree. Difficult as it is Olivier, when he's playing his great performances, *Othello* or *Macbeth*, enjoys it. I know he does. Obviously at certain performances he thinks, 'Oh, I've got to get through all these climaxes', but the enjoyment is there, the power is there. And in comedy it is much more essential to bubble. I don't mean that it's got to be champagne all the time, but it's got to look as though you yourself are amused by what you're doing. The prime example of that was darling Yvonne Arnaud, who was one of the most brilliant comediennes I ever saw. She could look at a script, read through the lines and decide: titter, laugh, drag, slight titter, big laugh, before she even started rehearsing. Her favourite thing was a bad Saturday matinée, a lot of old ladies who were rather comatose and wishing for their madeira cake and their tea. She'd say to herself, 'I'll get you by the end of the afternoon', and she always did.

In comedy the audience are practically a character in the play, aren't they?

Can't do without them; you can't do a play without an audience.

So you've got to get them into the mood where they'll come and act with you, as it were.

Yes, and sometimes they have to be goosed a bit. I nearly always play the first act of a comedy very quickly. I don't mean gabble; the difference between speed and pace. If you play quickly and articulately, it doesn't give them time, you throw away laughs; throw them away in the first act, pull them in in the last. When you've got your audience where you want them, you can then afford to take some leisurely effects. But in the first act you've got to get their attention quickly and therefore play it quickly. If there are big laughs, stop them, except for the very big ones. In all plays I've been in, with Gertie and with Alfred and Lynn, we'd know whoever was on first, how a certain line went. If it got a laugh we'd say, 'Ha! We're home – nice, warm audience.' If it got a titter, tricky. If it got silence, get to work, chaps. I used to give Gertie the wink because I played the first scene in *Private Lives* with Adrianne Allen, and when I came off, Gertie was just going on with Larry, and I used to go, quick; and she'd know, and be on it like a greyhound, and by the end of the first act we'd got them.

It would be interesting if you could give an example of some of the ways you varied your performance when you were playing with Alfred Lunt and Lynn Fontanne.

If you remember, in the third scene of the second act of *Design for Living* there is a big drunk scene, and we get drunker and drunker. One night, by accident, Alfred said one of my lines, and I gave him a quick look, and replied with his line, and with one glint he knew. It wasn't fooling on the stage, this was not jolly jokes; I wanted to do some of the bits of business that he'd put in, because I admired them, and the same with him, he'd seen little bits that he fancied. We switched roles. It didn't matter psychologically because we were both drunk. So we played the whole scene reverse-wise, from different sides of the stage, playing each other's parts. Lynn happened to be standing at the side of the stage and was sweating with fear; she thought that we'd dry up, that we'd fluff, that we'd giggle. We did none of these things. Only at the very end of the scene there was a moment when I had to do rather a discreet little belch, and I knew Alfred couldn't do a belch. When we got to that moment, and I was thinking on all levels at once, I thought 'What am I to do?' So I answered his line and said mine quickly and got back, did my little belch, and the curtain came down. And people out in front who had seen the play before never noticed the difference. It was absolutely nerve racking and very exciting. It was a challenge and both of us being accomplished performers it worked; but we never did it again.

We were talking earlier on about this problem of shedding certain aspects of yourself in order to get to a character. This must have presented itself in the film 'In Which We Serve', in which you played the naval captain and also directed.

That was the most difficult thing I ever did.

Playing a man of the navy and yet using yourself and your own emotions about the navy and what you'd experienced.

And using other people's hands. You see I've got to be awfully careful. I act a great deal with my hands and naval officers do not. I was clasping my hands behind my back, doing anything rather than do a Noël Coward gesture. I remember the farewell scene. I think it came out all right in the end, but it was very difficult to play. It was a track shot and I had to do it, knowing the camera was coming near me and, as it approached, seeing out of the corner of my eye all the sailors being whisked away, so that I was left with no audience, talking to the air. Oh, very tricky. I wasn't, then, terribly accustomed to screen

plate 160a

technique; I'd only done one picture before that, *The Scoundrel*, which was many years before. I found it very difficult to adapt myself and not to use too much emotion. I had to have the emotion inside and do as little with my face as possible, because if, as I did in the first take of the farewell scene, I looked emotional, it was the one thing I didn't want to do. I had a great deal on my side. To start with I had real sailors who had all been in action. They knew what I was talking about; I had an audience that knew. And at the

plate 160c

end, I had to stand still and say goodbye to each one of them. I had written some lines but I tore up my script and said, 'Please, chaps, say what you think you would have said in this situation.' And this I could hardly take. Each one of them said their own line like 'Good Luck Sir', you know, 'Chin up Sir', all these perfectly trite ordinary phrases spoken from the heart. Marvellous. Talk about improvisation; it was nothing to do with acting.

They were being, but then it was only a film, only a take; I doubt if they could have got that amount of emotion into it if they had been playing it eight times a week.

You haven't done a great deal of filming? Is this because on the whole you don't really like it as a medium?

I do like it as a medium, I find it very interesting, but in small doses. Having been in the theatre all my life, I still cannot help loving it best. I've found certain film experiences fascinating. I loved working with Carol Reed in *Our Man in Havana*, and he helped me enormously because, you see, what I always have to do, as a stage actor, when I go back into a film studio, is to unlearn in a day or two everything I've been carefully studying for years. I have to remember in a close-up not to use my lips, and I'm not a particularly adroit film actor, technically I mean – I don't pay particular attention to the camera. Carol used to say to me, 'I shouldn't do that if I was you', and I'd say 'What was I doing?' And he said, 'Well, your mouth. Your underlip in this shot is a foot wide.' I was pitching to get to the back of the gallery. And you don't have to sustain in a picture. You have to sustain a character if you've got any sense, but you haven't got a long scene to play.

plate 160b

Not like that first act of 'The Apple Cart' in which you had to sustain a speech of thirteen minutes.

Yes, sitting upstage, if you remember, with every light in London focused on my kisser. We arranged that. I studied that part for at least three months, and we had a conversation and I said, 'I warn you, Michael, I am of the school that believes in being absolutely word perfect at a first rehearsal', and you said that you didn't quite agree because there were certain actors whom it didn't fit, and I said, 'Over to you, pal. I will be word perfect.' And there is no seagull in Jamaica that doesn't know that thirteen-minute speech, because I did it hundreds of times. But I can't start to rehearse a play properly unless I know the words.

plate 158c

During the process of rehearsal you'll agree that a tremendous amount grows. Rehearsal is a process of exploration, one finds out much more about the play, one finds out what one's going to do with every moment of it, and so on.

But how can you find out something about what you're going to do, if your mind is fluttering with anxiety about what you're going to say next?

I entirely agree.

I believe that learning the part and each cue with a postcard over the page, which I do relentlessly, is the most horrible drudgery. And if I make one mistake on a page I go right back to the beginning again, until I've not only learnt it with this part of my mind, but with that part. I don't worry about whether I'm getting at the right meaning at this point. When I get up on the stage, the words give me the meaning; you can't know it better than the words. It's not only knowing it by heart, it's more than that. It's knowing it inside, getting to what the Lunts call the silky stage. There comes a moment half-way through rehearsals when suddenly not only have you not got the book but – a certain feeling becomes injected. I cannot afford, and I am adamant about this, to take time off at rehearsals to learn words. I think those should be learned before you start. When I've finished a long day's rehearsal, which is awfully tiring, I like to go to the cinema or to the theatre or to have dinner with a friend. I don't want to think about the play until next morning. If I have to go back and study after working hard all day and giving out vitality rehearsing, it makes it terribly difficult. I can't understand actors who leave it to the last week of rehearsals and say, 'Oh, I don't remember the last act; I must go home and study.' This only results in panic.

This was a huge move, wasn't it, from your own plays and the modern comedies, to playing Shaw.

It was very, very good for me, and I found it intolerably difficult at first. Playing Bernard Shaw is a completely different experience for an actor. In those long speeches I had to remember my scales, because you cannot do a long Shavian speech in a monotone. You must use your voice, without sounding theatrical, but it must hit this note, that note, that note, this note – you must go up and down without appearing to. But this is not done by just standing on the stage and doing it. When you're reading it and learning it, you've got to decide where you're going to take your voice up, where you're going to lower it, where you're going to do this; and the result has got to look as though you were doing it off the cuff.

It never seemed as though you were finding it difficult at rehearsals.

Ah, because I knew the words, but I did not know how to say them quite accurately. It was you who gave me the clues. I could have played that part off my own bat very effectively, but without you I couldn't have played it true. You told me the one thing that was important; you said, 'Keep this in your mind; remember that this is basically a sad man'; and I don't believe that even Bernard Shaw was aware of that. I wish he'd seen it, I loved him so. I hope he would have approved of me. But I wouldn't be certain because we played that last act with sentiment, and in the original production there was none.

But Shaw was not a man who lacked heart.

On the contrary. He was so kind when I was a young writer. He corrected my scripts for me, before I'd even met him. He took trouble to help a young playwright and he wrote me a postcard saying, 'Never read anything of mine again, so long as you live.'

In training young students to be professional actors I have a problem. They all start as what I call enthusiastic amateurs, and it's a tremendous struggle, when they're very talented and tremendously enthusiastic, to turn them into professionals, and to explain the difference between doing it for its own sake and doing it as a job by which you earn your living.

There's a new theme running through the theatre of which I have no part. I'm perfectly ready to admit that it's very valuable in the theatre that certain aspects of it should be subsidized by the government, such as the National Theatre, Covent Garden and, maybe, one or two others; but you must remember that I belong to the commercial theatre. I started humbly in the theatre with the intention of earning my own living, and though I've tried to keep my work up to a high standard, my highest accolade has been when the audience fills the theatre. It has given me no particular pleasure to have rave notices, and then for the play to close in sixteen days. If I can be good enough, and get whatever I want to say over to a large audience, then I've succeeded. Why is it so bad to have a rattling success with the House Full boards out? This is a curious snobbism and I disapprove of it. I think you should say to your students, 'Remember, one of the most important parts of your job is to please a large number of people and the larger the better. You don't have to be vulgar in order to do it, you don't have to act badly.'

In fact you just have to act well.

Yes, you've got to act well. The public must not be underrated. They're not all that silly, and the reason so few go to the theatre now is that they're bored stiff by plays that are too long, and with the general atmosphere of 'down'. That is not what people go to the theatre for, unless it's done with genius, and it seldom is.

Just recently there's been another very interesting experience for you, the production of 'Hay Fever', which you directed for the National Theatre. It's rather fun to think that you're now a classic.

Yes, it's really very curious, isn't it? Shakes me a bit, when I think that I originally directed it forty years ago.

With Marie Tempest.

plate 159a

Darling Marie, yes.

And now with Edith Evans and an entirely different generation of actors. The comparison must be very interesting.

plate 159b

Comparison between the two stars is completely impossible to make, because they were utterly different. Marie Tempest was a great comedienne and I absolutely loved her. I was very nervous at the age of twenty-five showing Miss Marie Tempest how to act. Quite early on in rehearsal she called me up on the stage and said, 'Come up here, boy, you wrote this scene and know how to play it, I didn't write it and don't.' And to my horror I found myself saying, 'Well, I think you should lift the cup when you say that.' She said, 'Quite right boy, thank you very much'; and from then onwards all was well, and of course she gave a twinkling comedic performance. I consider Edith to be a great actress and she had, in a curious way, more stature. Edith's comedy, when she is sure of what she is doing, is perfection.

Before you did this production of 'Hay Fever' with the National Theatre you'd been in America for quite a time. How did it feel coming back to the theatre in England?

It was very curious. I must just preface this by saying that in the old days, before the war, in the twenties and the thirties, whenever I was about to do a new production in England I always used to go to New York for a fortnight, and stay at the Astor Hotel, and go to every single play; because the tempo and the wonderful speed and vitality of the American Theatre was far superior to the English, then. Since the war the theatre in America has deteriorated enormously. There are still some very fine actors and admirable directors, but the supporting players don't have an interest. Here in England we have the National Theatre, the Aldwych, the Royal Court: all theatres with a different style. We also have a number of admirable repertory theatres all over England. So that young people have a chance of playing to audiences and are able to develop some of their theories, whereas in America they only have acting schools, which are not enough. Some of them are quite good, but then, they've also been caught by this awful solemnity bug – that the whole thing's so sacred.

And very, very personal and me, me, me.

Me, me, me. Yes, and they also fly like rabbits to the psychoanalyst's couch to have their own problems straightened out, but that's nothing to do with acting at all. I think they ought to get up on the stage and do it. Now in England the standard is immensely high, today, amongst young actors. But owing to the dearth of playwrights – I mean light comedy playwrights, not good playwrights – there are several fine playwrights in

England – and too much emphasis being placed on the lower orders of life, the young people have lost a certain style that we had in the old days.

You see, in my early days in the theatre, the actor-manager's time, which is certainly going back a bit, I would never go into a theatre belonging to Charles Hawtrey or Gerald du Maurier or Sir George Alexander or Sir Herbert Tree without being spick and span, whatever I was going to play. If I were going to play a dustman I would have my suit pressed for rehearsals out of respect for the theatre itself, the edifice, the building. You couldn't see a lot of people in denims and blue jeans and dirty old sweaters walking about the stage of the St James's. I don't know why I feel like this. I suppose it's old hat and sentimental. It isn't entirely.

No, it isn't; it's a respect for the work.

It's discipline too. I don't believe that you can rehearse easily a highly articulate comedy, if you're dressed in a slovenly manner. A young creature of twenty-one thinks it's perfectly all right to come slouching in, without thinking of his poise, without thinking of his line, his head, stance; and when suddenly he's put into the clothes, he doesn't quite know how to wear them. I don't blame him, I blame the directors. I think a slovenly appearance indicates, in some way, a slovenly mind, and I don't think you can afford to have a slovenly mind even if you're playing *The Caretaker*.

Particularly not, because it's a precise play.

Such a precise work that, although you may look like a dirty, filthy old tramp, your mind must not be. And there I think is a style in its own.

From all I've heard of Pinter, when directing, he is as precise and demanding as you are.

An absolutely meticulous director. Every pause is professionally timed and the net result is, I think, remarkable. I think he's not only a very extraordinary writer but also a remarkable theatre man.

I wish I could only explain – it sounds almost pompous – but the decline of manners and the decline of elegance means that it is much more difficult for young actors to achieve range. I remember when I was playing *Present Laughter* in the afternoon and *This Happy Breed* in the evening, it was with a sigh of relief that I got down to old shirt-sleeves and slouched on looking anyhow. It's so easy to play natural, when you can scratch yourself. Even then it's got to be well done; but its much easier than being slick, timing every line, being very sharp-looking; and I think that's what they're missing a bit. There are certain of them who could do it, given the plays. I think that there's room for everything in the theatre, for a drama, or a comedy, or a play about kitchen sinks, or tramps if necessary. That's fine, providing they are good enough. There is still room for a charming, upper-middle class family, who have hearts and limbs, who feel and think, just the same as everybody else; and even dukes and duchesses, there are still a few extant.

They are all human beings, so therefore to be a good actor you must constantly better yourself. If you come from humble beginnings you must then think, Well obviously I can play cockney, I can play north country; now I must learn how to play proper English, improve my voice so that I've got range; then I can play *Henry VIII* one night and *The Caretaker* the next. That kind of range is what actors should aim for, and I think that ambition has rather faded. As a matter of fact this has been disproved, occasionally, by some of the National Theatre cast. This is, I would say, unquestionably the greatest cast I have worked with in my life. I've never had such response from a group of actors all of

plates 157c, 158b

176

whom were fine actors in their own right; and this is what I call professional, there was no fumbling about words with them, I'm glad to tell you. We were rehearsing *Hay Fever*, but they were also rehearsing *The Recruiting Officer* and the re-do of *Othello* and *The Dutch Courtesan* at the same time. So they would rehearse with me from ten o'clock in the morning till five in the afternoon, then they'd have a break for a cup of coffee, and pop on to do one of the other plays; and they kept all these different parts in their minds and were always fresh. When I saw the play after it had been on for some time they were playing it beautifully and lovingly and correctly.

This is an enormously hopeful prospect, isn't it. First of all it is nice that we've got a National Theatre, with Olivier at the head of it, and a company which is on the whole a young company, and then you come along of another generation, and work with them, and you all feel absolutely at home together. One has a tremendous sense of continuity in our profession.

The fact that the head of the National Theatre is Laurence Olivier, an actor from the top of his head to the soles of his feet, keeps up the standard. He has a very sharp eye, and he presents a marvellous example to the young ones, and he always gives them chances. Now Larry inspires these young people, he is the boss. He is treated with respect, as the big actor-managers were treated with respect, though in a slightly different way because the managers have changed a little; but he's respected all right, and what he says goes. And so, when I came in to work under him as a director, he was, of course, enchanting to me and gave me everything I wanted. But above all, he gave me the best staff, the best stage management, and the best cast I've ever had, and that is more encouraging. I think the quality of acting that I got out of those young people is the most exhilarating and happy thing that's happened to me, in the theatre, for many, many, many years.

TIME CHART

This chart shows all the parts played in the theatre by the subjects of this book. It does not include their film or television appearances, or single performances for charity matinées and so on. Nor does it include any plays directed by one of them, unless he also acted in it. In their early careers only the more important parts are listed by name.

The theatre background section gives the most important events which took place in the theatre at that time. The plays mentioned are first performances of plays selected for their importance in the theatre. The following abbreviations are used:

A.D.C. = Amateur Dramatic Club, Cambridge University
d. = died
dir. = directed
f. = founded
N.Y. = New York
O.V. = Old Vic Company
o. = opened
O.U.D.S. = Oxford University Dramatic Society
p. = production
R.S.C. = Royal Shakespeare Company

1903	1904	1905	1906	*Theatre Background*
Plans for a National Theatre published by Granville Barker and William Archer Abbey Theatre, Dublin f.	Barker-Vedrenne Season, Court Theatre (1904–7) Royal Academy of Dramatic Art f. by Sir Beerbohm Tree Barrie's *Peter Pan*	Henry Irving d. Bioscope Cinema, London's first public cinema, o. Shaw's *Man and Superman*	Galsworthy's *The Silver Box* Central School of Speech and Drama f. by Elsie Fogerty Ibsen d.	

SYBIL THORNDIKE *Born 24 October 1882*	**1904** Debut, *The Merry Wives* Appeared in *The Palace of Truth* *My Lord from Town*	**1904-7** U.S.A., playing in *Hamlet*, *The Tempest, Twelfth Night*, *A Midsummer Night's Dream*, *As You Like It, Merchant*	of *Venice, Everyman*, old comedies, etc. (112 parts in all)	*Sybil Thorndike*

1907	1908	1909	1910	*Theatre Background*
First Repertory Company in England o. in Manchester by Nancy Horniman Somerset Maugham's *Lady Frederick* Synge's *Playboy of the Western World*	Marlowe Society, Cambridge f.		First Repertory Season London o. by Charles Frohman	

1907 *His Japanese Wife*	**1908** *The Marquis* *The Subjection of Kezia* Gaiety Theatre, Manchester: *Marriages are Made in Heaven* *When the Devil was Ill* *Gentlemen of the Road* *The Charity that Began at Home* *His Helpmate* *The Silver Box* *Hippolytus* *Cupid and the Styx*	**1909** Manchester: *The Feud* *Trespassers will be Prosecuted* *The Vale of Content*	**1910** *Peg Woffington' Pearls* Columbine, *The Marriage of Columbine* Frohman's Rep. Co.: *The Sentimentalists* Emma Huxtable, *The Madras House* *Prunella* *Chains* Emily Chapman, *Smith*	*Sybil Thorndike*

1911	1912	1913	1914	*Theatre Background*
Liverpool Repertory Company f. Chekhov's *The Cherry Orchard* – first London p. Gordon Craig's *On the Art of the Theatre*	Granville Barker's p. of *The Winter's Tale*	Birmingham Repertory Theatre o. by Barry Jackson	First Shakespeare p. at the Old Vic (*Romeo and Juliet*)	

1911 Emily Chapman, *Smith* (North America)	**1912** Gaiety Theatre, Manchester: Beatrice, *Hindle Wakes* *The Question* *The Charity that Began at Home* *Revolt* *The Whispering Well* *Jane Clegg* *Prunella*	**1913** *Elaine* *The Pigeon* *Jane Clegg* *The Price of Thomas Scott* *Nothing Like Leather* *The Shadow* Portia, *Julius Caesar*	**1914-1918** Old Vic: Adriana, *The Comedy of Errors* Lady Macbeth, *Macbeth* Rosalind, *As You Like It* Portia, *The Merchant of Venice* Constance, *King John* *(continued on next page)*	*Sybil Thorndike*

(continued on next page)

NOËL COWARD *Born 1899* **1911** Debut as Prince Mussel, *The Goldfish* Appeared in *The Great Name* *Where the Rainbow Ends*	**1912** *An Autumn Idyll*	**1913** *Hannele* *War in the Air* *A Little Fowl Play* Slightly, *Peter Pan*		*Noël Coward*

EDITH EVANS *Born 1888*	**1912** Debut as Cressida, *Troilus and Cressida*	**1913** Martin, *Elizabeth Cooper*	**1914** Queen, *Hamlet* Appeared in *The Ladies' Comedy* *Acid Drops* *My Lady's Dress* *Milestones*	*Edith Evans*

179

	1915	1916	1917	1918
Theatre Background	Lena Ashwell organized companies to entertain troops in France	Entertainment Tax imposed on theatre tickets Brighouse's *Hobson's Choice*	Beerbohm Tree d.	Nigel Playfair management, Lyric Theatre, Hammersmith (1918–32)
Sybil Thorndike	**1914-1918** *continued* Beatrice, *Much Ado* Imogen, *Cymbeline* Chorus and Katharine, *Henry V* Julia, *Two Gentlemen of Verona* Ophelia, *Hamlet* Queen Margaret, *Richard III*	Mrs Ford and Rugby, *Merry Wives* Prince Hal, 1 *Henry IV* The Fool, *King Lear* Ferdinand, *The Tempest* Launcelot Gobbo, *The Merchant of Venice*	Lady Teazle, *The School for Scandal* Kate Hardcastle, *She Stoops to Conquer* Lydia Languish, *The Rivals*	Peg Woffington, *Masks and Faces* Columbine, *The Sausage String's Romance* Nancy, *Oliver Twist* *The Profiteers* *The Kiddies in the Ruins*
Noël Coward	**1915** Slightly, *Peter Pan* *Where the Rainbow Ends*	**1916** Charles Wykeham, *Charley's Aunt* Basil Pyecroft, *The Light Blues* Jack Morrison, *The Happy Family*	**1917** Ripley Guildford, *The Saving Grace*	**1918** Courtney Borner, *Scandal*
Edith Evans		**1916** *The Conference* *The Man who stayed at Home*	**1917** *Her Husband's Wife* *Collaborators*	**1918** *The Dead City* Toured with Ellen Terry in scenes from Shakespeare *Manfred*

	1919	1920	1921	1922
Theatre Background	Phoenix Society f. for presentation of Old English Dramatists	Coward's *I'll Leave it to You*		
Sybil Thorndike	**1919** *The Hostage* *The Chinese Puzzle* *The Great Day* Hecuba, *The Trojan Women* *Napoleon* Sakuntala, *Sakuntala*	**1920** Hecuba, *The Trojan Women* Candida, *Candida* Medea, *Medea* *Tom Trouble* *The Showroom* *The Mystery of the Yellow Room* Celine, *The Children's Carnival* Grand Guignol Company, 1920–22: played 25 parts	**1921** Mother Sawyer, *The Witch of Edmonton* Lady Macbeth, *Macbeth* (Paris) Evadne, *The Maid's Tragedy*	**1922** Hecuba, *The Trojan Women* Jane, *Jane Clegg* Charlotte Feriol, *Scandal* Medea, *Medea* Beatrice, *The Cenci*
Noël Coward	**1919** Ralph, *The Knight of the Burning Pestle*	**1920** Bobbie, *I'll Leave it to You* Ralph, *The Knight of the Burning Pestle*	**1921** Clay Collins, *Polly with a Past*	**1922** Sholto, *The Young Idea* (on tour)
Edith Evans	**1919** *The Player Queen* *The Return from Parnassus* Nerissa, *The Merchant of Venice*	**1920** *From Morn to Midnight* Captain Dumain, *All's Well* *My Lady's Dress* *Wedding Bells* Aquilina, *Venice Preserv'd*	**1921** *Daniel* Mrs Van Zile, *Polly with a Past* *The Witch of Edmonton* *Mother Eve* *Out to Win* Lady Utterword, *Heartbreak House*	**1922** *The Wheel* Cleopatra, *All for Love* *I Serve* Cynthia Dell, *The Laughing Lady* Ruby, *The Rumour*
		JOHN GIELGUD Born 14 *April* 1904	**1921** Debut as Herald, *Henry V* Appeared in *King Lear*, *Wat Tyler*, *Peer Gynt*	**1922** *The Wheel*
	RALPH RICHARDSON Born 19 *December* 1902	**1921** *Jean Valjean* *The Farmer's Romance* Banquo and Macduff, *Macbeth* *The Moon-Children* Tranio, *The Taming of the Shrew* Malvolio, *Twelfth Night* *Oliver Twist* *Tale of Two Cities* Lorenzo, *Merchant of Venice* Guildenstern and Bernardo, *Hamlet* A Pedant, *The Taming of the Shrew*	**1921** *continued* Soothsayer and Strato, *Julius Caesar* Oliver, *As You Like It* Scroop and Gower, *Henry V* Angus and Macduff, *Macbeth* Francisco and Antonio, *The Tempest* Lysander, *A Midsummer Night's Dream* Curio and Valentine, *Twelfth Night*	**1922** Banquo, *Macbeth* Lysander, *A Midsummer Night's Dream* Horatio, *Hamlet* Decius Brutus and Octavius Caesar, *Julius Caesar* Fabian, *Twelfth Night* Lucentio, *Taming of the Shrew* (London debut) Sebastian, *Twelfth Night*
			LAURENCE OLIVIER Born 22 *May* 1907	**1922** Debut, Shakespeare Festival Theatre as Katharina, *The Taming of the Shrew*

1923	1924	1925	1926	Theatre Background
O'Casey's *The Shadow of a Gunman*	First broadcast of a play by BBC	Shakespeare Memorial Theatre receives Royal Charter	Shakespeare Memorial Theatre burnt down	
1923 April Mawne, *Advertising April* Imogen, *Cymbeline* Elinor Shale, *The Lie*	**1924** Gruach, *Gruach* Joan, *Saint Joan* Sonia, *Man and the Masses* Rosalind, *As You Like It* Hecuba, *The Trojan Women*	**1925** Joan, *Saint Joan* Phaedra and Artemis, *Hippolytus* Claire, *The Verge* Daisy Drennan, *The Round Table* Elinor Shale, *The Lie* Medea, *Medea* Queen Katharine, *Henry VIII*	**1926** Beatrice, *The Cenci* Joan, *Saint Joan* The Duchesse, *Israel* Gertrude, *Hamlet* Judith, *Granite* Helen Stanley, *The Debit Account* Lady Macbeth, *Macbeth*	*Sybil Thorndike*
1923 Sholto, *The Young Idea* *London Calling*	**1924** Nicky Lancaster, *The Vortex*	**1925** Nicky Lancaster, *The Vortex* (N.Y.)	**1926** Lewis Dodd, *The Constant Nymph*	*Noël Coward*
1923 Marged, *Taffy* The Serpent, Oracle, and She-Ancient, *Back to Methuselah* (Birmingham Rep.) Mistress Page, *The Merry Wives*	**1924** Mrs Millament, *The Way of the World* *The Adding Machine* Suzanne, *Tiger Cats* Mrs Collins, *Getting Married* The Serpent and She-Ancient, *Back to Methuselah* Helena, *A Midsummer Night's Dream*	**1925** *The Painted Swan* Evadne, *The Maid's Tragedy* Old Vic: Portia, *Merchant of Venice* Margaret, *Richard III* Katharina, *The Taming of the Shrew* Mariana, *Measure for Measure* Cleopatra, *Antony and Cleopatra* Mistress Page, *The Merry Wives* Kate, *She Stoops to Conquer* Portia, *Julius Caesar* Beatrice, *Much Ado* Rosalind, *As You Like It* Margery Eyre, *The Shoemaker's Holiday* Nurse, *Romeo and Juliet*	**1926** Maude Fulton, *Caroline* Rebecca West, *Rosmersholm*	*Edith Evans*
1923 Felix, *The Insect Play* Robert E. Lee, *Charley's Aunt*	**1924** Romeo, *Romeo and Juliet*	**1925** Castalio, *The Orphan* Nicky Lancaster, *The Vortex* Trofimov, *The Cherry Orchard* Konstantin, *The Seagull* Sir John Harrington, *Gloriana* Robert, *L'Ecole des Cocottes*	**1926** Ferdinand, *The Tempest* Tusenbach, *The Three Sisters* George Stibelev, *Katerina* Lewis Dodd, *The Constant Nymph*	*John Gielgud*
1923 Cassio, *Othello* Antonio and Gratiano, *The Merchant of Venice* Mark Antony, *Julius Caesar* Sir Lucius O'Trigger, *The Rivals* Bobby, *The Romantic Age*	**1924** Henry, *Outward Bound* Fainall, *The Way of the World*	**1925** Richard Coaker, *The Farmer's Wife*	**1926** *The Cassilis Engagement* *The Round Table* *He Who Gets Slapped* Lane, *The Importance of Being Earnest* *Devonshire Cream* Albert Prosser, *Hobson's Choice* Mr Dearth, *Dear Brutus* *The Land of Promise* *The Barber and the Cow* The Stranger, *Oedipus at Colonus* Arthur Varwell, *Yellow Sands*	*Ralph Richardson*
	1924 Professional debut as Suliot Officer, *Byron*	**1925** Thomas of Clarence and Snare, *2 Henry IV* *Henry VIII* *The Cenci*	**1926** 1926–1928 with Birmingham Rep. in many parts including Guy Sydney, *Something to Talk About* Vanya, *Uncle Vanya* Parolles, *All's Well* Tony Lumpkin, *She Stoops to Conquer* Richard Coaker, *The Farmer's Wife*	*Laurence Olivier*
		PEGGY ASHCROFT *Born December 1907*	**1926** Debut at Birmingham Rep. as Margaret, *Dear Brutus*	*Peggy Ashcroft*

Theatre Background	1927	1928		1929
	First talking picture shown in London (*The Jazz Singer*)	Ellen Terry d.		British Actors' Equity f. Malvern Festival f.

| Sybil Thorndike | **1927**
Nadejda, *The Greater Love*
Angela Guiseley, *Angela*
Medea, *Medea* (Paris)
Joan, *Saint Joan* (Paris)
Old Vic:
Katharina, *The Taming of the Shrew*
Portia, *The Merchant of Venice*
Beatrice, *Much Ado*
Chorus and Katharine, *Henry V* | **1928**
Judith, *Judith of Israel*
Everyman, *Everyman*
Queen Elizabeth, *The Making of an Immortal*
Rosamund Withers, *The Stranger in the House*
1928–1929, South Africa:
Elinor Shale, *The Lie*
Jane, *Jane Clegg*
Chorus and Katharine, *Henry V*
Beatrice, *Much Ado* | **1928**
Lady Macbeth, *Macbeth*
Joan, *Saint Joan*
Mrs Phelps, *The Silver Cord* | **1929**
Barbara, *Major Barbara*
Lily Cobb, *Mariners*
Jane, *Jane Clegg*
Medea, *Medea*
Lady Lassiter, *The Donkey's Nose*
Madame de Beauvais, *Madame Plays Nap* |

| Noël Coward | | **1928**
Clark Storey, *The Second Man*
This Year of Grace (N.Y.) | | |

| Edith Evans | **1927**
Mrs Sullen, *The Beaux Stratagem*
The Lady in Law
Mrs Millament, *The Way of the World* | **1928**
Serpent and She-Ancient, *Back to Methuselah*
The Tragic Muse
Napoleon's Josephine | | **1929**
Florence Nightingale, *The Lady with a Lamp*
Orinthia, *The Apple Cart*
Lady Utterword, *Heartbreak House*
Wills and Ways |

| John Gielgud | **1927**
Dion Anthony, *The Great God Brown*
The Constant Nymph (on tour) | **1928**
Grand Duke Alexander, *The Patriot* (N.Y.)
Oswald, *Ghosts*
Gerald Marlowe, *Holding Out the Apple*
Captain Allenby, *The Skull*
Felipe Rivas, *The Lady from Alfaqueque*
Alberto, *Fortunato*
John Marstin, *Out of the Sea* | | **1929**
Fedor, *Red Rust*
Henry Tremayne, *The Lady with a Lamp*
Trotsky, *Red Sunday*
Old Vic:
Romeo, *Romeo and Juliet*
Antonio, *The Merchant of Venice*
Cleante, *The Imaginary Invalid*
Richard II |

| Ralph Richardson | **1927**
Arthur Varwell, *Yellow Sands* | **1928**
Zozim and Pygmalion, *Back to Methuselah*
Gurth, *Harold*
Tranio, *The Taming of the Shrew*
Prejudice
The First Performance
Ben Hawley, *Aren't Women Wonderful?*
Arms and the Maid
The Runaways | | **1929**
South Africa:
The New Sin
Monsieur Beaucaire
Joseph Surface, *School for Scandal*
David Garrick |

| Laurence Olivier | | **1928**
Young Man, *The Adding Machine*
Malcolm, *Macbeth*
Martellus, *Back to Methuselah*
Harold, *Harold*
The Lord, *Taming of the Shrew*
Gerald Arnwood, *Bird In Hand*
Captain Stanhope, *Journey's End* (Stage Society) | | **1929**
Michael (Beau) Geste, *Beau Geste*
Prince Po, *The Circle of Chalk*
Richard Parish, *Paris Bound*
John Hardy, *The Stranger Within*
American debut as:
Hugh Bromilow, *Murder on the Second Floor*
Jerry Warrender, *The Last Enemy* |

| Peggy Ashcroft | **1927**
London debut, Bessie, *One Day More*
Mary Dunn, *The Return*
Eve, *When Adam Delved*
Betty, *The Way of the World* | **1928**
Anastasia Vulliamy, *The Fascinating Foundling*
Mary Bruin, *The Land of Heart's Desire*
Hester, *The Silver Cord*
Edith Strange, *Earthbound*
Kristina, *Easter*
Eulalia, *A Hundred Years Old* | | **1929**
Lucy Deren, *Requital*
Sally Humphries, *Bees and Honey*
Constance Neville, *She Stoops to Conquer*
Naomi, *Jew Suss* |

1929	1930	1931	1931	
	Stage Society (f. 1899) wound up	Lilian Baylis reopens Sadler's Wells (*Twelfth Night*) La Compagnie des Quinze (Michel Saint-Denis) visits London		*Theatre Background*
	1930 *The Devil* *To Meet the King* Phèdre, *Phèdre* (in French) *The Fire in the Opera House* Mrs Alving, *Ghosts* Emilia, *Othello* On tour: Dolores Mendez, *The Squall* Mrs Alving, *Ghosts* Jess Fortune, *The Matchmaker's Arms* Judith, *Granite*	**1931** Marcelle, *The Medium* Joan, *Saint Joan* Eloise Fontaine, *Marriage by Instalments*		*Sybil Thorndike*
	1930 Stanhope, *Journey's End* (Singapore) Elyot Chase, *Private Lives*	**1931** Elyot Chase, *Private Lives* (N.Y.)		*Noël Coward*
	1930 *The Humour of the Court* Mrs Sullen, *The Beaux Stratagem* Delilah, *Delilah*	**1931** *O.H.M.S.* *Tiger Cats* Laetitia, *The Old Bachelor* Florence Nightingale, *The Lady with a Lamp* (N.Y.)		*Edith Evans*
1929 Old Vic: Oberon, *A Midsummer Night's Dream* Mark Antony, *Julius Caesar* Orlando, *As You Like It* The Emperor, *Androcles and the Lion* Macbeth Hamlet	**1930** Hamlet John Worthing, *The Importance of Being Earnest* Old Vic: Hotspur, *1 Henry IV* Prospero, *The Tempest* Lord Trinket, *The Jealous Wife* Antony, *Antony and Cleopatra*	**1931** Old Vic: Malvolio, *Twelfth Night* Sergius, *Arms and the Man* Benedick, *Much Ado About Nothing* King Lear ———— Inigo Jollifant, *The Good Companions* Joseph Schindler, *Musical Chairs*		*John Gielgud*
	1930 *Silver Wings* Roderigo, *Othello* Old Vic: Hal, *1 Henry IV* Caliban, *The Tempest* Harry Beagle, *The Jealous Wife* Bolingbroke, *Richard II* Enobarbus, *Antony and Cleopatra*	**1931** Toby Belch, *Twelfth Night* Caliban, *The Tempest* Bolingbroke, *Richard II* Bluntschli, *Arms and the Man* Don Pedro, *Much Ado about Nothing* Kent, *King Lear* David Regan, *The Mantle* Malvern Festival: Matthew Merrygreek, *Ralph Roister Doister* Mr Courtall, *She Would If She Could*	**1931** Malvern Festival: Viscount Pascal, *The Switchback* Nicholas, *A Woman Killed with Kindness* Old Vic: Faulconbridge, *King John* Petruchio, *The Taming of the Shrew* Bottom, *A Midsummer Night's Dream* Henry V	*Ralph Richardson*
	1930 Ralph, *After All* Victor Prynne, *Private Lives*	**1931** Victor Prynne, *Private Lives* (N.Y.)		*Laurence Olivier*
	1930 Desdemona, *Othello* Judy Battle, *The Breadwinner*	**1931** Pervaneh, *Hassan* (O.U.D.S.) Angela, *Charles III* Anne, *A Knight Passed By* Fanny, *Sea Fever* Marcela, *Take Two from One*		*Peggy Ashcroft*

	1932		1933	1934
Theatre Background	Shakespeare Memorial Theatre reopens Priestley's *Dangerous Corner* Regent's Park open-air theatre o. (*1 & 2 Henry IV*)			Eliot's *Murder in the Cathedral* Pinero and William Poel d.
Sybil Thorndike	The Citizen's Wife, *The Knight of the Burning Pestle* (O.V.) Julie, *The Dark Saint* Egypt, Palestine, Australia: Joan, *Saint Joan* Lady Macbeth, *Macbeth* Madame de Beauvais, *Madame Plays Nap*	Lady Cicely Waynflete, *Captain Brassbound's Conversion* April, *Advertising April* Judith, *Granite* Kitty Fane, *The Painted Veil* Gertrude Rhead, *Milestones*	Evie Millward, *The Distaff Side* Mrs Siddons, *Mrs Siddons*	Victoria Van Brett, *Double Door* Nourmahal, *Aureng-Zebe* 'Z', *Village Wooing* Evie Millward, *The Distaff Side* (N.Y.)
Noël Coward			Leo, *Design for Living* (N.Y.)	Chaucigny-Varennes, *Conversation Piece*
Edith Evans	Nurse, *Romeo and Juliet* Emilia, *Othello* (O.V.) Viola, *Twelfth Night* (O.V.) Lady Utterword, *Heartbreak House* Irela, *Evensong*		Irela, *Evensong* (N.Y.) May Daniels, *Once in a Lifetime* Gwenny, *The Late Christopher Bean*	Duchess of Marlborough, *Viceroy Sarah* Nurse, *Romeo and Juliet* (N.Y.)
John Gielgud	Richard II, *Richard of Bordeaux* (dir.)		*Richard of Bordeaux*	Roger Maitland, *The Maitlands* Hamlet (dir.)
Ralph Richardson	Old Vic: Ralph, *The Knight of the Burning Pestle* Brutus, *Julius Caesar* General Grant, *Abraham Lincoln* Iago, *Othello* Toby Belch, *Twelfth Night* Ghost and the First Grave-digger, *Hamlet*	Malvern Festival: Matthew Merrygreek, *Ralph Roister Doister* Face, *The Alchemist* Oroonoko, *Oroonoko* Sergeant Fielding, *Too True to be Good* Collie Stratton, *For Services Rendered*	Dirk Barclay, *Head-on Crash* Nicholls, *Wild Decembers* Sheppey, *Sheppey* Mr Darling and Captain Hook, *Peter Pan*	MacGregor, *Marriage Is No Joke* Appleby, *Eden End*
Laurence Olivier			Steven Beringer, *Rats of Norway* Julian Dulcimer, *The Green Bay Tree* (N.Y.)	Richard Kurt, *Biography* Bothwell, *Queen of Scots* Anthony Cavendish, *Theatre Royal*
Peggy Ashcroft	Juliet, *Romeo and Juliet* Stella, *Le Cocu Magnifique* Salome Westaway, *The Secret Woman* Cleopatra, *Caesar and Cleopatra* (O.V.) Imogen, *Cymbeline* (O.V.) Rosalind, *As You Like It* (O.V.) Fraulein Elsa, *Fraulein Elsa*		Old Vic: Portia, *Merchant of Venice* Kate Hardcastle, *She Stoops to Conquer* Perdita, *A Winter's Tale* Mary Stuart, *Mary Stuart* Juliet, *Romeo & Juliet* Lady Teazle, *The School for Scandal* Miranda, *The Tempest* — Inken Peters, *Before Sunset*	Vasantesena, *The Golden Toy* Lucia Maubel, *The Life that I Gave Him*
Michael Redgrave	**MICHAEL REDGRAVE** 20 *March* 1908 Played many parts at the A.D.C., Cranleigh School, and Guildford Rep., including		Cranleigh School: Hamlet Prospero, *The Tempest*	Lear (Cranleigh) Professional debut as Roy Darwin, *Counsellor at Law* Appeared in *The Distaff Side* *A Sleeping Clergyman* *The Perfect Plot* *Sheppey* *Heaven on Earth*

1935	1936	1937	1938	
	Rattigan's *French without Tears* Stanislavsky's *An Actor Prepares* (in English) BBC Television o.	Barrie, Forbes-Robertson, and Lilian Baylis d. John Gielgud's Queen's Theatre season (Sept.–May)		*Theatre Background*
1935 Blanche, *Grief Goes Over* Lady Bucktrout, *Short Story* Lisha Gerart, *The Farm of Three Echoes*	**1936** Mary Herries, *Kind Lady* On tour: Mrs Gascoigne, *My Son's My Son* Lady Maureen Gilpin, *Hands Across the Sea* Doris Gow, *Fumed Oak* 'Z', *Village Wooing* Aphrodite and the Nurse, *Hippolytus*	**1937** Betsy Loveless, *Six Men of Dorset* Ann Murray, *Yes, My Darling Daughter* Hecuba, *The Trojan Women*	**1938** Mrs Conway, *Time and the Conways* (N.Y.) Volumnia, *Coriolanus* (O.V.) Miss Moffat, *The Corn is Green*	*Sybil Thorndike*
1935 *Tonight at 7.30*	**1936** *Tonight at 8.30* (& N.Y.)			*Noël Coward*
1935 Agatha Payne, *The Old Ladies* Nurse, *Romeo and Juliet*	**1936** Arkadina, *The Seagull* Old Vic: Lady Fidget, *The Country Wife* Rosalind, *As You Like It* Mother Savage, *The Witch of Edmonton*	**1937** Rosalind, *As You Like It* Katharina, *The Taming of the Shrew* Sanchia Carson, *Robert's Wife*		*Edith Evans*
1935 Noah Mercutio and Romeo, *Romeo and Juliet* (dir.)	**1936** Trigorin, *The Seagull* Hamlet (N.Y.)	**1937** Mason, *He Was Born Gay* (dir.) Richard, *Richard II* (dir.) Joseph Surface, *School for Scandal*	**1938** Vershinin, *Three Sisters* Shylock, *Merchant of Venice* (dir.) Nicholas Randolph, *Dear Octopus*	*John Gielgud*
1935 Cornelius, *Cornelius* Mercutio & Chorus, *Romeo and Juliet* (N.Y.)	**1936** Delbar, *Promise* Sam Gridley, *Bees on the Boat Deck* (co-dir.) Clitterhouse, *The Amazing Dr Clitterhouse*	**1937** Agardi, *The Silent Knight* Bottom, *A Midsummer Night's Dream* (O.V.)	**1938** Othello (O.V.)	*Ralph Richardson*
1935 Peter Hammond, *Ringmaster* Richard Harben, *Golden Arrow* (dir.) Romeo & Mercutio, *Romeo and Juliet*	**1936** Robert Patch, *Bees on the Boatdeck* (dir.)	**1937** Old Vic: Hamlet Toby Belch, *Twelfth Night* Henry, *Henry V* Macbeth Hamlet (at Elsinore)	**1938** Old Vic: Iago, *Othello* Vivaldi, *The King of Nowhere* Coriolanus	*Laurence Olivier*
1935 Therese Paradis, *Mesmer* Juliet, *Romeo and Juliet*	**1936** Nina, *The Seagull*	**1937** Lise, *High Tor* (N.Y.) Queen, *Richard II* Lady Teazle, *The School for Scandal*	**1938** Irina, *Three Sisters* Portia, *The Merchant of Venice* Yeliena Talberg, *The White Guard* Viola, *Twelfth Night*	*Peggy Ashcroft*
1935 *Biography* *Villa for Sale* *Libel* *Flowers of the Forest* Horatio, *Hamlet* *Too Young to Marry* *The Matriarch* *Counsellor at Law* *Youth at the Helm* *Barnet's Folly* *Cornelius* *Miss Linley of Bath* *The Copy* *A Hundred Years Old* *The Wind and the Rain* *Circus Boy*	**1936** *Boyd's Shop* *And So To War* Richard II, *Richard of Bordeaux* Richard Burdon, *Storm in a Teacup* *Painted Sparrows* Malvolio, *Twelfth Night* Old Vic: Ferdinand, *Love's Labour's Lost* Mr Horner, *The Country Wife* Orlando, *As You Like It* Warbeck, *The Witch of Edmonton*	**1937** Laertes, *Hamlet* (O.V.) Orlando, *As You Like It* Anderson, *The Bat* Chorus, *Henry V* (O.V.) Christopher Drew, *A Ship Comes Home* Larry Starr, *Three Set Out* Bolingbroke, *Richard II* Charles Surface, *School for Scandal*	**1938** Tusenbach, *Three Sisters* Alexei Turbin, *The White Guard* Aguecheek, *Twelfth Night*	*Michael Redgrave*

	1939	1940	1941	1942
Theatre Background	Frank Benson d. BBC Television closed down ENSA f. by Basil Deane	Council for the Encouragement of Music and the Arts (C.E.M.A.) f.	Old Vic Theatre bombed	Alec Clunes's Management, Arts Theatre, London (1942–53)
Sybil Thorndike		**1940** 1940–1942 toured mining villages for C.E.M.A.: Lady Macbeth, *Macbeth* Medea, *Medea* Candida, *Candida*	**1941** Constance, *King John* (O.V.) Medea, *Medea*	**1942** Further tour for C.E.M.A.: Lady Macbeth, *Macbeth* Medea, *Medea* Candida, *Candida* Rebekah and Chorus, *Jacob* Georgina Jeffreys, *The House of Jeffrey*
Noël Coward				**1942** Charles Condamine, *Blithe Spirit* (and on tour) Garry Essendine, *Present Laughter* (on tour) Frank Gibbons, *This Happy Breed* (on tour)
Edith Evans	**1939** Lady Bracknell, *The Importance of Being Earnest*	**1940** Muriel Meilhac, *Cousin Muriel* Epifania, *The Millionairess* *Diversion*	**1941** *Diversion No. 2* Katherine Markham, *Old Acquaintance*	**1942** Lady Bracknell, *The Importance of Being Earnest* Entertaining troops
John Gielgud	**1939** John Worthing, *The Importance of Being Earnest* (dir.) Hamlet (& Elsinore)	**1940** King Lear (O.V.) Prospero, *The Tempest* (O.V.) ENSA tour: Henry Gow, *Fumed Oak* Gilpin, *Hands Across the Sea* Svetlovidov, *Swan Song*	**1941** Will Dearth, *Dear Brutus* (dir.)	**1942** Macbeth (dir.) John Worthing, *The Importance of Being Earnest*
Ralph Richardson	**1939** Johnson, *Johnson Over Jordan*			
Laurence Olivier	**1939** Gaylord Easterbrook, *No Time for Comedy* (N.Y.)	**1940** Romeo, *Romeo and Juliet* (dir.) (N.Y.)		
Peggy Ashcroft	**1939** Isolde, *Weep for the Spring* (on tour) Cecily Cardew, *The Importance of Being Earnest*	**1940** Dinah Sylvester, *Cousin Muriel* Miranda, *The Tempest* (O.V.)	**1941** Mrs de Winter, *Rebecca*	**1942** Cecily Cardew, *The Importance of Being Earnest*
Michael Redgrave	**1939** Lord Harry Monchensey, *The Family Reunion* Henry, *Springtime for Henry*	**1940** Macheath, *The Beggar's Opera* Charleston, *Thunder Rock*		**1942** Gribaud, *The Duke in Darkness* (dir.)

1943	1944	1945	1946	
		Theatre Workshop f. by Joan Littlewood C.E.M.A. becomes The Arts Council of Great Britain	BBC Television resumed Company of Four, Lyric Theatre, Hammersmith (1946–53) Granville Barker d.	*Theatre Background*
1943 Dublin: Mrs Alving, *Ghosts* Lady Cicely Waynflete, *Captain Brassbound's Conversion* Mrs Hardcastle, *She Stoops to Conquer* ——— Lady Beatrice, *Queen Bee* Mrs Dundass, *Lottie Dundass* Queen of Hearts and White Queen, *Alice*	**1944** Old Vic: Aase, *Peer Gynt* Catherine Petkoff, *Arms and the Man* Queen Margaret, *Richard III* ——— Queen of Hearts and White Queen, *Alice*	**1945** Old Vic: Marina, *Uncle Vanya* Mistress Quickly, *1 & 2 Henry IV* Jocasta, *Oedipus Rex* The Justice's Lady, *The Critic*	**1946** Mrs Woodrow Wilson, *In Time to Come* Clytemnestra, *Electra*	*Sybil Thorndike*
1943 Garry Essendine, *Present Laughter* Frank Gibbons, *This Happy Breed*		**1945** A few appearances in *Sigh No More*		*Noël Coward*
1943 Hesione Hushabye, *Heartbreak House* (and touring troops)	**1944** Entertaining troops	**1945** Gwenny, *The Late Christopher Bean* (India) Mrs Malaprop, *The Rivals*	**1946** Katerina, *Crime and Punishment* Cleopatra, *Antony and Cleopatra*	*Edith Evans*
1943 Louis, *The Doctor's Dilemma* Valentine, *Love for Love* (dir.)	**1944** Arnold Champion-Cheney, *The Circle* Valentine, *Love for Love* (dir.) Hamlet Oberon, *A Midsummer Night's Dream* Ferdinand, *The Duchess of Malfi*	**1945** Hamlet (Burma) Charles Considine, *Blithe Spirit*	**1946** Raskolnikov, *Crime and Punishment*	*John Gielgud*
	1944 Old Vic: Peer Gynt, *Peer Gynt* Bluntschli, *Arms and the Man* Richmond, *Richard III* Vanya, *Uncle Vanya* (& Europe)	**1945** Old Vic: Vanya, *Uncle Vanya* Falstaff, *1 & 2 Henry IV* Tiresias, *Oedipus Rex* Burleigh, *The Critic* & 1946 (N.Y.)	**1946** Inspector Goole, *An Inspector Calls* Cyrano, *Cyrano de Bergerac*	*Ralph Richardson*
	1944 Old Vic: Button-Moulder, *Peer Gynt* Sergius, *Arms and the Man* Richard, *Richard III* Astrov, *Uncle Vanya* (& Europe)	**1945** Old Vic: Hotspur, *1 Henry IV* Shallow, *2 Henry IV* Oedipus, *Oedipus Rex* Puff, *The Critic* at Comédie Française in: *Peer Gynt* *Arms and the Man* *Richard III*	**1946** Appeared in New York in the five last-mentioned parts Lear, *King Lear* (O.V.; dir.)	*Laurence Olivier*
1943 Catherine Lisle, *The Dark River*	**1944** Ophelia, *Hamlet* Titania, *A Midsummer Night's Dream* The Duchess, *The Duchess of Malfi*			*Peggy Ashcroft*
1943 Rakitin, *A Month in the Country* Lafont, *Parisienne* (dir.)	**1944** Harry, *Uncle Harry* (co-dir.)	**1945** Colonel Stjerbinsky, *Jacobowsky and the Colonel* (dir.)		*Michael Redgrave*

	1947	1948	1949	1950
Theatre Background		Fry's *The Lady's Not for Burning*	National Theatre Bill passed	Shaw d. Old Vic Theatre reopened
Sybil Thorndike	**1947** Mrs Fraser, *Call Home the Heart* Isobel Linden, *The Linden Tree*	**1948** Mrs Jackson, *The Return of the Prodigal*	**1949** Isabel Bracken, *The Foolish Gentlewoman* Aunt Anna Rose, *Treasure Hunt*	**1950** Lady Randolph, *Douglas* (Edinburgh Festival)
Noël Coward	**1947** Garry Essendine, *Present Laughter*	**1948** Max Aramont, *Joyeux Chagrins* (Paris)		
Edith Evans		**1948** Old Vic: Lady Wishfort, *The Way of the World* Ranevsky, *The Cherry Orchard*	**1949** Lady Pitts, *Daphne Laureola*	**1950** Lady Pitts, *Daphne Laureola* (N.Y.)
John Gielgud	**1947** U.S.A. & Canada: Valentine, *Love for Love* John Worthing, *The Importance of Being Earnest* Jason, *Medea* (dir.) Raskolnikov, *Crime and Punishment*	**1948** Eustace Jackson, *The Return of the Prodigal*	**1949** Thomas Mendip, *The Lady's Not for Burning*	**1950** Stratford: Angelo, *Measure for Measure* Benedick, *Much Ado About Nothing* Cassius, *Julius Caesar* King Lear Thomas Mendip, *The Lady's Not for Burning* (N.Y.)
Ralph Richardson	**1947** Old Vic: Face, *The Alchemist* John of Gaunt, *Richard II* (dir.)	**1948** Marcus, *Royal Circle* (dir.)	**1949** Sloper, *The Heiress*	**1950** Preston, *Home at Seven*
Laurence Olivier		**1948** Australia and New Zealand with Old Vic: Teazle, *The School for Scandal* (dir.) Richard, *Richard III* Mr Antrobus, *The Skin of our Teeth* (dir.)	**1949** Old Vic: Richard, *Richard III* Teazle, *The School for Scandal* (dir.) Chorus, *Antigone* (dir.)	**1950** Duke of Altair, *Venus Observed* (dir.)
Peggy Ashcroft	**1947** Evelyn Holt, *Edward, My Son*	**1948** Evelyn Holt, *Edward, My Son* (N.Y.)	**1949** Catherine Sloper, *The Heiress*	**1950** Stratford: Beatrice, *Much Ado* Cordelia, *King Lear* Old Vic: Viola, *Twelfth Night*
Michael Redgrave	**1947** Macbeth	**1948** Macbeth (N.Y.) The Captain, *The Father*	**1949** The Captain, *The Father* Etienne, *A Woman in Love* (dir.) Berowne, *Love's Labour's Lost* (O.V.) Marlow, *She Stoops to Conquer* (O.V.) Rakitin, *A Month in the Country*	**1950** Hamlet (O.V. & Elsinore)

1951	1952	1953	1954	
Whiting's *Saint's Day*			Beckett's *Waiting for Godot* (first London p.)	*Theatre Background*
1951–52 Mrs Whyte, *Waters of the Moon*		**1953** Laura Anson, *A Day by the Sea*	**1954** Australia, New Zealand, Tasmania, India, Hong Kong, Malaya: Scenes from the Classics	*Sybil Thorndike*
		1953 King Magnus, *The Apple Cart*		*Noël Coward*
1951 Helen Lancaster, *Waters of the Moon*			**1954** Countess, *The Dark is Light Enough*	*Edith Evans*
1951 Leontes, *The Winter's Tale*	**1952** Benedick, *Much Ado* (dir.)	**1953** Mirabell, *The Way of the World* (dir.) Jaffeir, *Venice Preserv'd* Richard II (Rhodesia) Julian Anson, *A Day by the Sea* (dir.)		*John Gielgud*
1951 Vershinin, *Three Sisters*	**1952** Stratford: Prospero, *The Tempest* Macbeth Volpone, *Volpone*	**1953** Greenwood, *The White Carnation* Farley, *A Day by the Sea*		*Ralph Richardson*
1951 Antony, *Antony and Cleopatra* Caesar, *Caesar and Cleopatra* (& N.Y.)		**1953** Grand Duke, *The Sleeping Prince* (dir.)		*Laurence Olivier*
1951 Old Vic: Electra, *Electra* Mistress Page, *The Merry Wives*	**1952** Hester Collyer, *The Deep Blue Sea*	**1953** Stratford: Portia, *The Merchant of Venice* Cleopatra, *Antony and Cleopatra* (& London)	**1954** Cleopatra, *Antony and Cleopatra* (Europe) Hedda, *Hedda Gabler* (& Oslo)	*Peggy Ashcroft*
1951 Stratford: Richard II Hotspur, *1 Henry IV* Chorus, *Henry V* Prospero, *The Tempest*	**1952** Frank Elgin, *Winter Journey*	**1953** Stratford: Shylock, *The Merchant of Venice* King Lear Antony, *Antony and Cleopatra* (& London)	**1954** Antony, *Antony and Cleopatra* (Europe)	*Michael Redgrave*

	1955	1956	1957	1958
Theatre Background	ITA inaugurated	English Stage Company f. by George Devine Osborne's *Look Back in Anger* Brecht's *The Good Woman of Setzuan* (first Brecht p. in English) Brecht d.	Entertainment tax removed	Belgrade Theatre, Coventry, o. Pinter's *The Birthday Party* Wesker's *Chicken Soup and Barley*
Sybil Thorndike	Australia: The Grand Duchess, *The Sleeping Prince* Mrs Railton-Bell, *Separate Tables*	Lady Monchensey, *Family Reunion* Mrs Callifer, *The Potting Shed* (N.Y.)	Australia, 1957–1958: Mrs St Maugham, *The Chalk Garden*	
Noël Coward				
Edith Evans		Mrs St Maugham, *The Chalk Garden*		Queen Katharine, *Henry VIII* (O.V. & Paris)
John Gielgud	London & Europe: Benedick, *Much Ado* (dir.) King Lear	Sebastien, *Nude with Violin* (dir. with Coward)	Stratford: Prospero, *The Tempest* (& London)	James Callifer, *The Potting Shed* Wolsey, *Henry VIII* (O.V. & Paris)
Ralph Richardson	Australia and New Zealand: Grand Duke, *The Sleeping Prince* Mr Martin and Major Pollock, *Separate Tables*	Timon, *Timon of Athens* (O.V.)	General St Pé, *The Waltz of the Toreadors* (N.Y.) Cherry, *Flowering Cherry*	Cherry, *Flowering Cherry*
Laurence Olivier	Stratford: Macbeth Titus Andronicus Malvolio, *Twelfth Night*		Archie Rice, *The Entertainer* Titus Andronicus (& Europe)	Archie Rice, *The Entertainer* (N.Y.)
Peggy Ashcroft	Beatrice, *Much Ado* (& Europe)	Miss Madrigal, *The Chalk Garden* Shen Teh, *The Good Woman of Setzuan*	Stratford: Rosalind, *As You Like It* Imogen, *Cymbeline*	Julia Rajk, *Shadow of Heroes*
Michael Redgrave	Hector, *Tiger at the Gates*	Grand Duke, *The Sleeping Prince* (N.Y.)		Philip Lester, *A Touch of the Sun* Stratford: Hamlet (& Russia) Benedick, *Much Ado*

1959	1960	1961	1962	Theatre Background
Mermaid Theatre o. by Bernard Miles (*Lock up your Daughters*) Arden's *Serjeant Musgrave's Dance*	Royal Shakespeare Company at Aldwych Theatre, London Bristol University inaugurated first chair of Drama	Barry Jackson d.	Olivier appointed director of National Theatre Chichester Festival Theatre o. Rudkin's *Afore Night Come*	
1959 Dame Sophia Carrell, *Eighty in the Shade* Mrs Kittridge, *Sea Shell*	**1960** Lottie Bainbridge, *Waiting in the Wings*	**1961** Teresa, *Teresa of Avila*	**1962** Miss Crawley, *Vanity Fair* Marina, *Uncle Vanya* (Chichester)	*Sybil Thorndike*
				Noël Coward
1959 Stratford: Countess of Rousillon, *All's Well* Volumnia, *Coriolanus*		**1961** Margaret, *Richard III* Nurse, *Romeo and Juliet*		*Edith Evans*
1959 *The Ages of Man*	**1960** Prince Ferdinand Cavanti, *The Last Joke*	**1961** R.S.C.: Othello (Stratford) Gayev, *The Cherry Orchard*	**1962** Joseph Surface, *School for Scandal* (U.S.A.; dir.)	*John Gielgud*
1959 Victor Rhodes, *Complaisant Lover*	**1960** Edward Portal, *The Last Joke*		**1962** Peter Teazle, *School for Scandal* (& U.S.A.)	*Ralph Richardson*
1959 Coriolanus (Stratford)	**1960** Berenger, *Rhinoceros* Becket, *Becket* (N.Y.)	**1961** Henry II, *Becket* (N.Y.)	**1962** Fred Midway, *Semi-Detached* Chichester: Astrov, *Uncle Vanya* (dir.) Bassanes, *The Broken Heart* (dir.)	*Laurence Olivier*
1959 Rebecca West, *Rosmersholm*	**1960** Stratford: Katharina, *The Taming of the Shrew* Paulina, *The Winter's Tale*	**1961** R.S.C.: *The Hollow Crown* The Duchess, *The Duchess o, Malfi* Emilia, *Othello* (Stratford) Madame Ranevsky, *Cherry Orchard*		*Peggy Ashcroft*
1959 H.J., *The Aspern Papers*	**1960** Jack Dean, *The Tiger and the Horse*		**1962** Vanya, *Uncle Vanya* (Chichester) Victor Rhodes, *The Complaisant Lover* (N.Y.) Lancelot Dodd, *Out of Bounds*	*Michael Redgrave*

	1963	1964	1965	1966–7
Theatre Background	Last p. by Old Vic Company (*Measure for Measure*) First p. by National Theatre Company (*Hamlet*) Nottingham Playhouse o.	First World Theatre Season (Aldwych)	Yvonne Arnaud Theatre, Guildford, o. George Devine d. Gordon Craig d.	R.S.C.'s p., *Us* Stoppard's *Rosencrantz and Guildenstern are Dead*
Sybil Thorndike	**1963** Lady Beatrice, *Queen Bee* (on tour)	**1964** Countess of Lister, *The Reluctant Peer* Anne Storch, *Season of Goodwill*	**1965** Mrs Tate, *Return Ticket* Abby Brewster, *Arsenic and Old Lace*	**1966** Abby Brewster, *Arsenic and Old Lace* **1967** Claire, *The Viaduct*
Noël Coward				**1966** *Suite in Three Keys* George Hilgay, *Shadows of the Evening* Verner Conklin, *Come into the Garden Maud* Hugo Latymer, *Song of Twilight*
Edith Evans	**1963** Violet, *Gentle Jack*	**1964** National: Judith Bliss, *Hay Fever*	**1965** Mrs Forrest, *The Chinese Prime Minister*	
John Gielgud	**1963** Julius Caesar, *The Ides of March* (dir.)	**1964** Julian, *Tiny Alice* (N.Y.)	**1965** Ivanov, *Ivanov* (dir.)	**1966** Ivanov (N.Y.) **1967** National: Orgon, *Tartuffe*
Ralph Richardson	**1963** Father, *Six Characters*	**1964** South America and Europe: Shylock, *The Merchant of Venice* Bottom, *A Midsummer Night's Dream* Father, *Carving a Statue*		**1966** Waiter, *You Never Can Tell* Anthony Absolute, *The Rivals* **1967** Shylock, *The Merchant of Venice*
Laurence Olivier	**1963** National: Captain Brazen, *The Recruiting Officer* Astrov, *Uncle Vanya* (dir.)	**1964** National: Halvard Solness, *The Master Builder* Othello, *Othello*	**1965** National: Tattle, *Love for Love*	**1967** National: The Captain, *Dance of Death*
Peggy Ashcroft	**1963** R.S.C.: Margaret, *Henry VI, Edward IV* and *Richard III* (Stratford)	**1964** Margaret, *Henry VI, Edward IV* and *Richard III* (R.S.C.; Stratford & London) Madame Arkadina, *The Seagull*		**1966** The Mother, *Days in the Trees* (R.S.C.) **1967** Mrs Alving, *Ghosts* (R.S.C.)
Michael Redgrave	**1963** Chichester: Vanya, *Uncle Vanya* National: Claudius, *Hamlet* Vanya	**1964** National: Hobson, *Hobson's Choice* Halvard Solness, *The Master Builder*	**1965** Guildford: Rakitin, *A Month in the Country* (& London) Samson, *Samson Agonistes*	